Moodle 1.9
Testing and Assessment

Develop and evaluate quizzes and tests using
Moodle modules

Jason Myrick

PUBLISHING

BIRMINGHAM - MUMBAI

Moodle 1.9 Testing and Assessment

First published: December 2010

Production Reference: 1071210

Published by Packt Publishing Ltd.
32 Lincoln Road
Olton
Birmingham, B27 6PA, UK.

ISBN : 978-1-849512-34-3

www.packtpub.com

Cover Image by Filippo (filosarti@tiscali.it)

Credits

Author
Jason Myrick

Reviewers
Jac Gubbels
Nitin Parmar

Acquisition Editor
Dilip Venkatesh

Development Editor
Meeta Rajani

Technical Editor
Paramanand Bhat

Copy Editor
Laxmi Subramanian

Indexer
Hemangini Bari

Editorial Team Leader
Aditya Belpathak

Project Team Leader
Lata Basantani

Project Coordinator
Rebecca Sawant

Proofreaders
Susan Stevens
Chris Smith

Graphics
Nilesh R. Mohite

Production Coordinator
Melwyn D'sa

Cover Work
Melwyn D'sa

About the Author

Jason Myrick is interested in testing and assessments and computer delivery methods for testing. He has spent many hours playing with Moodle and teaching colleagues how to deliver tests with it. He decided that instead of a piecemeal approach, he would write a book that contained the basics of how to use Moodle to deliver tests and assignments for assessment. He is currently developing a research proposal for a PhD in testing with a focus on computerized assessments.

I want to thank all the wonderful people at Packt Publishing for giving me the opportunity to write this book. This book would not have been possible without the work of Dilip, Vincila, Priya, and all the others who have helped me along the way.

I also want to thank my editors, Jac, Julian, and Meeta, for all the feedback they provided. It was through their comments and corrections that the book came to be what it is.

Finally, I want to thank my family and friends for their continued support.

About the Reviewers

Jac Gubbels is a Technology teacher currently working in Luanda International School (Angola). After acquiring a masters in Artificial Intelligence and a few years of working as a web developer, Jac has held teaching posts in international schools abroad combining teaching with the responsibility for educational technologies. His love and support for the free software movement has led him to adopt Moodle as platform of choice to set up Virtual Learning Environments. Jac originally comes from the Netherlands.

Nitin Parmar is responsible for exploring, promoting, and supporting the use of a range of e-learning tools at the University of Bath. He is particularly interested in the management of change within education with respect to the implementation of applications to support technology-enhanced learning and teaching.

For the majority of the 2009/10 academic year, Nitin's role encompassed the operational management of the institutional VLE, where he project-managed colleagues to deliver a high-quality professional service. Within this scope, he coordinated and delivered the first ever Moodle Development Plan and chaired the newly formed Moodle Advisory Group.

www.PacktPub.com

Support files, eBooks, discount offers and more

You might want to visit www.PacktPub.com for support files and downloads related to your book.

Did you know that Packt offers eBook versions of every book published, with PDF and ePub files available? You can upgrade to the eBook version at www.PacktPub.com and as a print book customer, you are entitled to a discount on the eBook copy. Get in touch with us at service@packtpub.com for more details.

At www.PacktPub.com, you can also read a collection of free technical articles, sign up for a range of free newsletters and receive exclusive discounts and offers on Packt books and eBooks.

http://PacktLib.PacktPub.com

Do you need instant solutions to your IT questions? PacktLib is Packt's online digital book library. Here, you can access, read and search across Packt's entire library of books.

Why Subscribe?

- Fully searchable across every book published by Packt
- Copy and paste, print and bookmark content
- On demand and accessible via web browser

Free Access for Packt account holders

If you have an account with Packt at www.PacktPub.com, you can use this to access PacktLib today and view nine entirely free books. Simply use your login credentials for immediate access.

Table of Contents

Preface

This book is a practical guide to testing in Moodle. You will initially learn to create different types of questions such as True/False, multiple choice, short answer, and so on. After you have learned how to create questions you will follow a step-by-step process to create complete tests by tweaking various options. Once you have gone through how to set up a complete Quiz, you will learn how to create and set up a Lesson, which can be used to create simple vocabulary or flash card tests or complex, multi-branched assignments.

Once you have finished with the Lesson module, you will learn to test and assess students through work submitted using the Workshop module. This module also provides an opportunity for self- and peer-assessment of student work. Once finished with Workshop, you will learn how to create a variety of skill-specific tests: listening, reading, speaking, and writing. After the skill-specific test section, you will learn how to set up and use Gradebook, Moodle's grading module.

By the end of this book, you should be familiar with a variety of ways to set up questions and test and assess your students using many of Moodle's modules and features.

What this book covers

Chapter 1, Testing with Moodle Quiz: In this chapter we will look at Moodle's Quiz module, introduce some of the main features, and learn to create True/False questions.

Chapter 2, Multiple Choice Quizzes: In this chapter we will continue to explore the Quiz module, develop multiple choice questions, and look at some question formatting issues.

Chapter 3, More Question Types: In this chapter we will look at all other question types available in the Moodle Quiz module, as well as how to create each one.

Chapter 4, Creating a Quiz: In this chapter we will learn how to create a complete quiz using the Quiz module, as well as use some new options.

Chapter 5, Using Lesson: In this chapter we will look at Moodle's Lesson module. We will look at the setup, details, and how to create a Lesson for use in your classes.

Chapter 6, Using Workshop: In this chapter we will look at the Workshop module. We will look at the setup, details, and how to create a Workshop for use in your classes.

Chapter 7, Listening Tests: In this chapter we will look at a variety of ways to test listening skills using Moodle. We will look at uploading audio files, adding listening tasks, and using Forums with audio.

Chapter 8, Testing Reading: In this chapter we will look at a variety of ways to test vocabulary and reading skills using Moodle. We will look at how to make a QuizPort reading test, creating timed readings, and how to make flashcards.

Chapter 9, Testing Speaking: In this chapter we will look at a variety of ways to test speaking skills using Moodle. We will look at Nanogongs, using Skype, and two new contributions, VoiceBoard and VoiceShadow.

Chapter 10, Testing Writing: In this chapter we will look at a variety of ways to test writing skills using Moodle. We will look at pre-writing activities, writing portfolios, and setting up writing assignments.

Chapter 11, Using Gradebook: In this chapter we will look at the Moodle Gradebook, how it is set up, used, and how to create one in your course.

What you need for this book

This book assumes that you have already successfully installed and set up a Moodle site for teaching. The version being used for this book is 1.9.7. It is intended for those with beginning to intermediate knowledge of Moodle.

Who this book is for

If you are a teacher, tutor, or Moodle Administrator who is responsible for developing and evaluating an online test using Moodle, or would like to utilize more features in Moodle for testing and assessment purposes, then this book is for you.

Conventions

In this book, you will find a number of styles of text that distinguish between different kinds of information. Here are some examples of these styles, and an explanation of their meaning.

New terms and **important words** are shown in bold. Words that you see on the screen, in menus or dialog boxes for example, appear in the text like this: "clicking the **Next** button moves you to the next screen".

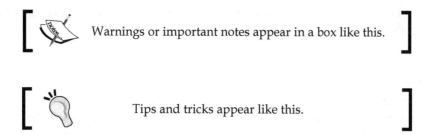

> Warnings or important notes appear in a box like this.

> Tips and tricks appear like this.

Reader feedback

Feedback from our readers is always welcome. Let us know what you think about this book—what you liked or may have disliked. Reader feedback is important for us to develop titles that you really get the most out of.

To send us general feedback, simply send an e-mail to feedback@packtpub.com, and mention the book title via the subject of your message.

If there is a book that you need and would like to see us publish, please send us a note in the **SUGGEST A TITLE** form on www.packtpub.com or e-mail suggest@packtpub.com.

If there is a topic that you have expertise in and you are interested in either writing or contributing to a book, see our author guide on www.packtpub.com/authors.

Customer support

Now that you are the proud owner of a Packt book, we have a number of things to help you to get the most from your purchase.

Errata

Although we have taken every care to ensure the accuracy of our content, mistakes do happen. If you find a mistake in one of our books—maybe a mistake in the text or the code—we would be grateful if you would report this to us. By doing so, you can save other readers from frustration and help us improve subsequent versions of this book. If you find any errata, please report them by visiting `http://www.packtpub.com/support`, selecting your book, clicking on the **errata submission form** link, and entering the details of your errata. Once your errata are verified, your submission will be accepted and the errata will be uploaded on our website, or added to any list of existing errata, under the Errata section of that title. Any existing errata can be viewed by selecting your title from `http://www.packtpub.com/support`.

Piracy

Piracy of copyright material on the Internet is an ongoing problem across all media. At Packt, we take the protection of our copyright and licenses very seriously. If you come across any illegal copies of our works, in any form, on the Internet, please provide us with the location address or website name immediately so that we can pursue a remedy.

Please contact us at `copyright@packtpub.com` with a link to the suspected pirated material.

We appreciate your help in protecting our authors, and our ability to bring you valuable content.

Questions

You can contact us at `questions@packtpub.com` if you are having a problem with any aspect of the book, and we will do our best to address it.

Testing with Moodle Quiz

1

Using computers to test is becoming commonplace. Computers are everywhere and they are able to speed up and do so many things that they have become necessary in many fields, and testing is no exception. The Moodle team has put together a variety of activities that allow us to create and deliver a variety of tests with ease, many of them graded automatically and with instant feedback, making Moodle Quiz a very useful tool.

In this chapter, we will:

- Talk briefly about testing
- Learn about the Quiz module
- Explore Basic options available with the Quiz module
- Explore True/False questions
- Make your True/False questions with the Quiz module

Moodle-based tests

Before going into a lot of detail about testing with Moodle, we need to ask the question, *What is a test?* A test is a series of questions or problems used to evaluate the abilities or skills of an individual or group. Pretty clear, right? There are all kinds of tests. There are aptitude tests, IQ tests, algebra tests, science experiments, and the list could go on and on. Achievement, cognitive, diagnostic, placement, and proficiency are all different kinds of tests in various fields. There are also different varieties of these tests: direct and indirect, discrete and integrated, norm- and criterion-referenced, objective and subjective tests. Tests!

Our purpose in this book is not to teach you about theories on what is a *good* test or how and why tests are important, although we will cover some important considerations related to computer-based testing later in the chapter?. Our goal here is to show you how to use Moodle for testing and offer a practical guide to doing it.

Now, if you are reading this book, chances are you are already using Moodle in some way in your classroom, school, or program. You will already understand some or many of the features Moodle has available for enabling administrators and educators to enhance classroom activities, improve the quality of education, and help student-teacher communication. Moodle also allows the teacher to set assignments anytime, allows students to upload files, allows for student-to-class communication, and so much more. The focus of this book is one of these *more's*. This book will help you understand how to use Moodle for testing and assessment and walk you through some of the features of Moodle that relate to testing and assessments.

Using Moodle to start testing your students will be a big change for them and for you. Some of the things you want to consider before making the change are as follows:

- What you are planning to test
- Item types that you plan on using
- Student access and familiarity with computers and the Internet
- Moodle experience
- Online learning experience
- Physical resources

The most important thing to keep in mind, regardless of the format your test takes, is that it is still a test. It needs to be developed, edited, revised, evaluated, and the student's answers need to be assessed just like a paper-based test. You need to give the students taking the test clear instructions and specific rules to follow, and you also need to make sure that the student understands how to use all the features you included in the test.

What is Moodle Quiz?

The Quiz module is one of the core components of the Moodle **VLE** (**Virtual Learning Environment**). It is intended to help the instructors to develop tests quickly and easily and offer computer-based tests to their students inside their Moodle course. There are many types of items available for use in the tests including: True/False, Multiple Choice, Short Answer, Essay, Embedded Answer, and several others.

Moodle Quiz is a powerful tool for instructors with the ability to offer tests via the course, as well as providing a range of tools that help to research and develop better questions. Moodle Quiz can provide immediate, teacher-created feedback, as well as allow students to immediately see their test scores for most item types.

I have downloaded and installed Moodle version 1.9.7 for this book and I created a no-frills, topic-based course that we will use as a model when developing our Moodle-based tests. I did this for two reasons. The first is simplicity and showing how things are built over time. An unused course is fresh and empty, and will allow me to show you what we are going to do and how it will look without anything else interfering. The second reason is that I need to explain how to show hidden items, and install contributed and third party modules and blocks in Moodle. I have made one small change to the course. I have changed the default theme to make some of the screenshots look better. If you want to change the theme of your site, and you have administrative privileges, go to **Site Administration | Appearance | Themes | Theme Selector** and you will see a list of available themes. So, while your course may have different themes or modules, you will have the same functionality as I do.

Creating our first questions

In this chapter, we are going to work with Moodle Quiz to develop our first questions in the Quiz module. If you have been using Quiz , this section might be a little basic for you; however, you may find some new ideas or explanations of Quiz functionality that you were unaware of. I would recommend reading through this part even if you are comfortable with Quiz, as all the tests we develop from here on out will be done using the information here and will not be reviewed later in the book.

We'll be walking through the steps I took to create our first questions in a moment. We will be looking at three basic functions in the Quiz module: the Question bank, quiz creation, and previewing.

Quiz features

Before we get into the making of a quiz, I want to point out some of the more important options available when creating a Quiz. First, we will take a look at the Quiz page as it looks when you first open it.

To create a new Quiz, you will need to go to your course page and click on the **Turn editing on** button. Once this is done, you will see two drop-down menus in each of the topics. The one on the left-hand side is titled **Add a resource** and the one on the right-hand side is **Add an activity**. Clicking on the **Add an activity** drop-down menu will display the activity options available. One of the activities is **Quiz**. Selecting the **Quiz** option will open the Adding a New Quiz page, the one we see in the next screenshot. Once you have finished looking it over, We'll talk about why each section exists and what each of them does.

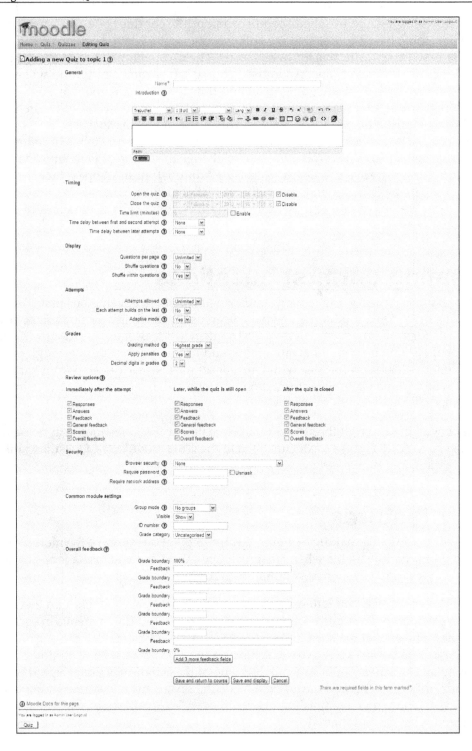

Don't worry! There is a lot of information there, and we are going to work through it together. You'll notice that there are nine basic fieldsets that can be modified. I want to describe them all to you now so we can begin the process with full knowledge of the possibilities in Quiz.

General

This section only has two separate fields, **Name** and **Introduction**. They are both simply explained, but very important for both students and teachers.

Name

While this may seem like a silly thing to mention, it isn't. The name of the quiz is important for several reasons. First, it allows the students to quickly and easily locate the quiz on the course page. The second reason is that the name of the test will mean much more a few weeks after it has been taken. A test called 'Test 4' doesn't mean as much to a student as 'Adding and Subtracting Fractions Quiz'. Finally, the score the student receives is recorded in the Moodle Gradebook with the same name, making it easier for the instructor and student to understand where he/she excelled or had troubles in the course.

It is important to note that overly long names can clutter the Gradebook display. You may want to view the Gradebook to see how the name has affected the view.

Introduction

This is the section where you can give instructions, explanations, as well as insert images, links, and tables. The person taking the test will only see the **Introduction** before the test starts, so this is also the only time before the test begins that you can give students last-minute advice or a reminder. The clearer this section is the better, so take your time when writing your introductions to your tests. This is also the place where you can communicate to your students what they need to study before taking the quiz.

Timing

This section allows you to set all the parameters related to the time frame for the test. You can set the time and date the student can access and take the test. If you don't have a specific time-frame in mind for the student to complete the test, in a self-directed study course, for example, you have the option to disable the time and date function. You are also able to determine the amount of time allowed for the test, and whether or not the student is allowed to take the test a second time. If you allow the student to take the test a second time, you can also set how much time they will need to wait until their second attempt.

Display

This option allows you to decide how many questions appear on each page of the test, or whether the test will simply be a scrolling single-page. It also allows you to give unique tests to all students by adding a bit of variety. This section allows you the option to shuffle question order, answer order, or both. In addition, inside individual questions, you have the option to override the option selected here.

Attempts

This option allows you to determine how many tries a student taking the test will get. It also allows you to create a test in which a student can work on the test, stop, and then come back to it later, starting where he/she left off. The final tool available in this section is what is termed Adaptive mode.

Adaptive mode is an interesting feature. It creates a **Submit** button next to each question, which when clicked, gives the answer and feedback to the student. If the student answers a question incorrectly, he/she can be given the same question again or asked a variation on the question. This question can either be a completely new form, such as going from a Multiple-choice item to a True/False one, or something simpler like rewording the question. In addition, we can apply penalties to adaptive items. For example, if a student answers a question incorrectly and is given an alternative one, he/she will lose a percentage of his/her grade. This happens each time they incorrectly respond to the question. This is a powerful tool and something that we will be using when we make our last test.

Grades

This option allows you to decide how to grade the student, basing grades on either the highest score, the first or last attempt, or the average of each of the student's attempts. It also allows you to apply penalties to adaptive tests based on the number of attempts made on the question. There is also an option that allows you to set the decimal place for the score if desired.

Review options

This section is built into Quiz for feedback purposes. It gives you the option of allowing students to see their responses, the correct answers, their grade, and teacher feedback. This option is also used to control when that feedback is given, it can either be immediate or delayed. Depending on your needs, there are a lot of options available here.

Security

This fieldset details security measures that can be taken in Moodle. It allows the teacher to add an additional layer of test protection by opening a browser with no navigation options. This will help stop cheating in some ways by not allowing students any browser options. It also has the capability of limiting access to the test by requiring a password or a specified IP Address. For example, if you want to make sure the test was taken in the school computer lab, you could use this feature.

While these two options are useful in some ways for stopping cheaters, they are not going to stop it all. Savvy students will be able to do things that, unfortunately, we cannot prevent. Ideally, high-stakes tests will be done in class, or in an environment that allows for proctors and student monitoring.

Common module settings

This section allows you to set up groups in a course, if you feel that is appropriate. You can have everyone in the class in the same group, or divide them however you see fit, for example, by level. Whichever method you choose, either using the option or not, will carry over to all aspects of the quiz.

Overall Feedback

This section lets you give a set feedback to the students. You are able to set grade parameters, say 90 percent to 100 percent, and if the student's score falls between those scores, they will receive the message you enter. This feedback is the same for all students taking the test. You are also given the option of adding additional feedback should you want to offer more comments based on a narrower range of student results.

All of these sections have default settings in place, one that many people find works for them. However, it is important for you to think about your needs and what you want from the test. Do you need to know whether a student is able to solve the equation in five minutes? Do you require that the student gets every question correct, no matter how many attempts it takes? It is impossible for me to know your situation, but think carefully about the choices you make in this section and your reasons for making them, because once the students begin working on the Quiz, you can't adjust the settings.

Creating a Quiz

Now, let's get down to business and create our first Quiz.

Step 1

The first thing that needs to be done is to make sure that you have all the editing and administrative access required to create and edit things in the course you are using. You should see a **Turn editing on** or **Turn editing off** button in the upper right-hand side corner, similar to the next image, if you have editing rights in the course:

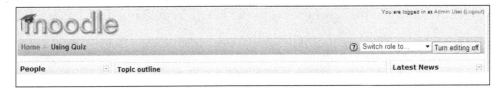

Once you have confirmed that you are able to add activities to the course, click on **the Turn editing on** button.

Step 2

Once the toggle is changed to **Turn editing on**, you will see two drop-down menus, one called **Add a resource** and one named **Add an activity** in each **Week** or **Topic** section of the course. The Quiz module is found under the **Add an activity** drop-down menu as seen in the next screenshot:

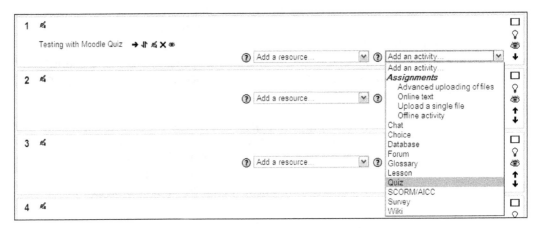

Once you have opened the Quiz module, you should see something like the following screenshot. I showed you a full page shot earlier, but you'll only see this part of the screen when you open the module.

Step 3

This is where we begin to add information and create the test. The first thing you see is the **General** section. Here, we will enter the name of the test and a brief introduction to the quiz. We will call the test **My First Quiz**. Under **Introduction**, we will write what the quiz is about:

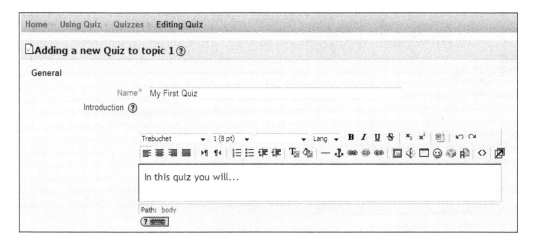

For the time being, we are not going to make any changes to the Timing, Display, or anything else. Our goal here is to show you how to set up the most basic test using the Quiz module. After entering the **Introduction**, scroll down to the bottom of the page and you will see three buttons: **Save and return to course**, **Save and display**, and **Cancel**. Click on the **Save and display** button.

Save and return to course

This option will save the test and bring you to the front page of your course.

Save and display

This option will show you what questions are in the test now.

Cancel

This option will clear any changes and erase the test unless you have saved it previously. It will also bring you back to the front page of your course.

Editing

You always have the option of going back in the test and making changes, which is done with the **Update this Quiz** button located in the upper right-hand side corner of the Quiz **Edit** tab, as you will see in the next image. So, if you decide that you want to change the name of the test, the test date, or other settings later, you can. For example, I've decided I don't like the name of the quiz I made, so I am going to change the name of My First Quiz to Testing with Moodle.

Step 4

Now that we have edited the name of the test, written a brief introduction, and clicked on **Save and display**, we have been taken to the **Editing Quiz** page. This page shows the **Question bank** on the right-hand side, where all the questions available are stored and where we can create new ones. On the left-hand side, we see the questions that are currently part of the test.

Note the **Update this Quiz** button on right-hand side of the screen. Clicking on it will bring you back to the Updating Quiz page where you can make changes to the global Quiz settings.

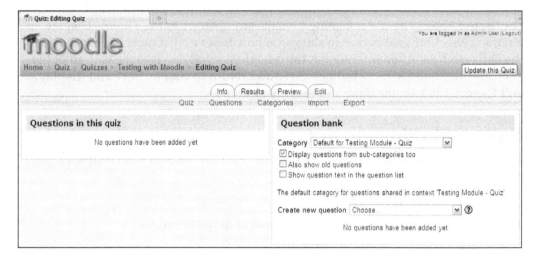

As you can see, there are several tabs, as shown in the previous screenshot: **Info**, **Results**, **Preview**, and **Edit**. Each of the tabs has a variety of options, which can help in many ways.

Info

Opening this tab will show information about the test. It will show us the test name, the introduction, the grading method, and a link to preview the test.

Results

As you can imagine, this is where we can look at the test results. We are able to see the general overview of the results on the first page. The other options available are **Regrade**, which allows us to go in and alter the grades; **Manual Grade**, which disables computer grading and allows us to go in and assign grades to everything; and **Item Analysis**, which gives us a variety of ways to look at the responses and analyze the quiz data.

Preview

This tab does as its name implies, it allows us to preview the entire test. We are able to see all the questions, look at the format of each question, take the test, and see the results, although, as a teacher, nothing is recorded. We go here to make sure there are no mistakes and everything is as it should be before we have our students take the test. Preview is a very useful tool and something I use every time I make a test in Moodle, and I hope you will use it for every test you make in Quiz too.

Edit

In the **Edit** tab that we are using, you can see **Quiz**, **Questions**, **Categories**, **Import**, and **Export**. We are currently looking at the **Quiz heading** and under this option, we can see the questions that have been added to the test and the bank of available questions to be added. As mentioned earlier, I specifically created this course because I wanted to build it up together with you; therefore, there are no questions in the bank yet. However, when we add questions, we will return here and talk more about some additional functions of the Question bank.

Under the **Question bank**, located at **Home | Quiz | Quizzes | Testing** with **Moodle | Editing Quiz** in the **Breadcrumbs** tab, you can see **Category** with its drop-down menu and several options related to what questions will be seen and how they will be displayed. You can also see the **Create New Question**, with its associated drop-down menu. This is what we are going to be working with now. We'll get back to the other functions once we have some questions built into the bank!

Now, before we move on, we need to know what a Question bank is. The Question bank is where all the questions available in the Quiz are made. The Question Bank allows you to make a variety of questions and edit and preview them. All the questions made in the Question bank are stored at the course level, but they can be made available for use site-wide, course-wide, or quiz Question bank specific, depending on your needs.

Step 5

Expanding the **Create New Question** drop-down will show the list of all the question types available. I'm going to briefly describe each of them for you, but for the first quiz, we will be using **True/False**, which is highlighted in the next screenshot:

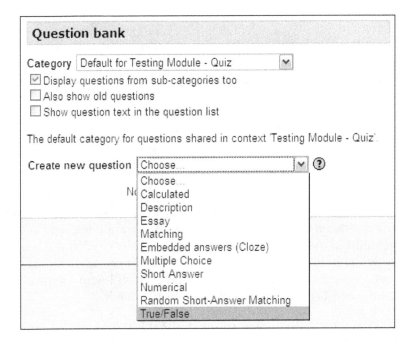

Item choices

We have looked at the general options available in the quiz module, but even more important are the question types. There are ten item types available in Quiz. The item choice you select for your test should be something that the students are familiar with and one that is appropriate to the subject material.

Calculated

These item types are particularly valuable to math and science teachers. They allow the teacher to input questions that need to be solved using a calculation. The teacher writes a formula in Moodle, adds a set of specific variables, and Moodle can draw on the variables to produce questions. This is a great tool, but it does have its limits. There are only certain types of calculations it is able to handle: many single-variable and a few multi-variable ones. This particular item type is a bit more complicated than some, because a formula needs to be input, but once you get the hang of formulating these types of questions, the process is fairly easy.

Description

These item types are not really questions, and they have no response options or grade component. They allow the instructor to add a piece of text, image, audio, or video related to questions that follow it in the test. Many people use Description questions for reading comprehension, graph or chart interpretation, and art-related questions.

Essay

This is the essay writing option included in Quiz, and mainly is used for open-ended responses. The student is required to read a prompt and write a response. The response can be written either in the test itself or in a separate word-processor and copy and pasted in, depending on your needs. This type of question is not graded by Moodle and requires you to read it and assign an appropriate mark based on whatever criteria you are using. You are also able to give individual feedback after reading the essay.

Matching

This option is the traditional matching item type. Students are given a list of items they need to match with another set. The questions and answers are placed in a mixed order. The answers are given in drop-down menus on the right-hand side of the screen. The results are marked by Moodle. If some answers are correct and some are wrong, Moodle will give a partial result based on the number of correct and incorrect matches.

Embedded Answers (Cloze)

This option is a fun item to work with. Using this item type, you can create a variety of fill-in-the-blank type questions and variations on multiple-choice questions. Cloze can handle numeric and written responses, and even allows hyperlinks to function inside of it. Embedded Answers (Cloze) however, isn't the easiest of the item types to use. It requires very simple coding to make the items look the way you want. The coding, which we will be demonstrating later, is fairly simple and limited to a few specific commands. Take it from me, a guy with only the most basic skills in this area, it's a breeze to learn. These questions are scored automatically by Moodle based on the parameters you set, so we need to be careful here and make sure we haven't made any mistakes.

Multiple Choice

This option is one of the most commonly used of the Quiz item types. It is easy to create quizzes with, allows for many different types of questions from text to image-based, and is familiar and easy to use. Questions can be made with single correct responses or multiple ones, and you can create any number of possible responses for each question. Responses can be shuffled, points can be awarded for multiple possible answers, penalties included for incorrect responses, and feedback given for individual items.

Short Answer

This is a fill-in-the-blank type of item. You create a question and the student must type in the correct answer. This item type can be a good tool for a variety of Test. Vocabulary and spelling are commonly tested using this item type, however there are multiple applications. You can include case sensitivity and what Moodle terms 'wildcards', search terms, which allow you to accept a variety of responses that include one of the set 'wildcard' phrases. For example, if students in an English language program were required to answer a question with the word 'color', you might add a wildcard with 'colour', since both spellings are considered correct.

Numerical

These questions are similar to questions of the 'short answer' type in that the student is required to type in a response The only difference is that with the Numerical item type, the answer needs to be a number. You may set a correct answer as an exact-only response, or you may allow anything that falls within a given set of numbers to be accepted. Again, like in Short Answer, the answer you expect might be 4.33, but you could make 4.3 or 4.35 acceptable answers, as well.

Random Short-Answer Matching

This item type looks just like Matching items to students, the difference is where the items are taken from. These items randomly take questions from the pool of Short Answer questions available in the category and mix up the answers to provide a matching-type question. This is a randomly generated test; therefore, students taking the test at the same time will not necessarily have the same questions. In addition, this type of item can be used as a test several times and, assuming the Question bank is large enough, students will be presented with a different test each time. This item type is also a way for you to have students review past material in no specific order or emphasis on the topic.

True/False

This is a simplified Multiple Choice item. Students are given a statement, question, reading, or some other prompt and asked to respond with either True or False. These tests have the advantage of being simple and fast to make, as well as helping with review situations. The drawback being, students have a high chance of guessing the correct answer without really knowing it.

These are all the item types Moodle has available in the Quiz module. There are also a few other question types available from third parties but they are not part of the core system.

Now, I'd like to continue showing you how to create a simple quiz using questions of the True/False type.

The True/False item creation screen is shown in the next screenshot:

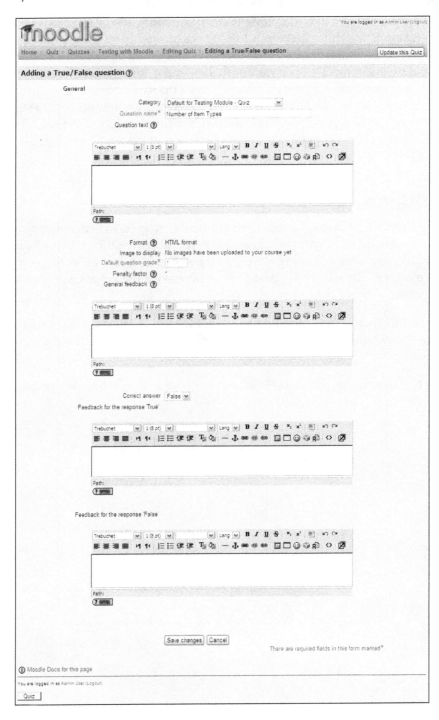

Each question type will contain several decisions for you to make. True/False is the simplest and has the fewest number of options, which is one of the reasons we are starting with it.

Options in True/False

As you can see from the previous screenshot, in True/False we are limited in the number of things that we can do. However, some of these options do carry over into other item types. A brief explanation of the information and options available in True/False is as follows.

Category

This drop-down menu tells us where the questions will be saved. When making tests in multiple courses, it is important to know where the questions can be found. Also, you may want to use some of these questions on a different test, so knowing the location of specific questions can be important. If you want to change the category the question is in, you can do so at a later time.

Question name

Simply put, this option is where you write the name of the question. The name can be of any length, although, only the first 256 characters are stored in the database.

Question text

This option is where you enter the text of your question. You may include images and links, as well. You can also adjust the font size and style. Remember, this text is what the students taking the test will see, so make sure it is of good quality and an appropriate font and size for them.

Format

This area is preset in the Quiz. You do have the option to change it, depending on how you are entering text and the browser you use. Moodle recommends that you leave the setting as it is. Beginning to intermediate users should ignore this setting, because, whichever setting it is on will work for what you are doing.

Image to display

If you have added any images to your course, you will be able to see which one will be displayed in the question. You can see in my course that I have yet to upload any images, so the screen states that **'No images have been uploaded to your course yet'**.

Penalty factor

This option is the number of points that will be deducted for each incorrect answer. However, the 'penalty factor' only applies when the question is used in a quiz using adaptive mode, that is, where the student is allowed multiple attempts at a question even within the same attempt at the quiz. If the penalty factor is more than zero, then the student will lose that proportion of the maximum grade for each successive attempt. For example, if the default question grade is 10, and the penalty factor is 0.2, then each successive attempt after the first one will incur a penalty of
0.2 x 10 = 2 points.

General feedback

Here is where the teacher can give some advice, background, or anything else related to the question asked. This option is often used to help the student understand what was being asked, to give some additional information, or some background. The student will not see the feedback until after the question has been answered. This feedback is shown to all students, regardless of their response. If this option is left empty, there will be no general teacher feedback.

Correct answer

Here is where the correct answer is selected from the drop-down menu. Since we are using True/False, you can choose either True or False. Clicking on your choice will display the correct response in the drop-down window.

Feedback for the response 'True'

Here you can give specific feedback to students who answered 'True'. If the answer is correct, it could be praise. If the answer is incorrect, it could be an explanation as to why it is incorrect. This option can be a very useful tool for teachers to give specific information to students regarding important course information. This option does not need to be filled in. If it is left blank, there will simply be no teacher-given feedback for that question.

Feedback for the response 'False'

This is identical to the **Feedback for the response 'True'** section except it relates to an answer of 'False'.

Step 6

Let's begin actually making the question now. We already have the page open, so from here, our first thing to deal with is the category. I am going to keep mine where it is because all the questions I am going to use are associated with the course I created; therefore, I'll use the **Course** setting. If you wanted the question available to a larger or smaller group, for example, all teachers using Moodle for just this Quiz, choose that setting.

Now we decide on the name of the question and what the question will ask. Curly decided to ask about the number of item types in Quiz, so I think I'll name my question Number of Item Types in Quiz.

Naming Your Questions:

When naming a question, it is much better to give it a name that makes it quick and easy to identify. Questions with names like 'Question 11' or 'Q4' are not very helpful. For instance, if you are testing vocabulary, the word being tested is a good option for the question name. You may also want to include a 'command' term like identify, evaluate, and others.

Once I have entered the name of the question and the text of the question in the appropriate places, I'll scroll down to just under the Question text, where I can see the **Format** option, images in the question, penalty points, for the correct response, and the **General feedback** area. I'm going to keep all of these the same for now and add some brief comments in the general feedback area.

Under the general feedback option, is a drop-down, which allows us to choose whether the response is **True** or **False**. After selecting the appropriate choice (I'm not telling what it is yet, you are going to have to try and guess!), move down to the True and False feedback options.

In both True and False, I enter some feedback. Once I have finished all my work, I go back to the top of the page and check to make sure everything is correct. Once this is done, at the bottom of the page, I click on the **Save changes** button.

After saving the question

Once the question has been saved, we are sent back to the page where all this started. Take a look at the **Question bank** area of the **Edit** tab. You will see here that the question has been saved and is now available to be added to the test. You will notice that the newly made question has a gray background, which makes it stand out and easy to find.

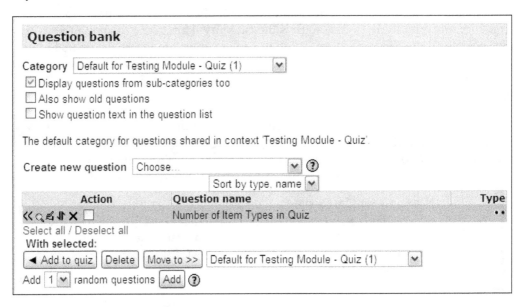

Question Options

Just under the **Create new question** drop-down, all of our newly available options for manipulating the question can be seen. Information and options about the question itself is displayed in three separate columns: **Action**, **Question name**, and **Type**.

Sort

This drop-down, directly under **Create new question**, allows you to determine how you are going to view your questions. You have three options here, Sort by name, type, or age. While this isn't that useful to us now, because we only have one question, later on it will become apparent how useful this option can be, especially when you are working in courses with hundreds of questions.

Action

This bar has five icons and a checkbox. These symbols are, in fact, buttons. You can use them to perform a variety of functions with the question they are associated with.

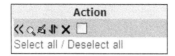

Add to quiz

This function will move your question into the quiz list.

Preview

This button will show you the question as it will look in your browser. It is useful, in that it gives you a way to check the question quickly to make sure everything is as it should be.

Edit

This button serves as an edit question button. It allows you to go in and make changes to the question if there are any problems.

Move

This button allows you to move the question to a different category. For example, if the question was in Course, but you wanted it to be in System, you could move it there.

Delete

This button is dangerous! It can completely delete any question you have entered. If you really want to get rid of the question, this is the button to use. Don't worry, if you make a mistake and click on it accidently, you will be prompted to confirm that you really want to erase it. Once you have deleted a question, you can't get it back.

Select

This button is useful in several ways. It allows you to select multiple questions to delete, move, or add to the test. Additionally, the check in the box makes it easy to see which questions you are working with.

Select all/Deselect all

Select all/Deselect all options are just below the single button actions. This feature allows you to choose all the questions in your Question bank to work with, as well as giving you the option to clear all the questions you selected and start over.

Below the **Select all/Deselect all** feature, there are three buttons that allow you to manipulate multiple questions. These buttons function just like the single button features mentioned previously, but they will allow you to add all the selected questions to the test, delete all the selected questions, or move them all to a different area. The **Move to** button has a drop-down menu alongside it, making it easy to select where you want to move the questions to. First select the destination, then click on the **Move to** button.

Question Name

Just like the title implies, this entry shows you what the question is called. A good naming scheme will save you hours in the long run, so start out with one.

Question Type

This part displays the type of question you are working with. Some of the icons are not immediately recognizable, but moving your pointer over them will show you what kind they are. Once you have used this module enough, these little icons will help you determine quickly what you are working with and help you discriminate between questions with similar names, but of different types. This is something you will encounter often.

Adding Questions to the Quiz

Now that we have the question in the Question bank, we're going to use one of the icons just mentioned. We're going to use the **Add to quiz** function. After we add the previously created question to the quiz, the **Questions in this quiz** section appears, as shown in the following screenshot:

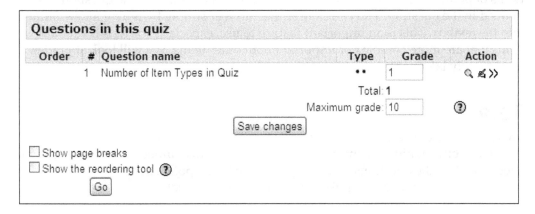

Looking at this, we can see a few new options.

Order

While you can see nothing here now, this is because there is only one question in the quiz. Once we add more questions, you will see up and down arrows. These arrows allow you to move the question position to a higher or lower place in the quiz.

#(Number)

This option shows the numeric order of the item in the test. The first item under '#' shows that this is the first item in the test.

Question Name

Here, we are able to see the question name, which allows us to confirm whether we moved the correct question to the test.

Question Type

We are also able to see the type of question it is, which helps us quickly determine the type of question and keep things organized. Also, placing your mouse over the icon will show its function, in case you have forgotten.

Grade

This entry allows us to set the number of points each question will be worth. The number entered into the textbox is how much this particular question is worth in terms of points in the test. By default, this number is the same as the question grade defined in the question. You can change this number simply by typing a new number into the textbox. This is an important feature to use, especially for tests containing items that are more complex or important than other items. We will look at grades more closely later in the book.

Total

This number shows the total possible points from questions in the test. You are not able to directly manipulate this number. If you want this number to change, you will need to look at the questions and make a change in the points assigned to each of them. Do not forget to click on **Save changes** after doing so!

Maximum Grade

This text box contains is the maximum possible points a student will be able to get in the test. This feature helps in grade scaling. You are able to adjust this value simply by typing a new number in the box. For example, if you give a weekly vocabulary quiz, and each quiz needs to be worth 5 percent of the student's grade, you might want to put a "5" in the box. Even if you have ten questions in the test, this option will scale the score to a maximum five-point total, so each question would be worth 0.5 points.

Action

There are three buttons here, each of which is the same as explained previously. There is a **Preview**, **Edit**, and **Move**.

Show Page Breaks and Show Reordering Tools

This function allows you to put pages into the quiz. If this option is selected, the **Questions in this quiz** pane will be divided. Once you select the **Show Page Breaks**, you will see a drop-down menu that allows you to set the number of questions that will be added to each page. Select the number you want and click on the **Go** button. You will now see that the quiz has been divided into a number of pages with each having the selected number of items. You are free to adjust the number of items per page later by using the **Move** icon located next to the Page Break line. You also have the option to delete the page breaks if you want.

Items Per Page
You should never have more than 10 items per page. This helps reduce the risk of page timeouts.

Since we only have one question right now, we'll get back to that function when we have a few more entries.

As seen previously, we can change the order of questions by clicking on the **Move** icon. However, if we enable the **Show Reordering Tool** option, we will see a new textbox under the **Order** column, on the left-hand side of the **Move** icons. Each of the boxes will contain a number ending in a "0", for example: 40, 100, 250. You can move items around quickly by placing the numbers in the boxes into an order you want. So, if you wanted to move a question with the number 50 to a spot between 20 and 30, you would simply need to enter some number between 20 and 30. Once you move the items, the numbers will automatically reset. You can move the items around this way as often as necessary.

If you decide to change any of the information, make sure you click on the **Save changes** button. If you don't, any work you did will be gone!

Preview the Test

What we want to do now is take a look at the question to see how it looks, and to give it one final review, which includes making sure that the answer is correct.

We can click on the **Preview** icon in the **Questions in this Quiz** pane to see the question. This action will create a pop-up window, as shown in the following screenshot:

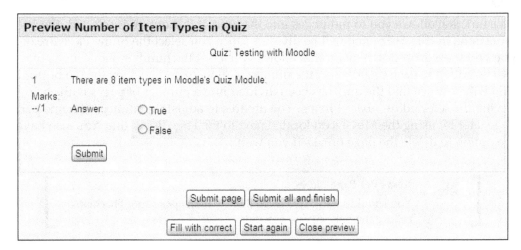

In the preview, we can see several pieces of information related to the question.

Question Name

At the very top of the pop-up window, you can see the question name.

Quiz Name

Just below the question name, you can see the quiz that the question is associated with.

Question

The question is displayed next. It includes the number of the question, the question text, the possible responses, and the point value assigned to the question.

Submit

This button allows the student to submit each answer as he/she finishes the question. It allows the student to immediately know if he/she got the answer correct or not. This feedback can be a useful feature, especially in tests that are completed over a period of time. However, in longer or timed tests, these buttons may be a problem because students might spend valuable test time reviewing their choices and not moving forward in the quiz. These buttons can be removed by going to the **Attempts** section in **Update Quiz** and selecting **No** in Adaptive mode.

Submit page

If you have multiple questions, and you have decided to use the Show Page Breaks option, this button will allow you to complete the questions and see the results for the page you are working on.

Submit all and finish

This button will allow you to submit all the questions in the quiz at once and close the test.

Fill with correct

This function will mark all the correct answer choices in the quiz. This is a useful function for teachers, because it helps make sure that the answers are correct without having to work through, or read, the items.

Start again

This feature will allow you to begin again. It will erase all selections made and move you to the beginning of the test.

Close preview

This option will close the Preview panel and you will return to the **Edit** page for the Quiz.

Now, let's attempt the question in Preview mode. I'll move my mouse over the checkboxes and choose the correct answer by clicking on them. How much do you remember about the Quiz? Look at the question, **There are 8 item types in Moodle's Quiz Module**. Is the **Answer True** or **False**?

I'll make my selection, and let's see the results.

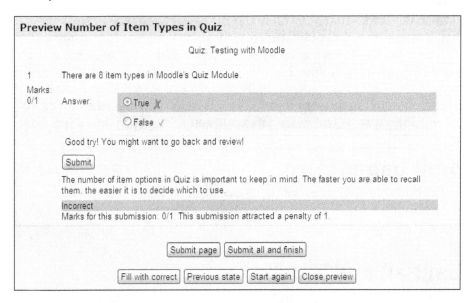

Now, we can see here that we have selected **True**, which is the wrong answer. The answer choice is highlighted, and there is a red **X** next to it. The correct answer has a green check beside it. This is what the students will see if the Adaptive mode is enabled.

Under the True and False radio buttons, , you can see that the feedback entered for an incorrect response has appeared. There button is another **Submit** button. This allows the student to change his/her answer if multiple attempts with a True/False test is allowed. This means that they only have to click on the other choice to get a correct response.

You can also see under the **Submit** button a message telling me the response was incorrect and the marks I received for this remained zero. The penalties applied note simply means that I will lose one point from the total possible in the test.

You also notice a new function has appeared at the bottom of the page, a button called **Previous state**. This functions as a Back button, allowing you to move back one step. This is useful if you are working through a set of questions and want to see how feedback is displayed, based on the response. This button is obviously only available in the teacher-preview mode.

Now, I'm going to select the correct response, so you can see how it would look.

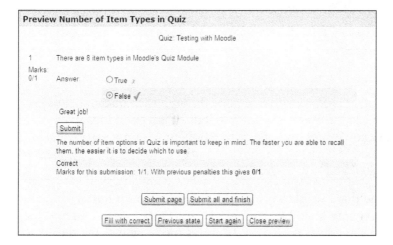

As you can see, I received both the correct answer and general feedback, and I was given one point for the answer. Note that the **Marks** in the preview under the question number didn't change. This is because we are in our second attempt. If we wanted the mark to be shown correctly, we would need to click on the **Previous state** button, which would mark this question correctly.

Step 7

Now that we have confirmed that the question is correct, we repeat the process. You can add as many questions as you like to the test, but for now, we're going to make four more. Here is how the entire test looks from the **Editing** tab with the new questions added.

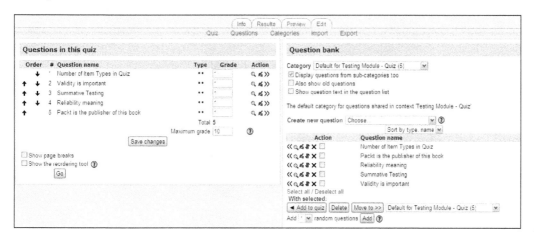

Take a quick look at **Order** in the **Questions in this Quiz** section. See the Up and Down arrows? These are the **Move** icons mentioned earlier.

Now that we have all the questions we want in place, we are ready to move on.

Step 8

Now, I know that we have already gone through each question, but just to make sure everything is just the way we want it to look, it is a good idea to sit down and take the test. Here you might find one or two hopefully minor errors that you overlooked earlier. We need to click on the **Preview** tab at the top of the page and we will see how the test looks from a student's point of view.

I have decided that I want to get rid of the small **Submit** buttons next to the questions. I'm going to go back to **Update this Quiz** button and find the **Attempts** section. Then, I'm going to turn off Adaptive mode by moving the choice to **No**. This means that whoever takes this test will need to answer all the questions and they will get their results at the end when they click on **Submit all and finish**.

We are only offering a single attempt at this quiz, but leaving on the Adaptive mode would allow the student to answer each question multiple times, even in a quiz with single attempt. This setting would also apply a penalty, if one were set, to the marks for each question incorrectly answered. Our updated test is shown in the following screenshot:

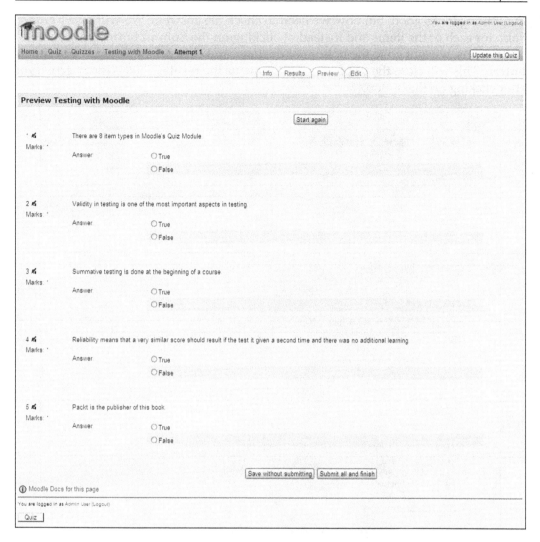

As you can see, changing the **Adaptive mode** option to **No** got rid of the **Submit** buttons and made the test look a little less cluttered compared to the earlier screenshot.

Careful with Arrow Keys

Arrow keys are really useful in navigating, but when you are taking a test in **Quiz**, they can move your selection. If you have selected an answer and it is still highlighted, and you click on the Down Arrow key for example, your answer will be changed. Make sure your students are aware of this!

Everything looks good, but now we need to check the answers. We will select True/ False for each of the items and instead of clicking on the **Submit** button next to each of the items, we will go to the bottom of the page and click on the **Save all and finish button**. This will close the test for us, and show us the results. This is the page we get after clicking on the button.

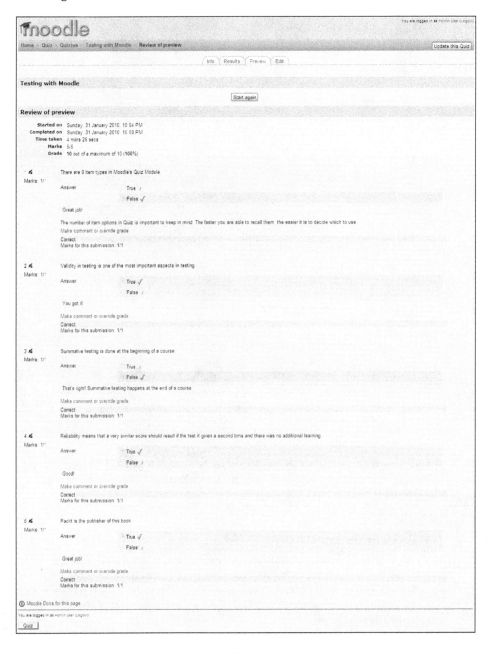

As you can see, all the answers are correct, and each received the proper number of points and feedback.

> **Teachers, Groups, and Quizzes**
>
> As a teacher, your marks will not be recorded when you are previewing the quiz. However, if you have added yourself as a teacher to a group, your results will be stored, even though you are a teacher. This action will prevent further testing of the quiz.

Also, look at the top left-hand side of the page. There is a small information section called **Review of preview**. This is a lot of very useful information. The information here tells us when the quiz was started, when it was completed, and the total time the person was taking the quiz. As the test developer, you are able to look at the time taken and possibly make decisions about how to time the test in the future. If the quiz time is simply too long, you might be able to cut some questions. If it is too short, you can create more. In addition, students will see this section once they finish the quiz.

You are also shown the number of points scored and the grade. These numbers are probably some of the most important pieces of information for most teachers, since we need this to ensure that all the correct responses are given the correct point value.

That is all there is to making a simple True/False test in Moodle Quiz. Now all that needs to be done is to make sure your students know where the test is and have them take it.

Your turn

Now that I've shown you how to create a True/False quiz, it's your turn to give it a try. I'm going to give you three statements and I want you to make a True/False quiz using them. The three statements are as follows:

1. Mice are smaller than cats.
2. Cats are smaller than dogs.
3. Dogs are bigger than horses.

Step 1

Go to the front page of your course and turn editing on by going to the upper right-hand side of the page. Make a new Quiz by going to the **Add an activity** drop-down in any of the topic sections and selecting **Quiz**.

Step 2

Now you will need to name the quiz and give it an introduction. Please call the quiz **My First Moodle Quiz** and repeat the name in the **Introduction** textbox.

Step 3

We are going to leave all the default settings as they are, except for one. We want to go down the page and locate the **Attempts** section. In this section, please find and turn off the **Adaptive mode**.

When you have done this, scroll down to the bottom of the page and click on the **Save and Display** button.

Step 4

We should now be in our quiz question creation area. Go to the category and change it to **Default** for **My First Moodle Quiz**. This will help us keep all our questions organized.

Once you have done this, find the **Create a new question** drop-down and select True/False.

Step 5

We will need to fill in all the required fields now. For Question name and Question text, enter **Mice are smaller than cats**. For correct answer, select **True**.

We will also include some feedback here. In the **Feedback for Response True** enter **Yes, mice are smaller than cats**. **In the Feedback for Response False** enter **Sorry, but cats are bigger than mice**.

Step 6

Scroll to the bottom of the page and click on **Save changes**.

Step 7

Repeat the process for the remaining two questions, including appropriate feedback for each.

Step 8

When you have all three questions created, move them to the quiz using the **Add to quiz** icon.

Step 9

Go to the **Preview** tab and look over the questions to make sure there are no mistakes. Answer all the questions correctly and then click on **Submit all and finish**.

When you finish all these steps, you should see the following screenshot:

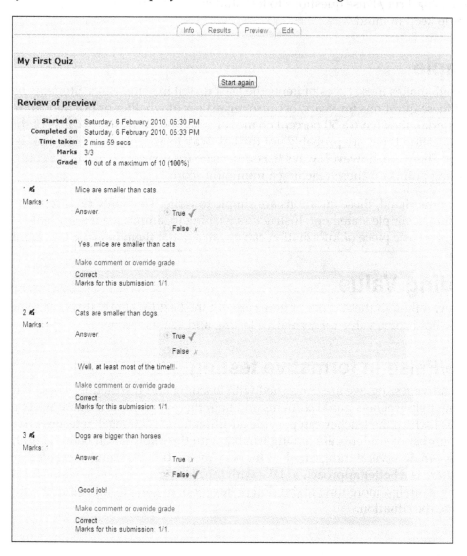

From here, you can see that I was able to put all the questions together into a quiz, the answers are all correct, and the score I received was a **100** %. You can also see the feedback each student receives from the correct answer.

I hope you were able to quickly and easily complete this little project. As I said before, if you were unsure of something, or got something other than I did, go back and review the chapter and make sure you followed all the steps outlined previously.

Testing with True/False

When using True/False questions to test students, there are a few assessment-related issues to keep in mind.

Simple

The math makes these types of items the least useful in some ways. Students have loved these questions for years, because regardless of whether or not they know the material, they have a 50 percent chance of guessing correctly. Because of this, these question types are probably not the best way to ask things in high-stakes types of tests. There are, however, ways to compensate for this problem, such as only awarding points for those reaching a minimum score.

On the other hand, these questions are simple to write. They only require, at minimum, a simple statement. Instructors wishing to simply see if a student is aware of a basic piece of information can create a list of them in just a few minutes.

Finding Value

Now, even though these types of items are not the best for summative assessment, they do hold some value for formative testing and self-assessment.

True/False in formative testing

In formative testing, we are concerned with teaching and instruction. These kinds of tests can help teachers guide students and help them determine student weaknesses or areas i which the teacher can provide additional instructions. If a teacher notices a large number of students are having trouble with the information being taught, the teacher can do several things: look at the way the material is being presented and see if there is a better approach to take with the class, give review sessions for those needing it, assign more time to the skill in question, or something else that will likely improve the situation.

By creating True/False tests in Moodle, which are fast and easy to produce, it is simple to create more formative tests, giving teachers an even easier way of checking on student progress. In addition, the use of the shuffle question and random question functions, which will be looked at later, allow any questions from the bank to be used. By creating a category based on a specific skill, you can load it with any questions you have based around that skill and Moodle will randomly generate tests for you. Assuming you are using the same types of questions focused on the same skill, you will be able to use the Quiz reporting tool to help you see any student improvement in that skill area.

Self-assessment

Self-assessment is about learning. It is about finding which areas you are weak in and working on improving them. Teachers that use this kind of activity are attempting to make their students become active and independent learners. Using True/False questions is a useful way to help students with this type of assessment. If you prepare a review quiz in Moodle using True/False question types, students can quickly see what they know and don't know. This knowledge will help dedicated learners decide how best to spend their time and energy.

Weaknesses in True/False

Even with the ability to compensate somewhat for guessing, with a 50 percent chance of guessing the correct answer at random, True/False itself is not the most effective item type available. In addition, students have no choice but to guess even if they don't know the answer. In fact, even if they don't want to answer because they know they don't know the answer, they are forced to either avoid clicking on either response option, or if they accidentally do click on an answer, make a guess. This situation is not all bad though, because there are some who argue that this process will force students to think carefully before selecting an answer. The problem is that there is no way to remove a response completely once one has been selected. An inclusion of a feature that would allow students to 'pass' if they didn't want to answer, I feel, would be a great addition. It could help in assessment and validity issues related to testing in Moodle.

Summary

In this chapter, we learned how to create True/False questions with the Quiz module. This introduction was, hopefully, an easy first step in learning how to use Quiz. We looked at many of the options available in generating a Quiz, using the Question bank, and we looked at every option available when creating a True/False item.

You should now be comfortable in making True/False questions in Quiz; however, I would like to caution you again about using these too often or for too many things. As mentioned earlier, these types of questions can be good for homework and review, because they are easy to develop and produce, and the results are easy to analyze. They are also useful as self-assessment tools, allowing students to see what they know and what they don't, quickly and easily. Students who are active learners and understand how to do self-assessment, will look at their results and make changes in their study habits or focus on the areas where they see a gap in their learning.

2
Multiple Choice Quizzes

Multiple choice is the second item type we will be looking at. It is one of the most common items found in tests today, and they have been a big part of small-scale and standardized tests since their inception. They are a common item type across a variety of subjects and fields, and from the sciences to the humanities, tests are filled with these types of questions. Moodle Quiz has them as well, and the majority of tests I've seen developed, for self-study, review, and assessment in Moodle are of this type exclusively, or contain a large number of them.

In this chapter, we will:

- Look at Multiple Choice questions
- Use some of the more advanced options available in Quiz
- See a Multiple Choice test in Quiz

Getting started

I hope you remember what we did in the previous chapter, but if you don't, do not worry. We need to get to the Question bank, as in Chapter 1. and Question Editing pages. One quick way to do this is through the Course Admin Menu. There is a link titled **Questions**, which will bring you to the correct place. All of the steps I am taking, from opening up my course and turning on editing, to getting to the bank of questions, is identical to what we did in the previous chapter.

The first thing we need to do is name the quiz. We are going to call this one Multiple Choice Quiz. For the introduction, we are just going to write the purpose of this quiz to teach you a few things about this item type. Once we click on the **Save and Display** button, we will see the **Question bank**.

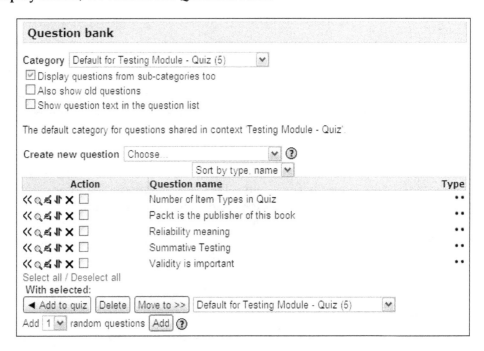

Notice the questions from the True/False quiz? They are there because the category they are associated with is Course. If I want to get rid of them so that they don't interfere with anything new I am doing, I have a few options.

Categories and contexts

I briefly mentioned categories earlier, but because I didn't have any way to show you what they did, I decided to wait to talk about them until we had some questions to work with. There are four default categories: System, Miscellaneous, Course, and Activity. The categories act like folders or directories, allowing the questions to be accessed at different levels or hierarchies. They are set up in what are known as contexts. Each context has its own question hierarchies, with the highest context being the Core System, moving down to Course Category, Course, and Activity. What this means is that you can select the context in which you can share your questions. By selecting the System option from the menu, any questions that have been created at this level will be available in all courses and for any quiz you have created on the site.

Miscellaneous/Course Category

The next level below System to store questions is Miscellaneous, like the Course Category. This category is where all the courses you are enrolled in are found.

The questions placed in this context are available to all courses and activities in the Course Category.

Course

This is where questions directly related to the course the quiz is being made for are stored.

Course is the default, and most Moodle users find this is a good place for their questions. Placing the items here allows you to create items specific to the course, based on exactly what was covered. It will also only use the questions developed in the course to draw on for random questions. You can also make a subcategory for questions you'd like to draw from. As long as questions are in one category, they can end up in a quiz that randomly draws questions from that category. Creating subcategories for different units in the course makes it easy to keep track of exactly which questions were used. It also helps in organization and administration of courses.

The drawback is that the questions are only able to be used in the course. So, looking at the previous graph, the Question bank in Course B would not be able to use anything from Course A. This does not mean we can't ever use them again; we will just need to export them to wherever we want to use them. We'll look at this activity later.

Activity

Creating items in the quiz Activity itself is also possible. This means that questions being created will only be available for the specific test being made.

The benefit to this is that you are assured that the questions are not available anywhere else, so, for example, if you want your test's questions to be completely isolated and unable to be used as random items in other formative or summative tests, this area would be a good place to place all the items.

The only real drawback is that the questions you spent all that time working on are limited to a single activity, a single exam.

I don't have the space here to go into how to use categories and contexts, but it isn't too hard to figure out. For a detailed and complete overview of how to create and use categories or contexts, check out these links: `http://docs.moodle.org/en/Question_categories` and `http://docs.moodle.org/en/Question_contexts`.

Multiple Choice item creation page

Since composing Multiple Choice items is nearly the same as creating True/False questions, we are going to be working on a few of them now. Once we have the hang of making them, we will look at a few options that we didn't use in the previous test and see how they work.

Returning to the Question bank, I go to the **Create New Question** drop-down and select **Multiple Choice**. As we talked about earlier, make sure you have the appropriate category selected.

When the Adding a Multiple Choice question page opens, you will notice that it looks very similar to the True/False question page. That's because it is. There are a few new options available here, but the page looks basically the same.

In the top section of the page, **General**, all the same information from True/False, such as item name and description are there. There are also three new options directly under the **General feedback** text area.

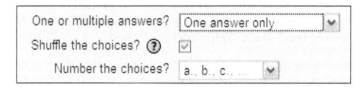

One or multiple answers

This drop-down option has only two choices. It enables us to either accept only a single response or more than one answer as a response. The two options in the drop-down menu are called **One answer only** and **Multiple answers allowed**.

Shuffle the choices

This option takes the possible responses and randomly orders them. This is useful for reducing cheating, and also allows each student to be given a slightly different version of the test.

This option will shuffle only if the Shuffle options for the quiz and the question are both turned on. The default is to shuffle or not based on the settings for the quiz module the Moodle administrator has set. These defaults can be overridden in the Quiz settings or here.

Number the choices

This section allows you to decide on how you want to mark the responses. You have four options: lowercase letters, uppercase letters, numbers, or nothing.

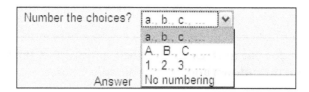

From here, we scroll down the page and we will see that we are offered five sections, called **Choice 1**, **Choice 2**, and others for entering the answers. These choices can be seen in the next screenshot:

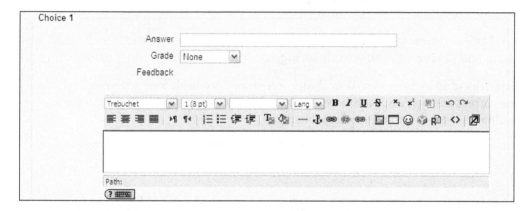

Here, we can enter our potential answers, the grade students will get for choosing the particular potential answer, and some feedback based on their response. Under the five answer sections, you have the option to create more choices using a button titled **Blanks for 3 More Choices**. Clicking on this button will create Choices 6 to 8.

There is no way to get rid of Choices, but it is possible to have fewer responses. If we only want to have three responses available, then all we need to do is fill in the three choices we want.

At the bottom of the page, we see the three feedback boxes: one is for correct responses, one for partially correct responses, and the final one for incorrect responses. As for choices, these can be filled or left empty.

Making a single response item

Now that we have looked over all the options for making a Multiple Choice item in Quiz, lets make one!

Step 1

In the Question bank for our quiz, as we've called it Multiple Choice Quiz, go to the **Create new question** drop-down and select **Multiple Choice**.

Step 2

We should be looking at the **Adding a Multiple Choice** question page. At the top, we need to make sure our **Category** is set to **Activity**, so we can keep all our questions separate from other areas.

We also need to create a name, the question text, give some general feedback (if we want), and decide on grades, numbering, shuffling, and the number of answers.

I have decided to ask a question about French history with four response options, one correct answer, and numbered: a, b, c, d. I also want to give some **General feedback**. Here is what this part looks like.

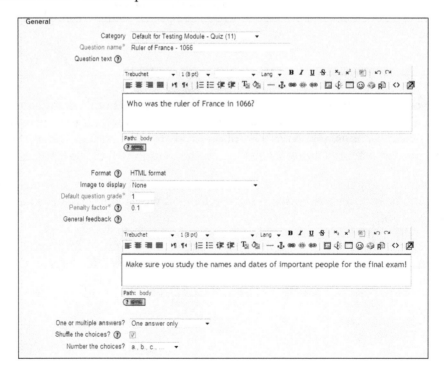

The grade for the correct response should be set to **100%**. This will give the student full points if it is answered correctly. The other options should be given as **None**, since they are all incorrect and are worth no points. Here are the first two question choices.

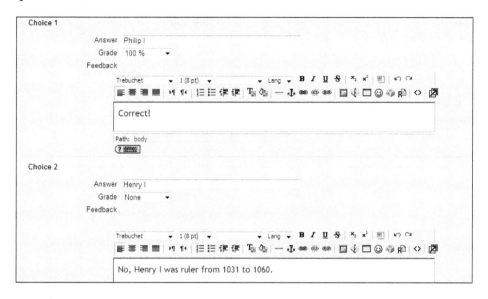

The final part of the page is the **Overall Feedback** section located at the bottom of the page seen here.

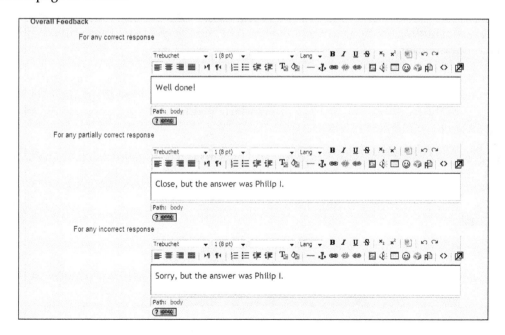

Once everything is completed, press the **Save changes** button to create the question.

The category this question will be placed in is set to **Activity**. I have created a name for the question and the question text has been entered. I have entered the possible responses, selected the correct answer by giving it a 100 percent grade, and set the numbering. I have also added some general feedback that all students will see, as well as added specific feedback depending on how the student answers the question.

Now, all we need to do is click on the **Save changes** button and the question will be created, added to the Question bank, and ready to use. To preview the question, click on the magnifying glass icon next to the question name. This is what our first multiple choice question looks like when created.

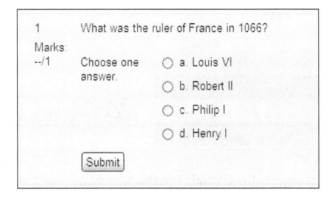

It looks pretty good, right? Do you notice anything about the item? The responses have been shuffled. Each time we look at or take the test the responses will be shown in a random order.

Now that we have the question created and ready to use, we need to make sure there are no spelling or content errors. This is all correct, so now I want to go and check to make sure the feedback and scoring are working properly. I'll just preview the test and answer each to make sure of this.

I'm going to turn off the Shuffle option, and go through each response to make sure everything looks like I want it to and is correct.

Making a multiple-answer item

Now, let's say we want to have an item that has a two-part answer, or two answers that are both required to answer the question. If this is the case, we need to create a multiple-response item. To do this, we follow the same basic pattern as we did in the basic, single-response item.

Step 1

First, we need to create a new multiple-choice question. Once this is done, we need to enter in all the same information as in the single response: question name, question text, and others.

The difference in this question is that, in the One or Multiple answers drop-down menu, I will select **Multiple answers allowed** instead of **One answer only**. Just so we can see how a different numbering system looks, this time I will use: 1, 2, 3, 4, and so on.

Numbering

If you are making a test, it is best to go with a single numbering system. If you are pulling in questions from multiple categories, simply go through and renumber everything so that they all match. If you don't keep everything the same, the students might get distracted by formatting, something we don't want to happen.

Now, I have created a new question, filled in all the general question information, written the question text, and given general feedback.

There are two new things that we need to look at before moving on.

Grade

When giving a grade in multiple-response items, you need to first determine how much each response is worth. You may base the percent you assign to the responses on several factors. For a question that requires two responses, those responses both being equally correct and required, a 50 percent grade for each correct selection would seem appropriate.

To select the score, I go to the **Grade** drop-down directly under the **Answer** text box, and select the score we want, in this case, we will select **50%** for both correct responses. The grades available are preset, so you can only work within these bounds. However, the selections are varied and should cover all needs.

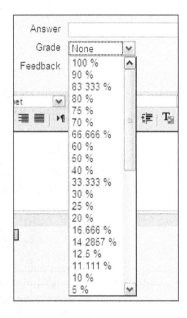

You are also able to take points away for mistakes. The grading scale goes down to a score of -100 percent, using an identical scale as the positive percentages.

If you select **Multiple answers allowed**, students can select all the responses they want. Note that Moodle does not give any hint as to how many options should be selected. There is no way to limit them to two or three choices. So, for example, if you have four possible responses in your question, students are able to select all of them and get a perfect score unless you take away points for incorrect responses.

In our question, I will be giving 50 percent for both correct answers and -50 percent for both incorrect answers. So, if the students make two selections and get both correct, they will receive a score of 100 percent. If they get select two answers and one is correct and the other is wrong, they will receive a score of 50 percent. If they choose two wrong answers, they will receive a 0 percent. It is not possible to give students negative scores for a question.

Now, some students might select three or four options. This is one reason to offer partial points for correct responses. For example, 50 percent for correct responses and -25 percent for incorrect ones. This would give the students a 25 percent if they answered one correct and one incorrect and 50 percent for selecting everything.

You can also select **NONE** from the **Grade** drop-down menu. If it is selected, you will not be given any points, nor will the student lose any points for selecting it. If you do not want to penalize students for incorrect responses, this is the way to do it.

Partially correct feedback

There is another feedback category that we haven't looked at yet called **For any partially correct response**. Here, we are able to give some feedback to students if they were only able to answer part of the question. Partial here means any score greater than 0 percent but less than 100 percent. This category can be useful to help direct the students to find the rest of the answer or show them where they made their mistakes.

Step 1

Now we need to go to the next section, **Choice 1**. As in the single-response multiple-choice questions, here is where we determine responses, grades, and item feedback.

First, we need to fill in a response to the question. The response can be as long or short as you like. Then we need to determine how much each response is going to be worth. Go to the **Grade** drop-down menu and select the percentage total for each of the responses. The default setting is **None**, and you may leave it like this if you like.

Step 2

Repeat Step 1 until you have all the responses you want. Remember, if you want to have only three options, you simply leave the answer area blank. In addition, if you want more response options, you can add more using the **Blanks** for three more choice buttons.

Step 3

Review the questions, answers, and make sure you have given every correct response a score.

Step 4

Preview the question. Look at the formatting to make sure it looks and works as it should. You should also make sure that the correct responses give the results you want.

Results

I've decided to create a question on the Japanese language. I want to confirm that my students are able to recognize two of the three scripts used in Japanese. I've created my question and responses following the steps mentioned previously. The result is shown in the next screenshot:

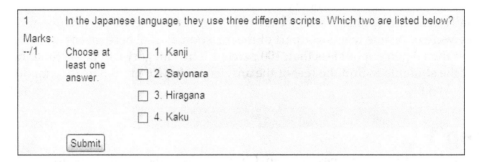

Looking at the previous screenshot, you can see that it looks almost identical to the single-answer multiple-choice question. The difference is that the radio buttons have become checkboxes, which allow us to select multiple answers.

That's how you make a multi-response question. Now, we will answer the question by clicking on the checkboxes and see the results.

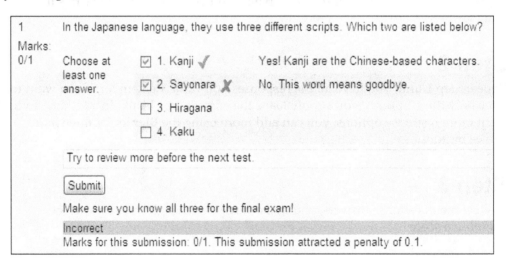

As you can see, we got one response correct and one wrong. We gave 50 percent for correct responses and -50 percent for incorrect responses, so my score is 0 percent. The scoring we entered is working properly.

The feedback I gave is located directly under choice 4. It is all spelled correctly, and looks the way I want it to. So, we can say sayonara to this part for now and move on to adding extras to multiple-choice questions.

Question design and formatting

So far, all we have done with our multiple-choice questions has been to create simple text questions. There is a lot more that we can do, and that is what we are going to learn about now. You will see the formatting and other options available in the rich-text editor in the next screenshot:

Basic text formatting

Looking at the previous image, you can see the basic features present in most word processors. You are able to use a variety of fonts, font sizes, headings, and languages. You are able to bold, italicize, underline, and strikethrough. You can align the text, add bullets and numbers, undo and redo, and use subscripts and superscripts. You can alter the background color and the color of the font, add tables, emoticons, anchors, special characters, and make the editor itself larger. You can even type in HTML code if you like. All these options are available in a standard word processor and are things you can use to help highlight important points in your tests, as well as make them easier to interact with.

Additional Fonts

If you want to use a font that is not already installed in the Moodle Text Editor, you can. It is a simple process, but you will need to ask your system administrator to do it for you, because it is a system-level change. You will also need to make sure the font is usable in your browser, or you won't be able to work with the font.

As a teacher, it is probably better to focus more on content than fonts, but the option is available if you want it.

Now, I'd like to go over a few of the options just to make sure we are all comfortable using them.

Adding images to multiple-choice questions

You are not going to always want simple text-based questions or answers. One common type of question that instructors frequently use is the image-based question. This item incorporates an image into the question.

These questions are easy to create and can offer new dimensions for questions, as well as make the questions and test much more interesting to students. You can add images to any question or any field that allows you to use the rich-text editor, but we are going to use a single-answer, multiple choice question. We will follow the same basic steps as before.

Step 1

We need to create a new multiple-choice question. When we are editing the question, we need to add the question name. We then need to add the question text. The question text we will be using for ours will be **Which holiday is this girl celebrating?**

Step 2

We now go to the toolbar and click on the **Insert Image** icon. It is the icon that looks like a framed picture of a mountain, located two places to the left of the smiley face icon.

Once we click on this icon, a pop-up menu will appear, as shown in the next screenshot:

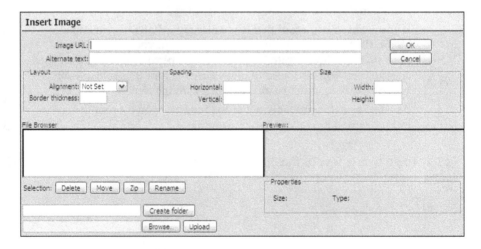

Here we have a few options in regards to how to use images and how they will be displayed in the question.

Image URL & Alternate text

If we use this option, we are able to take images directly from the Internet and use them for our tests.

To use it we first need to have the address where the image is found. We are not looking for the address of the site here, but just the image. If you simply link to the web page, it will not work. To get just the image address, click on the image and you should get a menu with one of the options being **View Image**. Select **View Image** and you will be taken to a different page with only that image. This is the address you want to use.

Once you have the image address, you copy and paste it to the **Image URL** text area. With the image address entered, we need to give the image a title in the **Alternate text** area. You can use anything you'd like here, but I tend to use the image name itself if it describes the image. If not, I create a short descriptive text of the image, something like "Girl celebrating Halloween".

After you have entered text in both the **Image URL** and the **Alternate text**, click on the **OK** button and the image will be added to your question. It is important to note that if the website you pulled the image from removes it or changes its location, it will not be available for the question. It is therefore advisable to download the image, so that it will always be available to you.

When you have finished adding responses and saving the question, you will see something like the following screenshot:

Source: Image: Tina Phillips / FreeDigitalPhotos.net

Now, looking back at the options available in the **Insert image** pop-up, you see three formatting options directly under the **Image URL** and **Alternate text** box where we were just working. They are called: **Layout**, **Spacing**, and **Size**.

Layout

In this fieldset, we are given ways to alter the **Alignment** and the **Border thickness**. Note that the image may be displayed differently on different browsers, although the CSS of the theme you are using will usually provide the appropriate margins and padding.

Alignment

There are several options available here that show how the text and the image will be displayed. The full list is shown in the next screenshot:

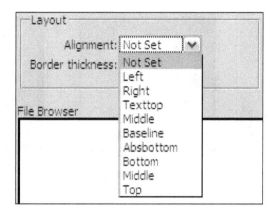

Most of these options are self-explanatory: **Left** will place the image to the left of the text, **Right** will place the image to the right of the text, and so on. However, there are a few possibly new terms. **Texttop**, **Baseline**, and **Absbottom** are HTML terms that many people might be unsure of. **Texttop** simply means that the very top of the tallest text (for example, l, b) will be aligned with the top of the image. This function works same as **Top** with some browsers. **Baseline** means that the imaginary line that all letters sit on will be aligned with the bottom of the image. In most browsers today, this functions the same as **Bottom**. **Absbottom** means that the letters that go below the baseline are aligned with the bottom of the image (for example, g, j). The top option, **Not Set** will place the image wherever the cursor is, without any special guide as to how it should be displayed.

Border thickness

The image you put into the question should look identical to the image you chose to use. If you are placing this image inside of text, or the edges are indistinct, or you simply want to frame it, use **Border Thickness**.

By placing a number in the **Border thickness** box, we will create a black border around the image. A small number will give a narrow border and a bigger number will give a thicker one.

Here are three images showing the difference in borders. The first is set with a border of 0, the second has a border of 5, and the third with 10. You will notice that the image size itself is the same, but the border causes the viewable area of the image to compress.

Source: Images courtesy of: freeimages.co.uk

Spacing

There are two spacing options available, **Horizontal** and **Vertical**. The larger the number entered, the more space there is between the text and the images.

Horizontal

This setting allows you to set the horizontal distance between the image and the text surrounding it. This option can be useful if you need to have the image set apart from the text in the question or explanation.

Vertical

This setting is like the horizontal setting. It allows you to set the vertical distance between text and the image. This option can be useful if you need to have set distances between the text or have multiple images in a list with text surrounding them.

Size

The two options here are **Width** and **Height**. These two settings allow you to alter the size of the image; smaller numbers will make the image smaller and probably easier to work with. Note that the actual images are not resized. For the best result, first resize the images on your computer to the size you want them to be.

Width

This setting allows you to alter the width of the image. Altering this setting without altering the height will produce narrow or wide images, depending on whether you adjust the value up or down.

Height

This setting allows you to alter the height of the image. This option functions just like **Width**, and will allow you to produce images that are vertically stretched or shrunk.

File Browser

In this space, you will see any images that have been uploaded to the course. As you can see in the previous screenshot, it is empty, which tells us that there aren't pictures available in the course yet. If you look below **File Browser**, you will see four options for images uploaded to the course. You can **Delete**, **Move**, **Zip**, or **Rename** any images that have already been uploaded into the course.

Preview

This is where you can view any images that have been added to the course. This feature can be useful if you have a lot of images and tend to forget which images are which.

Browse & Upload

This button, located underneath **File Browser,** is how we find images already on our computer. On my computer, this button automatically opens up **My Pictures**, which allows me to access all my images stored there. Your computer may be different, but most likely, it will do the same.

1. Once you are in your image collection folder, you need to select the image you want, click on **Open,** and the image location will be copied to the textbox beside the **Browse** button.

2. When the location of the photo has been added, click on the **Upload** button and the image will be added to the course.

Course Images

If you are planning on using a lot of images in your course, you might want to create a course pictures folder to hold them all in. By creating a folder, you can reduce the clutter and keep yourself better organized. To create an image folder, simply enter a name in the **Create Folder** textbox located in the **Insert Image** menu, in the bottom-left, and click on the **Create Folder** button. This will add the folder to the **File Browser** area.

The next question is going to be about a fruit, so I'm going to upload the photo of an apple. Here is what we have after it is has been added.

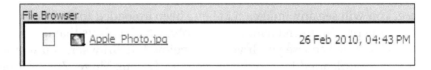

Now I am free to use this image in any question I want. There are two ways to do this.

The first and simplest method is the go to the question editing page and under the Question text, you will find a drop-down menu called **Image to display**. In this menu, you will see all the images currently available for the question. It will use the default settings to place the image. The screenshot is as follows:

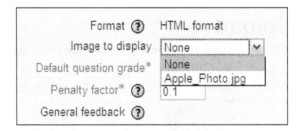

The second way we can add the image to our question is by simply clicking on the **Apple Photo.jpg** in the **File Browser** of the **Insert Image** window. This action will cause the image to appear in the **Preview** box on the right, and the directory location will appear in the **Image URL** at the top. We will also see the image **Size** and **Type** underneath the image **Preview | Properties**. We must add an **Alternate text** entry to the image, as well. Here is what the dialog box looks like before we click on **OK** and the image is added to our question.

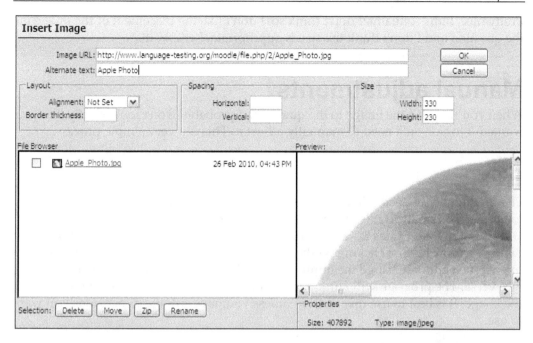

Source: Image Courtesy of: freeimages.co.uk

I have already prepared a question, and now adding this image to it produces the same outcome as the girl witch question, a question with an image. Here is what the question looks like, as shown in the next screenshot:

Source: Image courtesy of: freeimages.co.uk

Pretty nice, huh? Actually, I don't think so. I don't like the placement of the image in the question and I don't think the size is appropriate. Let's fix it!

Manual adjustments

When you first add the image to the question, it probably won't look exactly like you wanted it to, so you'll need to manually adjust it. This is a very simple process.

Size

The first thing you need to make sure of are the actual dimensions of the image. Is it too large? Too small? If it is, you need to go back to the question, open it for editing, and go to the **Insert Image** dialog window. Alternatively, you can re-enter this dialog window by first clicking on the image and then on the **Add Image** button in the rich-text editor. Change the numbers in **Width** and leave the **Height** blank, or vice versa. The program will automatically determine the other value and not stretch the image. It is best to use this method unless you have specific dimensions you want to use.

Once the dimensions are in place, save and preview the question.

If you first select the image, you will be ready to move on. If you did not first select the image, you will be creating an additional image in the question. You may want to delete the old image.

Layout

The actual location of the image on the page may not work or it may not look how you thought it would. This isn't a problem. The first thing you may want to do is switch to the full-screen editing mode, as your screen is more likely to have dimensions closer to those of your site.

You can see the image in the question. You are able to click and drag it to a different location in the question. You can also use the *Spacebar* or *Backspace* and enter to adjust left/right/up/down locations. However, reinserting is probably a faster route to altering the image location. When you have the image where you want it, preview the question to make sure you like the look of it.

Now, I have adjusted the previous image using my mouse to click and drag it to where I wanted it. The question looks better now. It took me about 30 seconds to make the changes to the previous item. Here is what we have now. Looks better, right?

1   What is this fruit called?

Marks: 1

Choose one   ○ 1. Pear
answer.
               ○ 2. Grape

               ○ 3. Cherry

               ○ 4. Apple

Source: Image courtesy of: freeimages.co.uk

Adding multiple images

Now, I mentioned earlier that if you didn't first select the image before adjusting the size, you will create an additional one and you will want to delete the old one. However, occasionally you may want to add more than a single image to a question.

The first thing you need to do is find the images you want. I have gone ahead and added a few more images to the course.

Create Folder

Now that we have uploaded several images to the course, I can show you about this function. **Create Folder** allows us to make different folders to hold our images. We now have several images related to fruits and vegetables, so we are going to create a folder titled **Fruits and Vegetables**.

The first thing we need to do is enter the name of our new folder into the textbox beside the **Create Folder** button. Once this is done, we click on the button and a new folder will appear above the images in the course, as seen in the next screenshot:

File Browser		
☐ 📁 Fruits_and_Vegetables	26 Feb 2010, 07:54 PM	
☐ 🖼 Apple_Photo.jpg	26 Feb 2010, 04:43 PM	
☐ 🖼 Carrot_Photo.jpg	26 Feb 2010, 06:50 PM	
☐ 🖼 Lemon_Photo.jpg	26 Feb 2010, 06:50 PM	
☐ 🖼 Tomato_Photo.jpg	26 Feb 2010, 06:50 PM	

To place our images in the folder, we need to check each of the boxes and click on the **Move** button. This will bring up a message stating **# files selected for moving**. Now go into the destination folder and click on **Move files here**. Now we need to check the Fruits and Vegetables link. This action will open up a directory with the **Move files here** button. Click on the button and the files will be moved.

Now when you go back to the **Insert Image** menu, you will no longer see the images, you will only see the folder containing them. This is a very useful function if you are working with different image types.

Now, I create a new multiple-choice question and go to the **Insert Images** menu. I select the image I want and add the **Alternate text**, make any adjustments to the **Size** (here, I will be using 150x150), and click on **OK**.

We repeat this process as many times as necessary to add all the images we want to our question. When you are adding new images, make sure the previous image is not selected or that image will disappear and the new one will take its place. Switching to the full screen editor really helps.

After writing the question and manually adjusting the image locations, add a letter next to each image and the result will be as shown in the following screen.

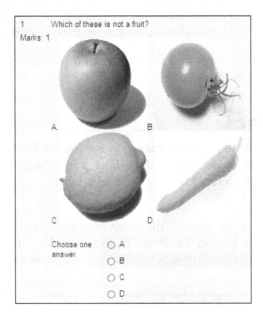

Source: Images courtesy of: freeimages.co.uk

For this particular question, I have turned off numbering, because it would be redundant to have the options numbered, as well as having single letter responses.

I have turned off the answer shuffling option, because it would be more confusing to students if the **A**, **B**, **C**, and **D** responses were in a different order than the images associated with the letters.

You can also use a table in the rich-text editor to keep the images looking good and in the right position. Just create a new table and set rows, columns, and spacing to look the way you want, then insert the images inside the cells.

Multi-image multi-response

If you want to include a question with multiple answers and with multiple images, you can. Make sure to change the One or Multiple answers drop-down menu from **One answer only** to **Multiple answers allowed**. This action will change the radio buttons to checkboxes and allow you to create multiple responses. I'm not going to give an example because of space constraint and the fact that I'm sure you can figure it out. If you decide to use this style, remember to make sure that you have given each of the responses a score!

Adding a Web Link (Hyperlink)

If you want your students to do some long reading comprehension assignments or if you want them to view a website or something else online, it is possible to insert a Web Link into the question text. While it is called a Web Link, this function can link to files online. This feature is especially useful for long passages or large images.

To add a link, you first need to write the text associated with the question. If you have no text, you can't create a link. So, first, we will write our question text. While we are writing the text, we will also fill in the answers and assign scores.

Now that we have our text, I select the word or words to be the link to our external information, image, web page, and other destinations. Once the words are highlighted, click on the **Insert Web Link** icon. When you click on it, an **Insert Link** window will appear.

Here, you need to enter the link to the URL you want to use. You also need to give the entry some kind of title, which will appear as a tool tip in standard-compliant browsers and can be used by screen readers for the visually impaired. Giving the link some kind of name to recognize where it will take you to is also a good idea. You can also choose the **Target**. There are several options here: new window, same window, and others. If you decide to use **Target**, choose one that works best for your needs. However, it may be better to let the user decide since setting a target goes against web-interface standards.

There is also the option for using an **Anchor**, if you have created any. An **Anchor** is a link within a page, and it allows you to jump quickly to an area by clicking on it. **Top** and **Bottom** are two common anchors, which quickly bring you to the top or bottom of the page you are viewing. These anchor spots first need to be defined by you before using the **Anchor** options.

Now, we are going to create a question about Brazil. We've found a web page we want our students to read over before they answer the question. We'll add the address to the reading in the **URL** line. For the **Title**, we are going to call it **Brazil Reading**, so the students, when hovering their mouse over the link, will see what it leads to. We are going to set a target here. For **Target**, we are going to select **New Window,** so the reading and test will be on two different pages. Do not forget to use New Window If you do, the quiz will effectively end when the page changes. This mistake is a No! Because we have not set an Anchor, there is no option for selecting anything in this box.

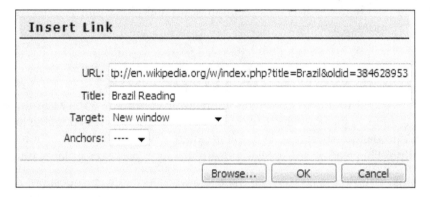

Scan the Wikipedia article about Brazil and then add the hyperlink to the Wikipedia article about Brazil. The question is now ready. The text I highlighted to be the link is now a link that will open a new window with the reading about Brazil. The students will click on the this article link, which will open the Brazil Reading, find the information, and then answer the question. Here is what the final product looks like.

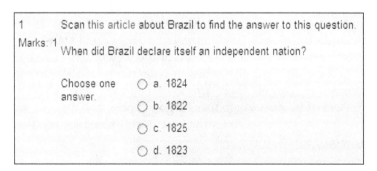

You can also link to files on your computer. Looking at the **Insert Link** window, you will see a **Browse** button to the left-hand side of the **OK** button. If you click on this button, you will be brought on the **Insert Link File Browser**. In this browser, you will see a list of files you have uploaded to the course. You can select one of these files to use, or you may upload a new file. If you want to use any of the files already in the **File Browser**, then simply click on one and it will be added as the URL. If you want to use a file not already uploaded, then you need to go to the **Browse** button at the bottom of the menu and find the file you want to upload. Click on the **Upload** button and the file will be added to the main course files directory. You will want to upload your files well in advance so that you can make good decisions about where you want the files located. Once the file is uploaded, you will be able to click on it and its location will be added to the URL. Then follow the same steps as before to make the question work the way you want it to.

Creating the Test

Now that we have created several multiple-choice questions, we simply need to move them to the test. To do this, we just repeat the process we used with the True/False questions. Back in the **Editing Quiz** page, click on the **Move** icon next to the question to move it from the Question bank to the Questions in this test. We have created six multiple-choice items, so there should be six in our test at this point. Note that for book spacing issues, I have eliminated one of the single image items.

Once we have all the questions added to the test, we need to go in and take it. I have gone through everything, and the test is functioning properly. Here is what our final test looks like as shown in the following screenshot:

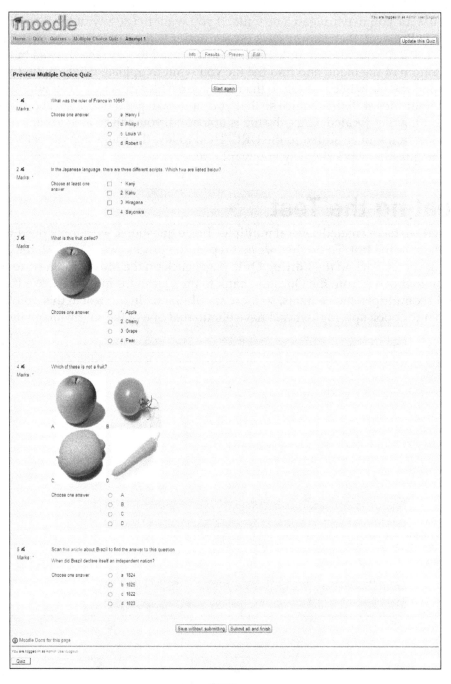

Well, that's it. We have created a variety of multiple-choice items and created a test. I'd just like to point out one issue that I feel needs to be addressed: feedback.

General feedback issues

Feedback is usually helpful and something that can help us grow as students or instructors. However, sometimes the different types of feedback that can be delivered with Quiz can be too much. Giving General Feedback, Item feedback, and Feedback for each correct or incorrect response puts a lot of information on the student's test, some of it too general to be of any real use. Look at this question, which is the same one we used in our first multiple-response question, and look at the Before feedback and After feedback screenshots:

Before feedback:

After feedback:

You can see all three feedback areas displayed here. Next to the answers, you can see the response feedback. This feedback is fairly useful, because it gives the correct meaning for each word. Under the responses, you can see the feedback for an incorrect response. "Trying to review more before the next test" might not be as useful as the concrete feedback given previously. Finally, under the **Submit** button, you can see the general feedback. This is the feedback all students receive and something that, by its very nature, must be general. This seems like a lot of feedback for a single item, and doesn't include the Quiz feedback based on score, which we haven't looked at yet.

You might note that there is no feedback for a correct response, or a partially correct response. Why do you think this is? You probably guessed it, but to get correct response feedback, the question needs to be 100 percent correct. To get a partial score, some percentage needs to be correct. For incorrect feedback, the result must be 0 percent. If you recall, in the question I used here we gave 50 percent for correct responses and -50 percent for incorrect responses. Therefore, the score on this question is 0 percent, giving me the incorrect response feedback text.

If you are the type of instructor who likes to give a lot of feedback, this approach may work for you. If you are the type who doesn't want to give too much feedback, then I would recommend using only what you feel you need. General feedback might be an overkill in many situations.

Often, a single piece of useful feedback to a student is worth more than many pieces that are vague. You need to decide how much you want to put there for your students, and also estimate how much they will absorb from each question. Remember that the feedback is available for each question, so a page full of feedback will likely be glanced at but not really absorbed.

Your turn

Now it is time for you to give this a try. What I want you to do now is to try and make each of the question types that we have talked about in this chapter and create a test. Your test should include:

- Single-response item
- Multiple-response item
- Item with an image
- Item with multiple images
- Item with Web Link

I'm going to walk you through creating the first one, but you will need to do the others on your own. If you get stuck, look back at the chapter to find out why. When you finish, preview each of your questions and the test.

Step 1

Create a new quiz and title it Multiple Choice Quiz. Use the same words for the **Introduction**.

Scroll down to the **Attempts** section and turn **Adaptive mode** to **No**.

Scroll down to the bottom of the page and click on the **Save and display** button.

Step 2

Click on the **Edit** tab. Change the **Question Category** to **Default** for Multiple Choice Quiz. Then go to the **Create new question** drop-down menu and select **Multiple Choice**.

Step 3

Now we are in the **Adding a multiple choice question** page. For Question name and Question text, please enter **Who was the first person to travel to the South Pole?** If you ever have a name that is too long, and this one is pretty close, simply use keywords that will help you identify it, something like: Identify first person South Pole.

Scroll down and make sure that the **One or multiple answers** drop-down is set to **One answer only**. Then make sure there is a check in the **Shuffle the choices** box. After that, change the numbering to **No numbering**. I usually use No numbering to keep my tests looking clean, but you may want to have letters or numbers next to your answer choices..

For Choice 1, enter Amundsen and give the Grade as 100 percent. In the feedback text add **That's right! He arrived at the South Pole December 14, 1911**.

We want to have a total of four possible responses, so for the remaining three choices enter: **Wilson, Scott, Ross** (all members of early South Pole expeditions). For each of these grades, leave the setting at **None**. For feedback, enter **Sorry, but it was Amundsen. He arrived at the South Pole on December 14, 1911**.

When you have finished, scroll to the bottom of the screen and click on the **Save changes** button.

Step 4

Now lets click on the **Preview** icon next to the question. Answer the question correctly and you should see something like the image shown in the following screenshot:

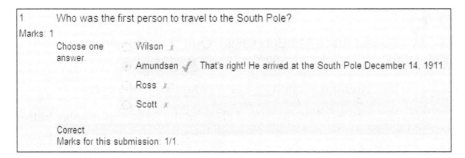

Step 5

If everything is correct, add the item to the test. If not, go back and fix any mistakes.

Now go back and create the remaining questions and add them to your test. If you run into any problems, review the chapter and look at the examples provided.

Just one final note on numbering before you make your test. I used all of the numbering systems available to give you an idea of how they looked. I would not recommend doing the same thing on a test. Choose one system, (personally, I prefer no numbering) and stick with it.

Summary

As you can see, the multiple-choice question format offers a lot of options. From simple text-based questions to multi-image ones, from single to multiple responses. There is a lot you can do with Quiz's multiple-choice question type. You will probably be using these questions a lot, so make sure to get used to them early.

Don't forget to make full use of all the options available in the rich-text editor and to review all your questions and answers multiple times. Once you have finished creating the test, take it to make sure it does what you want it to and the scoring comes out correctly.

Also, remember that categories are a useful tool, and they are there to help keep you and all your questions organized. Use them!

Finally, remember what I said about feedback. Too much can be frustrating and overwhelming. Keep it simple and direct. In the next chapter, we will look at more question types and how to create them.

3
More Question Types

We have already looked at True/False and Multiple Choice options in Quiz. Now, we are going to take a look at each of the remaining question types in Quiz. We will work together to create questions in each of them and then you will work alone to make questions for each format. Now, let's get to work and make some more questions.

In this chapter, we will:

- Look at the remaining question types
- Create questions for each item type
- Pursue Self-development activities
- Discuss considerations for each question type

Short Answer

Short Answer questions were briefly described earlier, but just so we all remember, short answer items are where the test taker writes a short response in a textbox. This option can be used either to answer a question or as a gap-fill activity. The test taker's response must be exactly the same as the one you entered or one of the alternative options you have made available, or the answer will be counted incorrect. In this section, we will look at how to make short answer items and use some of the options available. Once we have finished looking at how to set one up, you will create one on your own.

Gap-Fill Activity
If you are using Short Answer for a gap-fill type question, here is a good idea. Use underscores to show where the gap will be when writing your question title.

Step 1

First we need to go through the basic steps of creating a question, as we saw in *Chapter 1*. We need to go to the Question Bank page and create a new Short Answer item. If you have administration privileges, you can get directly to the Question Bank via the **Course Administration** block by clicking on the **Questions** link. Alternatively, you can open a previously created quiz and access the **Question Bank**. as we did in *Chapter 1*.

Step 2

Now, we need to complete the General section of the question. This process is identical to that of the previous questions we have created. We need to make sure the category is set to where we want the question located, give the question a name, and write the question text. Here, we also have the option of inserting any uploaded images, giving general feedback, or adjusting the points received for a correct answer to the question.

The question we are going to ask is, **Who was the first person in space?,** and we will use this text for both the question description and the question text. We won't be giving any general feedback and we won't be making any changes to the default settings.

There is one new option available in the General section of Short Answer. Is it called **Case Sensitivity**. This menu allows you to set whether you will require capitalization or not. This option is something you will have to decide for each question you create, depending on how important case is to you, your students, and what you are teaching. If case isn't that important, then you might want to leave it set to **No**, case is unimportant'. However, if you are working on something where the case is important, then you might want to have this option set to **Yes, case must match**. It all depends on your needs.

For our question, since we are talking about a person, the name should be capitalized, and so we could set **Case Sensitivity** to **Yes, case must match**. However, we are more concerned that the students know the answer, not whether they remember to capitalize, therefore, we're going to leave it set to **No, case is unimportant**.

Step 3

Now, we need to enter my answer into the **Answer** textbox. We type in the name of the person, **Yuri Gagarin**, in the **Answer** textbox, change the grade from **None** to **100%**, and we're going to give some feedback in the Feedback area. The only correct response for this item will be **Yuri Gagarin**, with the case being ignored.

This is all I have to do to create the question. Let's stop here and review the question to make sure we have done everything correctly and then save the changes.

We will now preview the question to make sure it looks the way we want it to. It looks fine, so we will go ahead and type in the correct answer first, then click on the **Submit all and finish** button. This sequence will show us the grade and feedback we get from the response, as shown in the next screenshot:

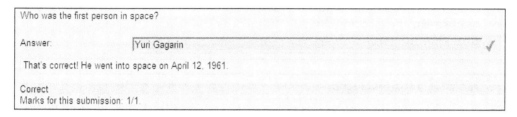

This question looks like what we want it to and we should be happy with the display and the feedback. However, some of the students might enter **Gagarin** instead of **Yuri Gagarin**. If they do this, their response will be marked incorrect. They also might enter **Y. Gagarin** or some other combination, which we need to consider and account for.

What we need to do now is go back to the Edit question page. Clicking on the **Edit** icon next to the question in the Question Bank will bring us to the Editing page. Now we can enter any other responses we are willing to accept. I have already gone back and entered several different variations on Yuri Gagarin's name, copied and pasted the feedback from the original response, and given a 100 percent score for each of the alternative responses. Now if a student responds with any of the variations of the name entered, it will be scored as correct, given full points, and receive correct response feedback.

We have entered seven variations of the Gagarin name; there may be one or more that we overlooked but feel should get credit. So, even though we have several different possible responses, students will still make mistakes, in spelling or simply enter the wrong person's name. Here is an example of a simple spelling mistake.

Who was the first person in space?

Answer: yuri garigin ✗

Incorrect
Correct answer: Yuri Gagarin
Marks for this submission: 0/1

As you can see, there is no feedback given for the incorrect answer. If we want to give feedback for a wrong response in Short Answer, we should create the final answer option with * in its **Answer** line.

The * symbol added to an answer textbox is what Moodle terms a **wildcard**. Wildcards are used to match a series of letters or characters and are also used for offering feedback for incorrect responses. We need to use wildcards because there may be spellings, combinations, or other factors you may not have considered. For example, let's say we entered a wildcard with letters on either side, **y*n**. This wildcard would match anything that began with a **y** and ended with an **n**: yon, Yuri Gagarin, Y. Gargin, yellow fan, and others. If we entered only one letter and a wildcard, say **s***, it would match anything beginning with an **s**: Silly, sad, Spain, ssssss, and so on. A wildcard entered without any characters attached allows us to set feedback for incorrect answers.

Incorrect response

Anything other than the correct responses you entered will be viewed as an incorrect response and will receive no grade. However, if you enter an * into the last **Answer** textbox, the feedback entered there will be displayed to anyone who does not respond with one of the correct options. It is important to note that the wildcard must be entered into the last answer, or it will not work properly.

Here is another example of a wrong response, but this time I have added the * to the final answer text and added some incorrect response feedback.

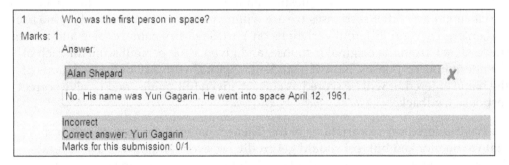

As you can see, now, when someone enters anything other than the correct response, he or she will receive the feedback shown in the previous screenshot.

Variations

Obviously, we can only enter a small number of variations into the system. It would simply take too long to enter a full range of variations on an answer. If we use the asterisk, or **wildcard** we are able to accept a range of responses as correct.

Spelling

The first way to use the **wildcard** is for spelling issues. If we aren't particularly worried whether or not a student can spell the response correctly, we can set up the response parameters to accept a variety of spellings.

If we have a question regarding polyhydroxyalkanoates (a linear polyester), maybe we aren't too worried if there is a mistake in spelling. What we can do is create an acceptable starting and ending point for the word. For example, we want them to have the **poly** correct and we feel they should be able to end with **ates**. If these were our requirements, we would simple enter **poly*ates** into the answer text. This would mean that students who wrote an answer that began with **poly** and ended with **ates** would have it marked correct.

Multiple response

This is a variation on the spelling rule outlined previously. If we ask the question, **What are the two main political parties in the US?,** we would expect the students to answer with something like **Democrats and Republicans**. However, they may write it in a different order, or with an ampersand (&), a comma, a space, or some other way. We are willing to accept several variations because the question is simply seeking to know whether the student knows the two major parties in the US political system. Our first option is not using the wildcard. This option forces us to manually enter several variations, and we also run the risk of missing some of the possible variations.

The other option is to use the wildcard. By creating the wildcard function, such as Democrats*Republicans, any variation will be accepted. Democrats and Republicans; Democrats & Republicans; Democrats, Republicans; Democrats + Republicans; and so on. It would even accept as a correct answer **Democrats are the best party available for the people (although I really wish there was a strong Independent Party) but unfortunately we still have to deal with the Republicans,** because, Democrats comes first and Republicans comes last. This function can be very useful, but it does have its limits, as you can see.

If you wanted to give credit for partial answers, you can do that as well. For example, you could set up your answers as follows:

- Democrats*Republicans — Answer 1 - 100%
- *Democrats* - Answer 2 — 50%
- *Republicans* - Answer 3 — 50%
- * — Answer 4 - 0%

It is important to enter your responses in the order you want them evaluated, because Moodle looks at the responses starting with Answer 1 and moves down the list until it finds one that matches. This is the reason why the wildcard is always located at the end of the answer options.

Creating Short Answer

We are going to prepare two Short Answer questions together. The first one will be a simple, single-word response. The second will use the wildcard feature.

Item #1

1. Create a new quiz with a title **Short Answer**. Leave all the settings to default but turn off the **Adaptive mode**.

2. Go to **Editing** tab and, in the Question Bank, make sure your category is set to **Default** for **Short Answer**.

3. Go to **Create a new question** and select **Short Answer** from the drop-down.

4. For Question name and Question text, enter the same thing: **What color are bananas?**

5. Leave all the settings as they are and make sure the **Case Sensitivity** is set to **No, Case is Unimportant**.

6. In Answer 1, write yellow in the **Answer** textbox. For grade, change **None** to **100%**. In feedback enter, **Yes, bananas are yellow!**.

7. We are only going to accept yellow and we are only going to accept it if it is spelled correctly. So, for Answer 2, please enter an * in the **Answer** textbox. Leave **Grade set** to **None**. In the feedback, enter: **'Sorry, but bananas are yellow**.

8. When you have finished, go to the bottom of the page and click on **Save changes**.

9. You will be brought back to the Question Bank and you will see your newly made question. Click on the **Preview** icon, the one that looks like a magnifying glass, and you will see the question we just made. It should appear as shown in the following screenshot:

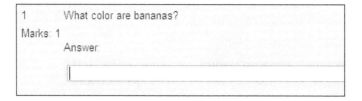

If you can see the previous screenshot in your preview, you have done everything correctly! Well done! Now, we want to check your responses to make sure they are the way you wanted them. The correct response will look like the next image on the left-hand side and any other response should look like the one on the right.

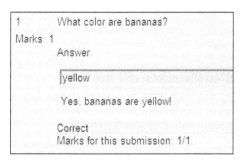 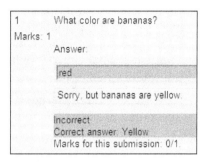

Item #2

For this one, we are going to use a wildcard to accept several different answers.

1. In the quiz we have already created, create a new Short Answer question.

2. Title it **Which two countries have the largest populations?** Use the same for the question text.

3. Leave all the options as default, except for **Case Sensitivity**. This time we want our students to use the correct case the names of countries are proper nouns. Change the setting to **Yes, case must match**.

4. Now we need to put our answers in the textboxes. We want to offer two possible correct answers to our students. In Answer 1's textbox, enter **China*India**. In Answer 2's textbox enter **India*China**.

5. This set-up will allow students to enter both countries in any order and with any conjunction, symbol, punctuation, or anything else separating the words.

6. We also need to change the grade for each of these options from **None** to **100%**. Also, for feedback, we will add a simple **Correct!**.

7. I have decided that we want to give half-credit if the students can get one of the answers. Go ahead and click on the **Blanks for 3 more choices** button towards the bottom of the page. In Answer 3 enter *China*. In Answer 4 enter *India*. This set-up will give partial credit if the student enters China or India.

8. For the grade, I will change the value from **None** to **50%**.

9. For Answer 3 feedback, we will write **India is one of them! The other is China**. For Answer 4 feedback, we will reverse the order.

10. In Answer 5, we will enter *. This wildcard value will give feedback to the students for any other response. The grade will remain as **None**, and for feedback, we will enter **China and India are the correct answers**.

11. We will also add a short note telling the students that if they forgot to capitalize the country names or spelled them wrong, the answer was counted incorrect. This explanation will also help cut down on students coming to you telling you they got the answer correct, but the computer marked it wrong. This text is what we will include in the Feedback: **Note: If you didn't capitalize the country names or if you misspelled them, you did not receive credit**.

12. Now click on **Save changes**. Preview the question and you should see the question and a blank textbox.

13. Now, answer the question using a correct response, a partially correct response, and an incorrect response.

14. The screenshot of the correct response is as follows:

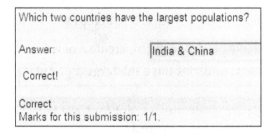

15. The screenshot of the partially correct response is as follows:

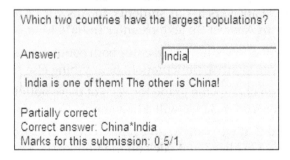

16. Finally, the screenshot of the incorrect response is as follows:

Which two countries have the largest populations?

Answer: |india and Chaina|

China and India are the correct answers.

Note: If you didn't capitalize the country names or misspelled them, you did not receive credit.

Incorrect
Correct answer: China*India
Marks for this submission: 0/1.

You can see that all forms are working as we want and the scoring and feedback is correct.

Short Answer considerations

Where should we use Short Answer? Well, we want to use Short Answer when we are looking for students to know an answer, and not just recognize it from a list of possible choices.

We also want to use simple answers in the Short Answer questions. If you create a long string of text, it is more difficult for students to get the correct answer, because the text might not match exactly or closely enough to the predetermined parameters. This situation is something to avoid. One-to two-word strings are probably most useful here; three is starting to push it. If the strings are longer, you run the risk of giving students inappropriate grades based on a slight difference in the response phrasing, for example, if a student had entered India, Russia, America, Turkey, China in the previous example, the answer would have been scored as correct, although, it is clearly wrong.

Additionally, after the student responds, he or she will see the correct response listed. The first correct response the system encounters will be used and displayed. So, using our previous example, if a student got the answer correct, he or she would see something like **democrat*republican** displayed in the Correct Response area. This point is not that important, but something you should be aware of as you may need to explain it to your students.

Numerical

These questions look very similar to Short Answer questions. The only difference is that these items allow for a bit of variation in the numerical responses. Let's look at how to make one.

Step 1

We are going to create a new test titled Numerical. We will change the category to **Default** for **Numerical** and then make a new Numerical question.

A Note on Categories

I am separating questions into distinct categories here; this may or may not be how you want to do it. I am doing using categories to keep all the questions in separate places for demonstration purposes. This style may not be appropriate for you and your situation.

Our question will be about area, and just for fun, we are going to add an image to the question. Once the question is created, title it **What is the area of the rectangle shown?**. In the Question text, enter the same thing.

Do you remember how to upload an image? Place your cursor in the appropriate place in the rich-text editor of the question text. Click on the **image** icon in the taskbar and the **Insert Image** menu will appear. We are going to take an image of a rectangle and upload it to the image folder. Once the image is there, we need to give it an Alternative Text; I'm calling mine **Rectangle**. Once these steps have been completed, we click on the **OK** button and the image will be placed in the Question HTML editor.

Step 2

Now we will scroll down to the **Answer** section. These items look very similar to the Short Answer items, except each has what is called an Accepted Error textbox.

Accepted Error

The Accepted Error textbox allows us to set a range of numbers that we will accept as correct. By entering a number in this textbox, we are giving a ± range of whatever number we enter in the box as correct. For example, if I have an answer of **50** and the Accepted Error is **five**, any number between 45 and 55 would be deemed correct and receive the full points for the question. If the Accepted Error is filled with a **0** or left empty, there will be no accepted variations in the answer.

We will now enter the correct answer in the **Answer** textbox. Our rectangle is **5** by **6**, so our Answer is **30**. This answer is worth full points, so we will make Grade 100 percent. We will not accept any variation on this response, so we will enter a 0 in the Accepted Error textbox. For feedback, we will enter **Well done!**.

For any other answer, we want to give incorrect feedback, so we will use the wildcard as in Short Answer and place an * in Answer 2, leaving the grade as **None**, and the Accepted Error blank. Once these steps are complete, click on the **Save changes** button.

Step 3

Now that our question has been created, we want to preview it. Click on the **Preview** icon and we see the following screenshot:

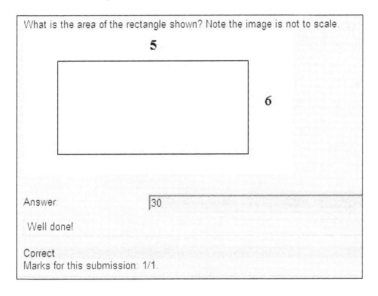

Two additional, and important, features of Numerical questions are the abilities to use units and multipliers.

You might want to use units of measurement in your response. If so, we need to enter the unit we want to use in the Unit textbox. For example, if you enter a unit of **cm** here, and the accepted answer is 15, then the answers **15cm** and **15** are both accepted as correct. It is important to also note that if a unit is entered, the unit used in the answer must be identical. For example, if you entered **GDP** and a student entered **G.D.P.**, it would be marked incorrect.

You can also specify a multiplier. This multiplier will help convert from one unit to another. So, if your main answer was 5500 with unit W, you can also add the unit kW with a multiplier of 0.001. This means that the answers **5500, 5500W** or **5.5kW** would all be marked correct. Note that the accepted error is also multiplied, so an allowed error of 100W would become an error of 0.1kW.

That is all there is to making a simple, Numerical item in Quiz.

Your turn

Now you are going to create a numerical item. Carry out the following steps and you shouldn't have any problems. If you do, go back to the Numerical section and look it over.

Make sure you are in the **Default for Numerical category** and create a new Numerical question.

1. For Question name and Question text enter **How many centimeters is (9-3)+(4*7)?**.

2. In the Answer 1 Answer textbox, enter **34**, give the Grade as 100 percent, and leave Accepted Error blank. In Feedback, enter **Correct!**.

3. In the Answer 2 Answer textbox, enter *****, leave the grade as **None**, and leave Accepted Error blank. In feedback, enter **Sorry. Check your work again!**.

4. Scroll down to Unit 1 and in the Unit textbox enter **cm**.

5. Save the question and preview it. Enter the correct answer and you should see the screenshot shown below. The incorrect answer will display the wildcard message.

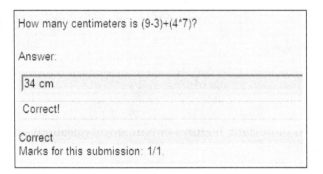

Numerical considerations

There are many uses for these questions and they are a valuable addition to the Quiz repertoire. There are two small things that need to be considered before using these items.

Variables and word problems

If you are interested in having an equation like (x+4)*y=?, you can do so by entering the variables in the HTML editor as part of the question. However, because this question type does not allow for variables, it may be better to use the Calculated item type described later in this chapter.

Another issue to consider is word problems. You are not able to enter words as answers in Numerical questions, so if you are interested in creating word problems, you will want to use the Short Answer question.

Matching

The Matching questions in Moodle are probably what you'd expect. They offer a list of names, items, questions, and other items on the left-hand side of the screen and the answers in the form of a drop-down menu on the right-hand side.

Matching is a very simple item to create and can be a useful addition to tests. Instead of wasting any more time talking about Matching items, let's show you how to make one.

Step 1

First, we're going to create a new quiz. We'll call it **Matching** in both **Name** and **Introduction**. We're going to leave all the options set to default except for the **Adaptive mode**, which we will turn to **turn off**.

In the Question bank, we'll make sure the category is set to **Default** for **Matching**. Once these steps are done, it is time to create a new Matching question from the new question drop-down.

Step 2

For this question, we're going to be asking our students to match a list of US Presidents to their time in office. **Match the US Presidents and their terms** is what we will use for both the name of the question and the question text.

We're going to leave all the options set as they are and go to the questions and answers section.

Step 3

This section is where we will enter the questions and answers. In our case US Presidents will fill the **Question** textbox and their time in office will fill the Answer textbox. An example of how the question looks is shown in the next screenshot:

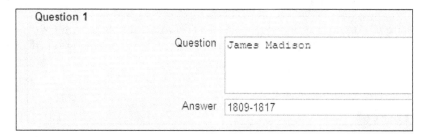

There is a note at the top of the section telling us we are required to, at minimum, enter two questions and three answers. The note also informs us that we are able to add more incorrect answers if we like, which can be very helpful if we are working with a small number of items.

As you can see, we have entered **James Madison** in **Question 1 Question** textbox and his term of office, **1809-1817**, in the **Answer** textbox. We will now go ahead and add two additional Presidents and their terms to the item. For Question 2 we are adding James Monroe, 1817-1825, and for Question 3, John Quincy Adams, 1825-1829.

We will also be using Question 4 to create an additional distractor by filling in its Answer with a term of office but no President. In the **Question 4 Answer** textbox, we will add **1829-1833**.

Now that we have entered all the information, we need to go back and make sure all our settings, spellings, and information is correct. Once we have confirmed that everything looks as it should, we'll click on **Save changes** and the question will be created.

You will notice that there is no place for feedback. This is one of the few places that we can't give direct feedback in Quiz. If we want to give feedback, we need to go to the General feedback and include whatever we'd like all the students to see. We could, for example, simply include the additional information about the answers or make a comment on the importance of knowing these dates for the course final exam.

We will simply enter the correct answers, just so we can see how it looks.

Step 4

Now we need to preview the question. We click on the **Preview** icon next to the question and see what it looks like. Here is the Matching question. Each of the drop-down menus contain the dates we entered in a random order, as you can see here.

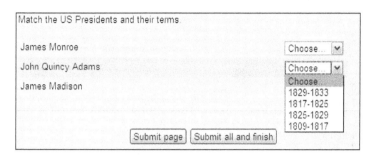

Now, I'll go ahead and answer the questions by putting everything in the proper place, then click on the **Submit all and finish** button. We can see an example of a correct response, a partially correct response, and an incorrect response.

The screenshot of a correct response is as follows:

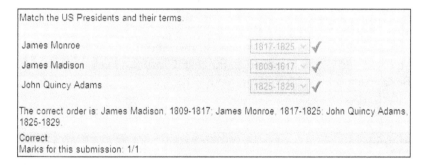

The screenshot of a partially correct response is as follows:

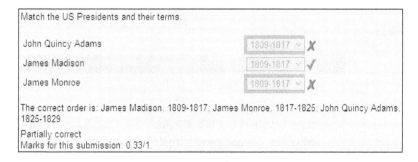

Finally, the screenshot of an incorrect response is as follows:

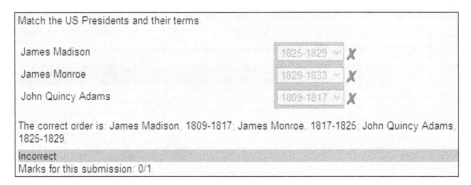

> ### Identical Responses
>
> Unfortunately, there is no way right now to keep your students from accidentally guessing the same option more than once or simply guessing the same option multiple times in, hopes of at least getting some credit. To deal with the former point, remember to tell your students to check their work before submitting. To deal with the latter, adding more options will lessen the chances that this kind of student will guess correctly.

Step 5

Now that we have checked everything and confirmed the question is correct, the final thing to do is move the question to the test. Close the **Preview** window. In the Question Bank, click on the **Move** icon next to the question and it will be placed in the Quiz.

Your turn

We are now going to make a matching question together. It will be a standard matching question. For this question, we will be asking about four currencies and the countries where they are used.

1. First, we need to create a new Quiz and in the **Name** and **Information** textboxes, call it **Matching**.

2. Leave all the settings as default, except for **Adaptive** mode. We want to turn that off. Once it is off, go to the bottom of the page and click on the **Save and Display** button.

3. In the new Quiz, click on the **Edit** tab. Change the **Category** to **Default** for **Matching**. Then go to **Create new question** and select **Matching**.

4. In Name and Question text, once again, we will be using the same thing. Enter the following text into both textboxes: **Match the currency to the country**.

5. Once finished, we will enter the correct responses into the General feedback textbox: The correct answers are: **Belize - Dollar; Brazil - Real; Colombia - Peso; Costa Rica - Colón.**

6. Now we will need to enter the countries into the **Question** textbox and the currencies into the **Answer** textboxes. There are currently only three Questions available, so we need to click on the **Blanks for 3 More Choices** button.

7. Once we have added the four countries and currencies, we will want to add a couple of more distracters. In the Answer 5 textboxes, please enter Quetzal (Guatemala's currency). In the Answer 6 textbox, please enter Bolívar (Venezuela's currency).

8. When we finish, we need to click on the **Save changes** button.

9. Preview the question and you should see something very similar to the following image. You can see all four countries and all six currencies.

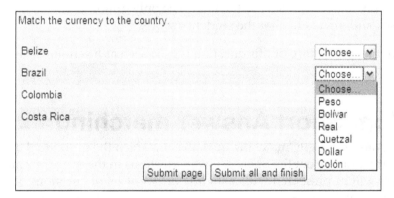

10. Check all the answers to make sure everything is where it should be, then move the question to the Quiz.

Special Textbox Characters

You can't enter special characters or symbols into textboxes. If you want to add a special character, such as an accent mark, you need to use its HTML entity code, for example, $#8364 for the Euro sign, copy and paste it from somewhere else, or you can find many listings online for the HTML entity code.

Matching considerations

As you can see, matching items are fairly easy to create and easy to use. However, there are two things that you should think about when adding these items to tests: shuffle and score.

The shuffle function can be a great feature for all kinds of questions, but sometimes it can cause more confusion in students. In Quiz, we have the option to shuffle the questions and the responses. In Matching, the responses are automatically shuffled. However, there is also a shuffle in Matching. If the **Shuffle with Questions** is selected at the quiz level, and if the box is checked, the questions or statements are shuffled, as well as the responses. There are times when this option can be useful and times when it will cause unnecessary distraction.

Also, in Matching, you might have noticed we didn't add a grade to anything. This is because each option is worth an equal percentage of the item score. So, if there were four possible options, each would be worth 25 percent of the total. A student getting two correct responses out of the four options would receive a 50 percent score for the item. This is normally considered a fair way of marking these types of items, but there may be times when you do not want to accept partially correct responses. There is no way to do this inside of the item. The only option you would have would be to go back and manually alter the student's score.

In addition, the only nature of this question type is seen as a serious disadvantage by many users.

Random Short Answer matching

These questions are simply matching questions in which the individual questions are drawn at random from the Short Answer questions in the question category, and each student will be presented with a slightly different set of questions. Random Short Answer matching takes the Short Answer question on the left-hand side of the page and takes correct answer from each, and makes it a choice for matching on the right-hand side of the page. These questions are very simple to create and so we will jump right in so you can see what they look like. Do this one with me.

Step 1

We are going to go back to our Short Answer quiz and inside it we are going to create a new question. We will select **Random Short-Answer Matching**.

Step 2

You will notice that the Question Name and Question Text have both been completed for us. If you want to change the name or text, you can. We are going to leave it as it is.

We are not going to leave any General Feedback, so we scroll down to the bottom of the page and we see a new function called **Number of Questions to Select** with a drop-down menu beside it. This drop-down menu gives us the option to select between two and ten Short Answer questions to be randomly added to the question and made into Matching items. We have already created four items, so we will select four from the drop-down menu and click on **Save changes**.

If you enter more questions than you actually have, you will see a message above the **Number of Questions to Select** drop-down menu, telling you that there are not enough questions available and that you will need to: choose a new category to use, add more questions, or reduce the number of questions you want to use.

Step 3

Now we will preview the question and then add it to our test. Here is what it looks like, as shown in the next screenshot:

1	For each of the following questions, select the matching answer from the menu.
Marks: 1	
	What are the two main political parties in the US?	democrat*republican ✓
	Who was the first person in space?	Yuri Gagarin ✓
	What color are bananas?	Yellow ✓
	Which two countries have the largest populations?	China*India ✓
	Correct	
	Marks for this submission: 1/1.	

Random Short-Answer matching considerations

These questions can be very useful if you want to create review sections on tests or simply want to drill students frequently over past questions in a quick and easy manner. However, as I am sure you can see in our item shown previously, there are some issues with creating these items.

The first issue is that creating a list of random questions from a wide variety of topic areas makes for an extremely easy quiz. Only the correct response is added to the matching, so if you decide to use these items, try to make sure that all the Random Short Answer items that are being drawn upon are in the same subject area and require the same type of answers (that is, if you have questions with dates as answers, put them all together in one category).

The other issue that is clear is the wildcard. If you intend to use these wildcards, you may want to go back to the Short Answer and create a new category specifically for the Random Short-Answer Matching and change the first correct answer to a specific response. For example, instead of using **democrats*republicans** as the first correct response, you could enter **democrats and republicans**. Doing this will ensure there is no hint or obvious difference between different responses.

Calculated

These questions are used to create problems with variables. They give you the ability to create an x+3=y type of problem by substituting random numbers into the **x** variable. Remember the wildcard mentioned previously? We will be using it again here to create what are called *datasets* from which the variables we use will be drawn from.

These items are particularly useful to math and science teachers, especially if you want your students practicing on the same formula multiple times. These items require a bit of practice, and are spread over three pages, but for the most part, they aren't too difficult to put together.

What we are going to do with this question type is create a simple problem with a single variable to have our students practice with.

Step 1

The first thing that we are going to do is set up a new quiz. We'll call it **Calculated**.

Once we have done that, we are going to create a new question. The Calculated question creation is similar to the other types, but there are some new options. In fact, the first thing on the page is a **Category** drop-down and a button called **Update the Category**. This function allows us to share wildcards from across categories, if any are available. We have not created any, so we have none to access. We will see how to this later.

Now, we need to give the question a name and write the question text. We're going to be starting with a very simple formula. Let's say we are teaching our students simple, single multiplication and we want them to practice their new skills. We'll name the question and enter the question text as the same thing, *What is {x}*2?*

Wildcard and Asterisk

We have talked about wildcards before. We use the asterisk to denote them. However, here the asterisk means multiply. I know this might be a bit confusing, but just remember here, the asterisk means multiply, not wildcard!

Step 2

Now that we have a question title and a question, we need to make an answer for it.

In the Answer section there are a few options available to us, all of which are new. Here is what the Answer section looks like and a brief description of each of the functions.

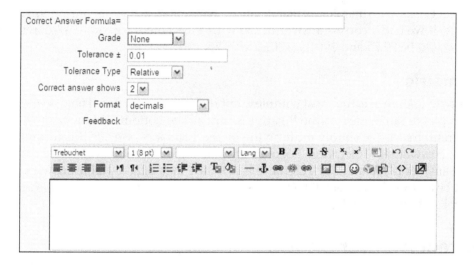

Correct Answer Formula

This is where we will put the formula for the correct answer. It will contain at least as many wildcards as there are in the question itself. **Do not include the equal sign in the formula**.

Tolerance

This setting allows us to enter a response tolerance range. By entering a number here, we set the range of answers that will be considered correct. The larger the number here, the larger the range of acceptable answers.

Tolerance Type

There are three Tolerance Types available in Moodle: **Relative**, **Nominal**, and **Geometric**.

Relative

Relative tolerance sets the upper and lower tolerance range by multiplying the correct answer by the number in the **Tolerance** (that is, Correct Answer*Tolerance). So, if our correct answer was 100, and our tolerance was .25, the result would be 100*.25=25. Therefore, the range of acceptable responses would be between 75 and 125 (100±25=75, 125).

Nominal

Nominal tolerance is very simple. It takes the Tolerance and adds and subtracts from the correct response (that is, Correct Answer±Tolerance). So, using our previous example, if we had a correct answer of 100 with a .25 **Tolerance**, our correct response range would be 99.75 and 100.25 (100±.25=99.75, 100.25).

Geometric

Geometric tolerance is the most complex, but it is still easy to use. The upper-end of the acceptable range mirrors the Relative formula. The bottom-end range, however, is different. Instead of simply multiplying by the Tolerance, we use this formula Correct Answer/(1+Tolerance). So, once again using our previous example, if our correct answer is 100 and our Tolerance is .25, the range of acceptable answers would be 80 to 125. (that is (100/(1+.25)=80) for the low range and the Relative Type formula for the high range.

Correct Answer Shows

This option shows the number of decimal places or the number of significant digits the answer will display, depending on the selection made in the following **Format** section.

Format

This drop-down menu has two options, **decimal** and **significant digits** which determines whether the answer will display decimals or significant digits. **Decimal** will leave the answers exactly as they are, up to the predetermined number of places selected. If **significant digits** is selected, the response will only give that number of digits, leaving all remainders as zeros. For example, 5.678534 with a format of decimal and a correct answer shows 4, will return with this: 5.678. If you had selected **significant digits** instead of **decimal,** the result will look like this: 5.678000.

Now that we understand the functions of each of these sections, we will begin to enter in the information. Our question again is basic multiplication with a single variable, **What is {x}*2?** In the **Correct Answer Formula=** we will enter **{x}*2**. All variables that need to be replaced by Moodle, such as **x** must be placed in curly brackets.

In the **Grade** drop-down, we want to give **100%**. In the **Tolerance**, we are going to change the default number to **0**, because there is only one correct answer and we are working with simple arithmetic. For the **Tolerance Type**, we are going to leave the setting at the default, **Relative**, because with the **Tolerance** set to **0**, this setting won't do anything. In **Correct answer shows** we are going to make it **0** and for **Format**, we will leave it at the default, **decimal**. Once all this information has been entered, we will see the following screenshot:

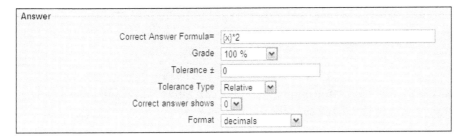

Multiplication

One quick note when using multiplication, if you enter {x}2, 2(x), 2x, or any other normally accepted multiplication form, the formula will not work. **You must use the '*' for all multiplication.**

We will now scroll down the page. The first thing we see is a button called **Blanks for 1 More Choices**, which will allow us to enter an alternative formula, if one is needed (I'm not a math teacher, but I'm sure there are many cases where this is done!).

You will also see a new section called **Unit 1**. You are able to enter in a unit of measurement here, such as grams, meters, or widgets. So, if the question is something like **What is the total length of Xm+Ym+Zm?** you could enter 'm' in the Unit textbox and a response of **XYZm** or **XYZ** would be accepted. There is also an option for more units to be added. So if we had a question like **What is the length of Xcm+Ymm+Zm?** we might want to allow students to answer in a variety of ways. We might want to add all three units (mm, cm, m) to allow the students to respond with whichever they want. For now, we are going to leave this option blank, but we will use it in our next question.

Now, we need to click on the **Next Page** button at the bottom of the page.

Step 3

After clicking on the **Next page** button, we will see a page called **Choose Dataset Properties**. This is where we need to select which dataset we will be using. What is a dataset? A dataset is the set of values that Moodle will use to replace the variable, in our case that means a set of numbers that will replace {x}. The larger the dataset you create, the less chance there is of question duplication. We don't need a huge dataset for our drill, so we are going to create one that has 20 possibilities.

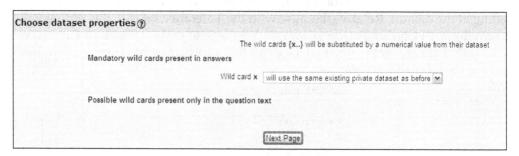

We really only have a simple choice here, we can either select **will use a new shared dataset** or **will use the same private dataset as before**.

If we choose **will use a new shared dataset** we will create a new set of numbers that can be used by the same variable, in our case **x**, in any other question in the quiz. This can be a useful feature, especially if you are creating a number of similar questions.

The second option is the **will use same private dataset as before**. This means that the numbers created for the variable will only be available for this question. We are going to select this option, simply because I want us to practice entering the datasets more than once. So, we select this option and click on the **Next Page** button at the bottom of the page.

Step 4

Now that was have decided on the dataset we want to use, we will be adding numbers to the {x} variable we created. There are two ways to do this in Moodle. One is manually adding numbers and the second is allowing Quiz to do the work for us. We'll look at both.

Now, looking at this page we see a lot of new options. It looks a little daunting at first, but don't worry, we'll go through it together. There are two sections on this page, one is called **Item to Add** and the other is called **Add**. Here is what the **Item to Add** section looks like, as shown in the next screenshot:

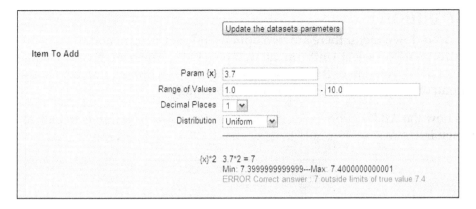

You might first notice the **ERROR** message at the bottom. This is because a randomly generated value, in this case **3.7**, has been given as **{x}**, and since we set our **Tolerance** and **Correct answer shows** options to **0**, this error message is normal. Now, let's take a look at the options here.

Update the datasets parameters

This button is located just above the **Item to Add** section. When clicked, it places a new, randomly generated number in the **Param{x}** textbox.

Param

Here, we can manually enter the numbers that we want to use. We simply need to type in the number that we want to use for the variable and click on the **Save changes** button at the bottom of the page. There is a limit of 100 entries.

Range of Values

Instead of manually inputting all the numbers, you are also able to supply Moodle with an acceptable range of numbers and it will randomly generate numbers within that range.

Decimal Places

This feature allows you to set the number of decimal places used in the question. It ranges from 0 to 10.

Distribution

In this drop-down menu there are two options, one is **Uniform** and the second is **Loguniform**. If you select **Uniform**, all numbers in the range are given an equal chance of being generated. If you select the **Loguniform** option, numbers at the lower end of the scale are more likely to be generated.

This is how the **Add** section looks. Again, there are a few new things to look at, as shown in the next screenshot:

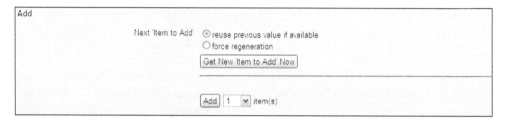

Next Item to Add

If you have deleted a number from your list of values, you can use the **reuse previous value if available** to replace the deleted number when creating new ones. Moogle will automatically add the deleted number and the new number to the dataset. We can't see the **Delete** button yet since we haven't created any items. Refer to individual items to use the fieldset just discussed.

The **force regeneration** function is used to automatically generate new values in the dataset.

When you have selected the option you want, click on the **Get New Item to Add Now** button and a new item will appear.

Add

This is the button you click on to create the new item. Next to the button you can see a drop-down menu. This menu contain the numbers 1 to 100 in multiples of 10. You can create one question at a time if you are using the manual way. You can create 10, 20, or more questions at a time if you are using the automated way.

The manual way

If you want to manually add in the numbers to be used, here is how you do it:

1. Type in the number you want in the **Param** textbox.
2. Go to the **Add** section below and click on the **Add** button. Don't change the number next to the button, leave it at **1**.

This is all you need to do to add a number to the variable. You can keep doing this until you have all the numbers you want.

The automated way (The easy way!)

If you want to make it easy on yourself, you should go ahead and use the **Range of Values**.This is how it is done:

1. Enter the lowest number in the acceptable range in the left box and add the highest number in the acceptable range in the right box.
2. Change the decimal places to suit your needs.
3. Select the **Distribution** you want.
4. Go to the **Add** section and in the **Next item to add** section change the button from **reuse previous value if available** to **force regeneration**.
5. Go to the **Add** button drop-down menu and select the number of variations you want.
6. Click on the **Add** button.

This is all you need to do to create a range of numbers for the variable.

So, what are we trying to do from here? Well, we want to create a simple, single-variable question. We are creating this question with a single variable for our students to drill basic substitution. We want to have 20 separate values for that variable. The easiest way for us to do this is using the automated way and having it create the 20 values we want for the variable {x}.

Step 5

Now we are going to determine the kinds of numbers we will allow to be added to the dataset. We don't want the results to be less than 2 or greater than 100. Because we are multiplying by 2, the lowest number we want to use is 1 and the highest is 50, because those numbers will deliver us a range of responses somewhere between 2 and 100.

We need to change the **Range of Values** to **1–50**. Then, we're going to change the **Decimal Places** to **0**. Next, we are going to set the **Distribution** to **Uniform**.

Once the new parameters are set, I will go back to the top of the screen and click on the **Update the datasets parameters**, which will place a new number, one within the newly outlined parameters, into the **Param** textbox.

Going to the **Add** section, we will set the **Next Item to Add** to **force regeneration**. We want a total of 20 values available, so we change the drop-down menu next to the **Add button** to **20**. Here is what our screen looks like.

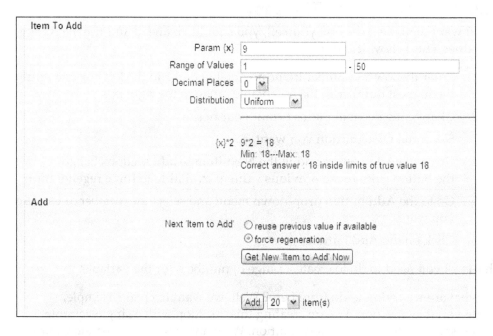

As you can see in the previous screenshot, the number **9** has been added to the **Param**. Under the **Distribution** drop-down, you can see that the number meets our requirements because it falls between the **Range of Values** that we have chosen.

Once this is done, we click on the Add button and 20 random items will be created directly below the **Add** button. The items are listed in reverse order, with the last number at the top. Here is what the newly created items look like:

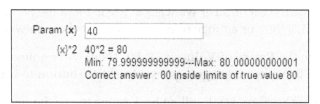

All of the numbers listed will be considered correct by Moodle. We will quickly scroll down to make sure they all are. When you do this on your own, you might notice a repeated number. If you want to change it to something else, simply type a new number in the **Param {x}** textbox.

Delete

Now that we have added some items, you will see a **Delete** button with a drop-down menu directly above the newly created items. This button will allow you to delete the items in the order they are listed, from last to first. You are also able to delete in multiples of 10.

Step 6

Now that we have created our question, we want to see how the variable substitution works. We will save our work and preview the question. We'll be given one of the 20 items we just created and we will need to multiply that number by two, as shown in the next screenshot:

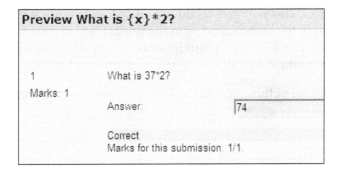

The item is working and we received the correct score. If you click on the **Start Again** button on the Preview menu, you will be given a new, randomly generated item from the list we created.

As you can see, we put together a single-variable item by creating a simple formula and dataset to replace the variable.

That is all there is to creating a single-variable, calculated item.

Creating a multi-variable item

Creating a multiple-variable item is almost the same as creating a single variable one. We will follow all the same steps as we did previously, with a few small changes so we can see some of the other functions in action!

Step 1

We will create a new question, making sure it is in the **Activity: Calculated category**. We are practicing dividing with decimals and measurements with our students, so we want to drill them on it. For Question name and Question text, we will enter **What is {x}/{y}?**

Step 2

In the **Answer** section, we will put {x}/{y} in the **Correct Answer Formula=** textbox. We will give a **100%** grade, a **Tolerance** of **.1** and set the **Tolerance Type** to **Nominal**. We will set the **Correct Answer Shows** to **2** and set the **Format** to **Decimals**.

Once these steps are done, we will go to the **Units** section and click on the **Blanks for 2 More Units** button. This will give us three unit spaces to work with. We will enter **cm** in the first, **mm** in the second, and **m** in the third. We will give each of these a different multiplier. Cm will have a multiplier of 1, mm will have a multiplier of 10, and m will have a multiplier of .01.

Once we have done all of this, we will click on the **Next Page** button at the bottom of the page.

Step 3

Now we need to select the type of dataset we want to use. We will select **will use a new shared dataset** for both variables.

Once the selections are made, we will click on the **Next Page** button.

Step 4

Here we will set the range of values for both {x} and {y}. We will set the **Range of Values** for both to **1–50**. We will set the decimal places at **1** and the **Distribution** to **Uniform**.

Once these steps are completed, we will click on the **Update the datasets parameters** button. Then we need to go to the **Add** section and select **force regeneration**. Once this is done, we will move to the **Add** button and select the number of items we want to create, in this case, we want to create 20. We will click on the **Add** button and 20 items will appear below.

After looking everything over and making sure there are no mistakes, we will click on the **Save changes** button.

Step 5

We will preview the question and make sure it works properly. Here is what we should have:

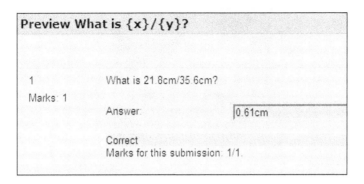

And that is all there is to making a multi-variable question.

Your turn

Now, you are going to make a multi-variable item! Just carry out the following steps and you shouldn't have any problems. If you run into a problem, look at your work and make sure there are no mistakes or any missing information.

1. Create a new calculated question. Name it **How many centimeters is ({a}+{b})/{c}?** Use this name for the Question text as well.

2. In the **Correct Answer Formula**, enter **({a}+{b})/{c}**. Change **Grade** to **100%**. Change **Tolerance** to **.1**. Change **Tolerance Type** to **Nominal**. For **Correct Answer Shows** make sure the setting is at **2** and that **Format** is set to **decimal**.

3. In the **Unit** section, add **cm** to the **Unit** textbox. When finished, click on the **Next Page** button.

4. Change the a, b, c wildcards to **will use a new shared dataset,** then click on the **Next Page** button.

5. Change the **Range of Values** from **1–10** to **1–20**. Make sure the **decimals** are set to **1** and the **Distribution** of **a** and **b** to **Uniform**. We are going to use the **Loguniform** for **c**, just to make it a little easier for the students.

6. In the **Add** section, click on the **force regeneration** radio button and change the **Add** drop-down to **20**. When you have done this, click on the **Add** button.

7. After checking over everything, click on the **Save changes** button.

8. Preview the question and you should see something like this (your numbers will probably be different):

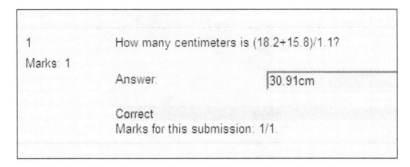

Calculation considerations

Calculation is not limited to basic arithmetic. There are a range of functions it can fulfil. The full list of current functions it supports is: abs, acos, acosh, asin, asinh, atan, atan2, bindec, ceil, cos, cosh, decbin, decoct, deg2rad, exp, expm1, floor, fmod, is_finite, is_infinite, is_nan, log10, log1p, log.max, min, octdec, pi(), pow, rad2deg, rand, round, sin, sinh, sqrt, tan, tanh.

When creating formulas in Calculate, make sure you are following the rules of math. If you make a mistake, forget a bracket or parenthesis, or neglect to include anything, your formula will not work as intended, if at all. So, be careful and take your time while creating these items.

One final note, if you are creating multiple levels or formulas inside of formulas, make sure to use all the parentheses you need. If you need to have a certain part of the problem calculated before another part, you need to use parentheses. If in doubt, use parentheses.

Embedded Answers (Cloze)

Cloze is a question type that uses the cloze procedure to test reading ability. It does this by deleting words from a text and having the reader insert them. Moodle's Embedded Answers (Cloze) offers three item types, short answer, numerical questions, and multiple choice, which are embedded in a sentence, paragraph, or other piece of text. Cloze is one of the more difficult question types available in Quiz because you need to use a mark-up language to create these item. In Embedded Answers (Cloze), that mark-up language is called CLOZE. The CLOZE mark-up language is used to tell Moodle what to do with the text and how to display it. Here you have to use Moodle auto-format. When you save your text, Moodle will do a number of things to automatically format your text for you. For example, URLs such as `http://yahoo.com` or even `www.yahoo.com` will be turned into links. Your line breaks will be retained, and blank lines will start new paragraphs. Smiley characters such as :-) will automatically become their graphical equivalents. You can also embed HTML code if you want and it will be retained.

Just to let you know, chances are you will make some mistakes when making these questions, especially if you are not familiar with Cloze. Don't worry, we'll walk you through the process and give you some tips on how to check your work.

There are two options for creating these questions: you can either write the code directly into the rich-text editor or you can import the files from somewhere else. We will start with the basics, showing the different formats for this item type and then we will show you how to import files.

Now, let's get started! For the first example, we'll be showing how to create a simple, fill-in-the-blank question inside a sentence, very similar to Short Answer.

Hot Potatoes

Many people feel that Hot Potatoes software is the easiest way to create Embedded answer (Cloze) questions. Once you have created your questions on your PC, you can then import them into Moodle's quiz module.

Hot Potatoes is a free software and allows for these questions to be created without learning all this syntax.

Short Answer—Cloze

Step 1

To start with, we want to create a new quiz. We'll call this test Embedded Answers (Cloze). We'll keep all the settings as default except for **Adaptive**, which we want turned off. We'll click on the **Save and display button**, which will bring us to the **Add Questions to Quiz** screen. In the Question Bank, we are going to switch the category to the new quiz we have just created, **Embedded Answers (Cloze)** and then go to the **Create a New Question** drop-down and select **Embedded Answers (Cloze)**.

Step 2

The first thing you might notice as you scroll down the page is that it is very short. There is very little for us to do here because all the information will be contained in the rich-text editor. All we really need to do outside the rich-text editor is provide the question name and offer general feedback.

For the question name, I am entering **Queen Isabella sent Columbus on his voyage**.

Step 3

Now, we are going to start entering the mark-up. All parts of the question text that are not part of the response are outside the curly brackets All the actual mark-up needs to be inside the curly brackets { **and** }. Because the question begins with an embedded answer, we start by adding {.

The next thing we need to address is the point values of the item. We want this question to be worth the same weight as any other question, so we want to start by entering a **1** at the beginning, which will give it the same value as all other questions on the test, assuming we have left all the other questions equal.

We also want to make this a Short Answer-type question, so the next thing we are going to enter is **SHORT ANSWER** (each of the question type designators in Embedded Answers must be written in all capital letters), which will create the blank in the text. Immediately after the colon, we need to begin entering the possible responses.

In the blank, we want our students to write Queen Isabella, so we need to make sure we give a 100 percent grade for that answer. We begin by entering `%100%Queen Isabella`, which will score this response as correct and give it full points. We also want to give some feedback, so after that we type `#Correct!`. The # signifies the feedback received. The code will look like this: `%100%Queen Isabella#Correct!`

Now, we also want to give credit if a student writes King Ferdinand. However, since he wasn't the main person involved, we only want to give half-credit for this response, as well as a bit of feedback. We enter the code like this: `~%50%King Ferdinand#He was partially involved`. Note the ~.This is used to separate answers.

Finally, we need to do something for feedback for all other responses. By entering `~*`, we are saying that the response is not worth any points. For feedback, we want to make sure the student knows the correct answer. The code looks like this: `~*#Wrong Answer. Queen Isabella is the correct answer.`

We have now added all the code we need for the response, so we need to close the code by adding a }. Now we need to finish the question by adding the rest of the text. After the } we type `sent Columbus on his voyage.`

Now, in the Question textbox we have the following CLOZE code:

```
{1:SHORTANSWER:100%Queen Isabella#Correct!~%50%King Ferdinand#He was
partially involved.~*#Wrong answer. Queen Isabella is the correct
answer.} sent Columbus on his voyage.
```

Copying from MS Word

Don't! When you copy and paste from Microsoft Word, some of that code comes along with it. It can cause your code to become corrupted and not function properly. If you don't want to use the Moodle HTML editor, use some kind of plain text editor.

Once we have entered this text, there is a button below titled **Decode and Verify the Question Text**. By clicking on this button, we will see if there are any mistakes. In fact, I purposely have made a mistake in the previous code so you can see what an error message looks like. Before you go on, look back at the previous code and see if you see anything that looks wrong. If you don't see it, not to worry. I purposely left off the % before Queen Isabella. By doing this, I created an error that the **Decode and Verify** button has picked up. The output is displayed in the next screenshot:

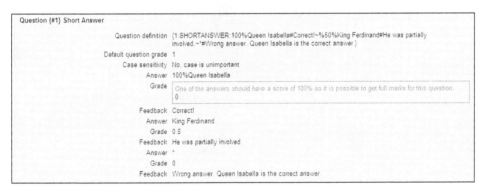

Looking at the red box around the Grade, we see the mistake. I have not given any answer the full possible points. 100%Queen Isabella is also clearly not a response I want to give credit for either. What I need to do is go back and add another % in front of the **100%Queen Isabella**. This change will score the question as a correct response with full points. Here is the corrected code.

```
{1:SHORTANSWER:%100%Queen Isabella#Correct!~%50%King Ferdinand#He
was partially involved.~*#Wrong answer. Queen Isabella is the correct
answer.} sent Columbus on his voyage.
```

Once we go back and add the %, the Decode and Verify message no longer gives any errors. This means we can move on.

Question (#1) Short Answer	
Question definition	{1:SHORTANSWER:%100%Queen Isabella#Correct!~%50%King Ferdinand#He was partially involved.~*#Wrong answer. Queen Isabella is the correct answer.}
Default question grade	1
Case sensitivity	No, case is unimportant
Answer	Queen Isabella
Grade	1
Feedback	Correct!
Answer	King Ferdinand
Grade	0.5
Feedback	He was partially involved.
Answer	*
Grade	0
Feedback	Wrong answer. Queen Isabella is the correct answer.

Step 4

Now that we have entered in the code and verified that the question is working properly, we can save the question. In fact, Moodle will not allow you to save the question if there are any errors.

Now we want to preview it to see how it looks and how the responses work. We will go to the preview button and try each of the responses. Here is what the question and the correct response looks like.

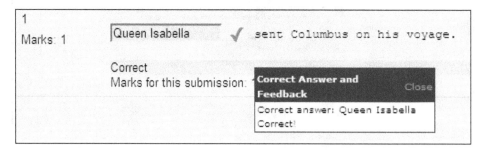

Notice the floating feedback? You only see the feedback you entered when your mouse hovers over the answer. Make sure your students understand this point.

After we have confirmed that the question is working and there are no mistakes in spelling or in any other information, we move the question to the test. This is all you need to do to make a Short Answer-type Embedded Answer question.

Numerical

Remember the Numerical questions discussed earlier? The Embedded Answer (Cloze) Numerical questions are very similar to the Numerical question type, but there are differences, mainly in the way they are created. Please be aware of this if you are using both types of questions.

The **Numerical** options in Embedded Answer (Cloze) are very similar to Short Answer. The difference is that any responses must be numerical and they may not include text.

Because this item is so similar to Short Answer, we will work through this together. I'll point out the differences as we come to them.

Step 1

First we need to create a new Embedded Answer (Cloze) item and name it **2+___=8**.

Step 2

In the Question text, we need to create a bit of code, just like we did previously in Short Answer. We will enter `2+{1:NUMERICAL:%100%6#Correct~*#Sorry , the answer was 6.}=8`. We will now scroll to the bottom of the page and click on **Decode and Verify**. Once we see that this formula is correct, we will save the question and then preview it.

As you can see, this is identical to the way we did Short Answer, except that I have entered **NUMERICAL**, which designates that the response must be numerical in nature. You may not enter non-numbers as the answer. If you do, the result will be considered incorrect.

Here is what the item looks like when completed correctly:

Here is what the question looks like when incorrectly answered. Note that the floating textbox is only visible if the incorrect answer is hovered over:

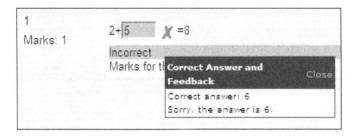

The other neat thing we can do with Numerical here, is just like what we did with the independent Numerical discussed previously. We can allow a margin of error in the responses. Work through this with me.

Step 1

First we need to create a new question. Once the question is made, we will title it **12*____=144**.

Step 2

Now, in the Question text we will enter the following {1:NUMERICAL:%100%12#Corr ect!~%75%12:1#Close! The correct answer was 12.~*#Sorry, the correct answer was 12.}=144.

See the %75%12:1? This 12:1 means that we have allowed a 1 number deviation from the correct response. So, a student entering 11 or 13 will get 75 percent if they guess either. We can create as many of these alternatives as we like, but for now, we're going to keep it simple.

Once we have entered this information, we will click on **Decode and Verify** to check the formula. Once we have confirmation that is it correct, we save it.

If a student responds with an **11** he would see the following screenshot. Note that if the student hovers the mouse over the **11**, he or she would see a floating menu with the **Correct Answer and Feedback** we entered. I have manipulated the image so it is seen separately in the screenshot:

Matching

Creating matching questions in Embedded Answers is similar to the Short Answer, although here they are called **MUITICHOICE**. We enter the text and code in a similar fashion as shown previously. Watch me work through putting one together for you.

Step 1

To start, we are going to create a new Embedded Answer question. In the question, we'll make sure the category is set where we want it (**Default for Embedded Answer**) and we'll title this one **Matching Weather and Seasons**.

Step 2

In the Question textbox, we want to enter four weather types and have our students match the weather to the season.

First, we tell the students: **Match the weather to the season.**

Then, we enter in the following:

1. Warm:{1:MULTICHOICE:%100%Spring#Correct!~Summer#No.~Fall#No. ~Winter#No}

This shows us **1. Warm:** is the prompt. In the code we can see that the question is worth 1 point. It is a Matching question. We also see that **Spring** is the correct answer and the feedback received from selecting **Spring** is **Correct!**. Students who select **Summer**, **Fall**, and **Winter**, will receive no points and they will see the simple feedback, **No**.

We will now repeat this process for each of the remaining three weather types.

2. Hot:{1:MULTICHOICE:Spring#No.%100%Summer#Correct!~Fall#No. ~Winter#No.}

3. Cool:{1:MULTICHOICE:Spring#No.~Summer#No.~%100%Fall#Correct! ~Winter#No.}

4. Cold:{1:MULTICHOICE:Spring#No.~Summer#No.~Fall#No.~%100%Winter #Correct!}

The following screenshot shows how the question appears:

Match the weather to the season.
1. Warm: {1:MULTICHOICE:%100%Spring#Correct!~Summer#No.~Fall#No.~Winter#No.}
2. Hot: {1:MULTICHOICE:Spring#No~%100%Summer#Correct!~Fall#No.~Winter#No.}
3. Cool: {1:MULTICHOICE:Spring#No.~Summer#No.~%100%Fall#Correct~Winter#No.}
4. Cold: {1:MULTICHOICE:Spring#No.~Summer#No.~Fall#No.~%100%Winter#Correct!}

= and %

You can use = to signify a correct response in both Matching and Numerical instead of %100%. However, for some reason, = does not work in Short Answer. So, in Short Answer this {1:MULTICHOICE:%100%Red#Correct!~Yellow#No.~Blue#No.~Green#No.} would work but {1:MULTICHOICE:=Red#Correct!~Yellow#No.~Blue#No.~Green#No.} would not. I use %100% for all questions, but feel free to substitute = if you'd like.

Step 3

Once I have entered the code, I'll want to go to the bottom of the page and use the **Decode and Verify** button to confirm everything is correct.

Because there are four possible grades in this question, we will receive feedback on each of the items. The feedback for Question {1} is shown in the next screenshot. Numbers 2, 3, and 4 all have a similar look.

Question {#1} Multiple Choice	
Question definition	{1:MULTICHOICE:%100%Spring#Correct!~Summer#No.~Fall#No.~Winter#No.}
Default question grade	1
Layout	Dropdown menu in-line in the text
Answer	Spring
Grade	1
Feedback	Correct!
Answer	Summer
Grade	0
Feedback	No.
Answer	Fall
Grade	0
Feedback	No.
Answer	Winter
Grade	0
Feedback	No.

We can see that the grades, responses, and feedback are correct, so we save the question. Now we want to preview it and answer all the questions correctly to make sure they are working properly. Let's look at the completed question in the following screenshot:

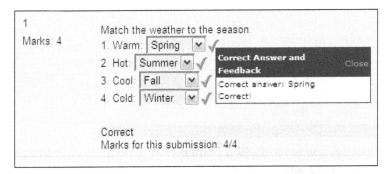

You can see that all the answers are correct, the feedback for the correct answer is there, and the total points (4/4) has been given.

If you wanted to create something like this in a sentence, you can. It takes a little more work, but it's not too hard.

The first thing you need to do is create a new question. After giving the question name in the question text, you could enter something like this: In the Spring it is {1:MULTICHOICE:Cold#Sorry, it is warm.~Hot#Sorry, it is warm.~%100%Warm#Correct!}.

Entering this will create a Multichoice in a sentence. The output is shown in the next screenshot:

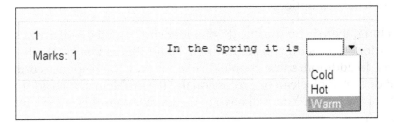

If you want to have multiple sentences connected, simply continue adding to the question text. Here, we have added to the original question text. The output of the following code is shown in the next screenshot:

```
In the Spring it is {1:MULTICHOICE:Cold#Sorry, it is warm.~Hot#Sorry,
it is warm.~%100%Warm#Correct!},
but in the Summer it is {1:MULTICHOICE:Cold#Sorry, it is
warm.~Warm#Sorry, it is hot.~%100%Hot#Correct!}.
```

Notice that this question is worth two points. That is because both Multichoice sections have been assigned one point each.

Embedded Answers (Cloze) considerations

These are not the easiest questions to begin with, but they get easier the more you use them. They can be a very useful addition to your tests, but there are a couple of things to consider before adding them.

Like in the previous Short Answer questions, Embedded Answers (Cloze) Short Answer will only accept the options you enter, so a spelling mistake, a slightly different word, a different phrasing, will all be counted wrong. You should follow the advice in Short Answer, keep the responses short and direct, and give clear instructions on what is expected. Alternatively, you can use wildcards, as shown earlier. The wildcard should be placed as the last answer option and used as a catch-all and feedback option.

In the Matching, there is no shuffle. If you enter choices, they will always be in that same order. Make sure you are thinking about this as you create the questions and answers. In addition, some people dislike the way the responses don't line up. They feel it doesn't look clean or professional. This problem can be addressed by making use of the editor. You will have to decide whether this is a problem or not yourself.

There is a lot more to this type of question that can be addressed here. For additional information about Embedded Answers (Cloze), you should check the context help for this in the question, as well as at http://docs.moodle.org/en/Cloze.

Essay

Essay questions are perhaps the easiest of the questions to create. These questions allow you to see what the student knows or feels about the question. One of the drawbacks to using Essay is that they require you to read each response individually and manually score them, something we will talk more about later.

Some people use Assignment to give essay questions. Assignment allows you to create essay questions in a faster, easier, and many say, better way. However, if it does have a place in your quizzes, that place is for when you want to time your students' writing, and this is something that can't be done with Assignment.

When creating Essay questions, it is important to clearly tell the students what you are looking for in the response. How many words you are looking for, that they must follow a specific essay format, and so on. If you are able to clearly spell out these types of things, the Essay format will be a valuable addition to your tests.

Step 1

We will create a new quiz and title it **Essay**. Then we need to make sure we are in the **Default** for **Essay** and then create a new essay question. We will call it **Should the government support more farmers?** and use the same for the question text. **Choose a position and support it with evidence from class discussions and readings**.

Under this entry, we see two feedback fields, **General Feedback** and **Feedback**. These are basically the same thing, they will show feedback to the student after we are ready and have graded the essay. The only difference between these two fields is that the **General Feedback** will always be shown and the **Feedback** will only be shown once. This action, of course, depends on your Quiz settings in the **Review Options**.

Once we have entered our feedback, if any, we click on the **Save changes** button.

Step 2

Preview the essay question and see if there are any mistakes or if there is anything you want to change.

Here is what the finished product looks like.

1	Should the government support more farmers? Choose a position and support it with evidence from class discussions and readings.
Marks: 1	
	Answer: I think that the government should...

That is all there is to making Essay questions in quiz. It is very easy to do. In fact it is so easy, I am not even going to make you create one!

Essay considerations

Essays can be a very useful addition to your tests, but are time consuming to mark. You will need to read over each one individually and manually grade it. Until you have gone in and added a grade, the student will have a zero for this question.

Also, when you have multiple essay questions on one page of a quiz, only the first will give the student access to the rich-text editor. Any remaining essay questions on the page will have plain-text areas only.

Depending on your teaching context and subject area, it may be simpler to have students use the Assignment activity or a word processor and print their work for you to look over and score. Not only does this process give you a hard copy of their work, it also allows you to physically write on the paper, which may allow more specific feedback to be given. Grades are automatically transferred into the Gradebook, students have feedback available to them online at any time, and you can allow the students to retake the quiz with their earlier answers available.

Description

I saved the easiest for last. In fact, Description questions are not even proper questions. There is no way to answer and there is no grade for them. They are mainly used to display text or images, and they can act as labels for different parts of your test.

One important thing to note is that if you decide to use descriptions, you must not use the quiz-shuffling question orders option. If you do this, descriptions will not appear in the order you want them to.

I use these items to display an image, scene, or reading that I want my students to write about or answer questions relating to it. If you use Descriptions, and you want the questions to directly follow it in the test, you need to turn off the **Shuffle questions** option in your quiz, or the item could appear anywhere in the test.

The item creation is extremely simple, and is just like Essay. You need to enter a Question name and Question text, image, table, or other item. There is a Feedback function as well, which can be used to give students additional information about the topic or why the material was added to the quiz.

Once you have completed adding all the material you want, click on the **Save** button to save the question.

Summary

We have looked at all the question types available in Quiz now. We have learned how to create each type and discussed several issues relating to each. Unfortunately, we haven't been able to cover every possibility here, only some of the basics.

Each of the question types here is useful and can be a valuable addition to your tests. I recommend that you work through each of the items we have looked at and practice making more. You will find that the more you make, the easier it gets to create them and alter them to fit your needs. All the effort you put into working with the Quiz module will be worth your while because of the auto-grading and recycling opportunities these features present.

In the next chapter, I will look at some complex questions and show how to develop a test using Quiz. I will also supply a few more tricks for you that weren't included here.

4
Creating a Quiz

In the previous chapters, we covered how to set up all the questions themselves. All this was leading us to where we are now, creating a full quiz in the Quiz module. We will look at the options in the quiz module more closely, use them, and then see how they work in a complete test.

In this chapter, we will:

- Create a complete test
- Use a variety of options we have not used before
- Discuss issues related to creating tests in Moodle

Getting started

As mentioned earlier, we have already seen and practised setting up a variety of question types, and we have moved them into a Quiz, but we have not really created a complete test. To do this, we will need to review the options we saw earlier and start using them. We will need to view the **Timing**, **Display**, and all the other options available to us if we want to create an effective test for our students.

To start with, we need to select a topic or theme for our test. We are going to choose general science, since the subject matter will be easy to incorporate each of the item types we have seen previously.

Now that we have an idea of what our topic is going to be, we will get started in the creation of the test. We will be creating all new questions for this test, which will give us the added benefit of a bit more practice in item creation. So, let's get started and work on making our first real test!

Let's open our Moodle course, go to the **Activity** drop-down, and select **Create a new Quiz**. Once it has been selected, we will be taken to the Quiz creation page and we'll be looking at the **General** section.

The General section

We have seen this section so many times that there really isn't much we need to discuss about it. The only thing we really need to do is give the test a name that describes what the test is going to cover. Let's call it 'General Science Final Exam' as it describes what we will be doing in the test.

The introduction is also important. Previously, we have simply copied the name and placed it in the description, mainly because we were just practicing and there really was no actual need to describe the test. However, this is a test students will take and an effective description of what they will be doing is an important point for them. It helps get their minds thinking about the topic at hand, which can help them prepare, and a person who is prepared can usually perform better. For our introduction, we will write the following, 'This test will see how much you learned in our science class this term. The test will cover all the topics we have studied, including, geology, chemistry, biology, and physics. In this test, there are a variety of question types (True/False, Matching, and others). Please look carefully at the sample questions before you move on. If you have any questions during the test, raise your hand. You will have 'x' attempts with the quiz.

We have now given the test an effective name and we have given the students a description of what the test will cover. This will be shown in the **Info** tab to all the students before they take the test, and if we want in the days running up to the test. That's all we need to do in this section.

Timing

In this section, we need to make some decisions about when we are going to give the test to the students. We will also need to make a decision about how long we will give the students to complete the test. These are important decisions, and we need to make sure we give our students enough time to complete the test. The default **Timing** section is shown in the next screenshot:

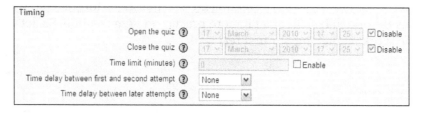

We probably know when our final exam will be. So, when we are creating the test, we can set the date that the test will be available to the students and the date it will stop being accessible to them. Because this is our final exam, we only want it to be available for one day, for a specified time period.

We will start by clicking on the **Disable** checkboxes next to **Open the Quiz** and **Close the Quiz** dates. This step will enable the date/time drop-down menus and allow us to set them for the test. For us, our test will start on **March 20, 2010** at **16:55** p.m. and it will end the same day, one hour later. So we will change the appropriate menus to reflect our needs. If these dates are not set, a student in the course will be able to take the quiz any time after you finish creating it.

We will need to give the students time to get in class, settle down, and have their computers ready. However, we also need to make sure the students finish the test in our class, so we have decided to create a time limit of 45 minutes. This means that the test will be open for one hour, and in that one hour time frame, once they start the test, they will have 45 minutes to finish it. To do this, we need to click on the **Enable** checkbox next to the **Time Limit (minutes)** textbox. Clicking on this will enable the textbox, and in it we will enter **45**. This value will limit the quiz time to 45 minutes, and will show a floating, count-down timer in the test, causing it to auto-submit 45 minutes after it is started. It is good to note that many students get annoyed by the floating timer and its placement on the screen. The other alternative is to have the test proctor have the students submit the quiz at a specified time.

Now, we have decided to give a 45 minute time limit on the test, but without any open-ended questions, the test is highly unlikely to take that long. There is also going to be a big difference in the speed at which different students work. The test proctor should explain to the students how much time they should spend on each question and reviewing their answers.

Under the **Time Limit (minutes)** we see the **Time delay between first and second attempt** and **Time delay between later attempts** menus. If we are going to offer the test more than once, we can set these, which would force the students to wait until they could try again. The time delays range from 30 minutes to 7 days, and the **None** setting will not require any waiting between attempts on the quiz. We are going to leave these set to **None** because this is a final exam and we are only giving it once.

Once all the information has been entered into the **Timing** section, this dialog box is what we have, as shown in the next screenshot:

Timing							
Open the quiz ⑦	20 ▾	March ▾	2010 ▾	16 ▾	55 ▾	☐ Disable
Close the quiz ⑦	20 ▾	March ▾	2010 ▾	17 ▾	40 ▾	☐ Disable
Time limit (minutes) ⑦	45			☑ Enable		
Time delay between first and second attempt ⑦	None ▾					
Time delay between later attempts ⑦	None ▾					

Display

Here, we will make some decisions about the way the quiz will look to the students. We will be dividing questions over several pages, which we will use to create divisions in the test. We will also be making decisions about the shuffle questions and shuffle within questions here.

Firstly, as the test creators, we should already have a rough idea of how many questions we are going to have on the test. Looking at the **Questions Per Page** drop-down menu, we have the option of 1 to 50 questions per page. We have decided that we will be displaying six questions per page on the test. Actually, we will only have five questions the students will answer, but we also want to include a description and a sample question for the students to see how the questions look and how to answer them' thus we will have six on each page.

We have the option to shuffle questions within pages and within questions. By default, **Shuffle Questions** is set to **No** and **Shuffle within Questions** is set to **Yes**. We have decided that we want to have our questions shuffled. But wait, we can't because we are using Description questions to give examples, and if we chose shuffle, these examples would not be where they need to be. So, we will leave the **Shuffle Questions** setting at the default **No**. However, we do want to shuffle the responses within the question, which will give each student a slightly different test using the same questions and answers.

When the display settings are finished, we can see the output shown in the next screenshot:

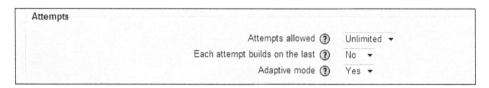

Attempts		
Attempts allowed ⑦	Unlimited ▾
Each attempt builds on the last ⑦	No ▾
Adaptive mode ⑦	Yes ▾

Attempts

In this section, we will be setting the number of attempts possible and how further attempts are dealt with. We will also make a decision about the Adaptive Mode.

Looking at the **Attempts allowed** drop-down menu, we have the option to set the number from 1 to 10 or we can set it to **Unlimited** attempts. For our test, we have already decided to set the value to 1 attempt, so we will select **1** from the drop-down menu.

We have the option of setting the **Each Attempt Builds on the Last** drop-down menu to Yes or No. This feature does nothing now, because we have only set the test to have a single attempt. If we had decided to allow multiple attempts, a Yes setting would have shown the test taker all the previous answers, as if the student were taking the test again, as well as indicating whether he or she were correct or not. If we were giving our students multiple attempts on the test, but we did not want them to see their previous answers, we would set this to **No**.

We are also going to be setting Adaptive mode to **No**. We do not want our students to be able to immediately see or correct their responses during the test; we want the students to review their answers before submitting anything.

However, if we did want the students to check their answers and correct any mistakes during the test, we would set the **Attempts Allowed** to a number above 1 and the **Adaptive Mode** to **Yes**, which would give us the small **Submit** button where the students would check and correct any mistakes after each question. If multiple attempts are not allowed, the **Submit** button will be just that, a button to submit your answer.

Here is what the **Attempts** section looks like after we have set our choices:

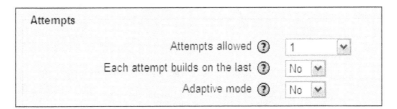

Grades

In this section, we will set the way Moodle will score the student. We see three choices in this section, **Grading method**, **Apply penalties**, and **Decimal digits in grades**; however, because we have only selected a single attempt, two of these options will not be used.

Grading Method allows us to determine which of the scores we want to give our student after multiple tries. We have four options here: **Highest Grade**, **Average Grade**, **First Attempt**, and **Last Attempt**. **Highest Grade** uses the highest grade achieved from any attempt on any individual question. The **Average Grade** will take the total number of tries and grades and average them. The **First Attempt** will use the grade from the first attempt and the **Last Attempt** will use the grade from the final attempt. Since we are only giving one try on our test, this setting has no function and we will leave it set at its default, **Highest Grade**, because either option would give the same result.

Apply penalties is similar to **Grading method,** in that it does not function because we have turned off Adaptive Mode. If we had set Adaptive Mode to Yes, then this feature would give us the option of applying penalties, which are set in the individual question setup pages. If we were using Adaptive Mode and this option feature set to No, then there would be no penalties for mistakes as in previous attempts. If it were set to Yes, the penalty amount decided on in the question would be subtracted for each incorrect response from the total points available on the question. However, our test is not set to Adaptive Mode, so we will leave it at the default setting, **Yes**. It is important to note here that no matter how often a student is penalized for an incorrect response, their grade will never go below zero.

The **Decimal digits in grades** shows the final grade the student receives with the number of decimal places selected here. There are four choices available in this setting: 0, 1, 2, and 3. If, for example, the number is set to 1, the student will receive a score calculated to 1 decimal place, and the same follows for 2 and 3. If the number is set to 0, the final score will be rounded. We will set our **Decimal digits in grades** to **0**.

After we have finished, the **Grades** section appears as shown in the next screenshot:

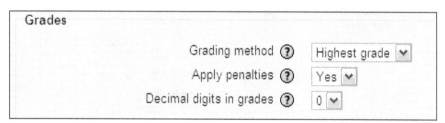

Review options

This sectopm is where we set when and what our students will see when they look back at the test. There are three categories: **Immediately after the attempt; Later, while quiz is still open;** and **After the quiz is closed.**

The first category, **Immediately after the attempt**, will allow students to see whatever feedback we have selected to display immediately after they click on the **Submit all and finish** button at the end of the test, or **Submit,** in the case of Adaptive mode. The second category, **Later, while quiz is still open**, allows students to view the selected review options any time after the test is finished, that is, when no more attempts are left, but before the test closes. Using the **After the quiz is closed** setting will allow the student to see the review options after the test closes, meaning that students are no longer able to access the test because a close date was set. The **After the quiz is closed** option is only useful if a time has been set for the test to close, otherwise the review never happens because the test doesn't ever close.

Each of these three categories contains the same review options: **Responses, Answers, Feedback, General feedback, Scores,** and **Overall feedback**. We have actually been looking at **Review options** throughout this book. We have seen all of these except for **Overall feedback**, which we will be using shortly. Here is what these options do:

- **Responses** are the student's response to the question and whether he or she were wrong or correct.
- **Answers** are the correct response to the question.
- **Feedback** is the feedback you enter based on the answer the student gives. This feedback is different from the General quiz feedback they may receive.
- **General feedback** are the comments all students receive, regardless of their answers.
- **Scores** are the scores the student received on the questions.
- **Overall feedback** are the comments based on the overall grade on the test.

We want to give our students all of this information, so they can look it over and find out where they made their mistakes, but we don't want someone who finishes early to have access to all the correct answers. So, we are going to eliminate all feedback on the test until after it closes. That way there is no possibility for the students to see the answers while other students might still be taking the test. To do remove such feedback, we simply unclick all the options available in the categories we don't want. Here is what we have when we are finished:

Review options ⑦		
Immediately after the attempt	Later, while the quiz is still open	After the quiz is closed
☐ Responses	☐ Responses	☑ Responses
☐ Answers	☐ Answers	☑ Answers
☐ Feedback	☐ Feedback	☑ Feedback
☐ General feedback	☐ General feedback	☑ General feedback
☐ Scores	☐ Scores	☑ Scores
☐ Overall feedback	☐ Overall feedback	☑ Overall feedback

Regardless of the options and categories we select in the **Review options**, students will always be able to see their overall scores. Looking at our settings, the only thing a student will be able to view immediately after the test is complete is the score. Only after the test closes, will the student be able to see the full range of review material we will be providing.

If we had allowed multiple attempts, we would want to have different settings. So, instead of **After the quiz is closed**, we would want to set our **Review options** to **Immediately after the attempt**, because this setting would let the student know where he or she had problems and which areas of the quiz need to be focussed on.

One final point here is that even a single checkbox in any of the categories will allow the student to open and view the test, giving the selected review information to the student. This option may or may not be what you want. Be careful to ensure that you have only selected the options and categories you want to use.

Security

This section is where we can increase quiz security, but it is important to note that these settings will not eliminate the ability of tech-savvy students to cheat. What this section does is provide a few options that make cheating a bit more difficult to do. We have three options in this section: **Browser security**, **Require password**, and **Require network address**.

The **Browser security** drop-down has two options: **None** and **Full screen pop-up with some JavaScript security**. The **None** option is the default setting and is appropriate for most quizzes. This setting doesn't make any changes in browser security and is the setting you will most likely want to use for in-class quizzes, review quizzes, and others. Using the fullscreen option will create a browser that limits the options for students to fiddle things. This option will open a fullscreen browser window with limited navigation options. In addition to limiting the number of navigation options available, this option will also limit the keyboard and mouse commands available. This option is more appropriate for high-stakes type tests and shouldn't be used unless there is a reason. This setting also requires that JavaScript is used. **Browser security** is more a safety measure against students pressing the wrong button than preventing cheating, but can help reduce it.

The **Require password** does exactly what you think it would. It requires the students to enter a password before taking the test. To keep all your material secure, I recommend using a password for all quizzes that you create. This setting is especially important if you are offering different versions of the quiz to different classes or different tests in the same class and you want to make sure only those who should be accessing the quiz can. There is also an **Unmask** checkbox next to the password textbox. This option will show you the password, just in case you forget!

Finally, we have the **Require network address** option, which will only allow those at certain IP Addresses to access the test. These settings can be useful to ensure that only students in the lab or classroom are taking the test. This setting allows you to enter either complete IP Addresses (for example. 123.456.78.9), which require that specific address to begin the test; partial IP Addresses (for example 123.456), which will accept any address as long as it begins with the address prefixes; and what is known as **Classless Inter-Domain Routing** (**CIDR**) notation, (for example 123.456.78.9/10), which only allows specific subnets. You might want to consult with your network administrator if you want to use this security option.

By combining these settings, we can attempt to cut down on cheating and improper access to our test. In our case here, we are only going to use the fullscreen option. We will be giving the test in our classroom, using our computers, so there is no need to turn on the IP Address function or require a password. When we have finished, the **Security** section appears as shown in the next screenshot:

Security	
Browser security (?)	Full screen pop-up with some JavaScript security
Require password (?)	☐ Unmask
Require network address (?)	

Common module settings

In this section, we have four options available to us: **Group mode**, **Visible**, **ID number**, and **Grade category**.

The **Group mode** doesn't affect the students, it is only for the teacher. When looking at the test results, the teacher will see them in smaller groups instead of as a whole. In the **Group mode** drop-down menu, there are three options. The first is the default setting, **None**. This setting means that the students taking the test are all part of the same group. The second option is **Separate groups**, which means that the students are part of their own group and take the test in that group. **Visible groups** means that students work in their own groups, but they are able to see the work of other groups. This setting, however, does not mean that they will see the other student's answers.

Using the **Visible** feature is identical to the Open/Closed eye in the course. This function will make the test visible or invisible to the students. It is a good idea to hide the quiz while you are developing it, just in case a student accidentally accesses it or takes it before you are ready. Note that invisible quizzes do not show up on the event calendar.

The **ID number** function allows you to set an ID for the quiz, which will help identify it for grading. You can develop an ID system for your course that will help you identify types of activities, quizzes, and others. For example, you could set up an ID system with the hundred's placeholder acting as an ID for quizzes, activities, and others. The ten's placeholder might act as a week identifier. The one's placeholder might be the numerical order of the assignments. So, using our idea, let's say we decide to use 300 as an identifier for quizzes. We are in our fourth week of class. This is the second quiz we have given that week. In our ID system this quiz would be 342, so that is what we would place in the ID Number textbox.

The **Grade category** function is used if you have set up grading categories in **Gradebook**. The default setting is **Uncategorised**, which will not place the results into any preset category. If you have created categories in **Gradebook**, you will see them here and you can select the appropriate category for the test results to be included in.

For our test, we will be leaving the **Group** set at **None**; changing **Visible to Hide**; setting **ID number** to **1**; and the **Grade category** will be set to **Uncategorised**, because we have not yet created any. Here is what the **Common module settings** looks like when we finish. Some users may have a **Show Advanced** button in this field that will allow them to restrict the quiz to particular groups.

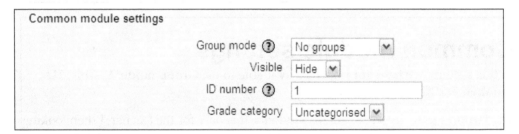

Overall feedback

In this section, we can give our students feedback based on the results of their test. These fields are set up with what is called a **Grade boundary**. A **Grade boundary** will give the students the feedback based on the range of scores in the boundary.

When setting up the **Grade boundary**, we can enter either numbers or percentages with a preset maximum grade of **100%** and a preset minimum grade of **0%**. By default, there are seven Grade boundaries, but we can set as many as we'd like, by clicking on **Add 3 more feedback fields**. Any fields that we do not want to use, we leave blank. Here is what we will enter as **Overall feedback** for our test:

As you can see, **Grade boundary 100%** has been given the **Feedback Excellent!**. The next **Grade boundary** is **90%**. This value means that a student who scores between 100% and 90% will receive 'Excellent!' as their Overall feedback. A student scoring **90%** to **80%** will receive **Good job!**; **80%** to **70%** will receive **OK!**; and **70%** or lower will receive **You need to review the material!**.

Saving the test

Now that we have entered in all of our requirements for the test, we need to save it. We have the option to either **Save and return to course**, **Save and display**, or **Cancel**. We will click on **Save and display** and we will be directed to the **Add questions to Quiz** screen, where we will begin making the questions for our first complete test in Moodle Quiz.

Designing the test

Now that we have the test parameters worked out, we need to start organizing the actual questions for the test. When designing a test, it is a good idea to give students an introduction to the test, clear instructions, and examples of how the questions work. It is also a good idea to give some easier questions at the beginning, to build up the students confidence.

For our test, we will be using all the types of questions we have worked with before. We will create six questions for each page, with each page containing a single question type. We want to give a Description question first, to explain what the section is about and we also want to give a sample of the question type.

Test introduction

On the first page of the test, we will use a Description question to give the students an overview of the test. On this page of the test, we will tell the students what types of questions to expect, how many questions they will have, the time limit, when they can check their results and see our feedback, and what to do if they have any questions.

Once we have created the text in the Description question, we **Save** and **Preview** it to make sure it looks like we want it to. The first page of the test is as follows:

Quiz: General Science Test

This is a test of all we have covered this year in our General Science class. The test will cover: Biology, Chemistry, Geology, Physics and a few other areas that we covered in this class.

The test is in 9 parts. Each part contains a description of what you need to do in the section and a total of 5 questions you need to answer. There will be a variety of question types including: True/False, Multiple Choice, Matching, Fill-in-the-Blank, and a few others.

You have 45 minutes to complete the test. When you finish the the test, press the Submit All and Finish button on the last page. When everyone has finished the test, your results and my feedback will be available.

If you have any questions during the test, please raise your hand and I will come help you.

Good luck!

Save without Submitting

This caution cannot be repeated enough! You can include it in your quiz introduction or verbally, but make sure your students are clicking on the **Save without Submitting** buttons every 5 to 10 minutes. If anything happens during the test, such as power loss or Internet failure, all their work will be lost unless they save their work. You must stress the need to do this to your students!

Section introduction

Now the real fun begins! We will start to create our questions for the test. On the second page, we will be asking True/False questions about Space.

To begin with, we will create a Description question explaining the section and the types of questions to expect. In the description, we will include a sample image of how the True/False questions look and some information about the section. The example we will show them is a screenshot of a True/False question that I have already prepared and uploaded to the image folder. Once we have finished writing the description of the section, we will use the **Add Image to Display** drop-down and select the already prepared image. Here is what the section introduction for True/False looks like when we've finished:

Instructions:

In this section, you will have to answer 5 True/False questions related to our study of space and planets. To answer a True/False question, you must read the statement and choose the correct answer by pressing the button next to the correct answer.

Here is an example of what a True/False question looks like. The correct answer has been selected.

This test is about science.

Answer: ⊙ True

            ○ False

Reading this section, the student quickly sees how many items they will have to answer, what the topic covered is, the type of items they will be working with, and a sample of exactly what they will be looking at. This is the kind of information we need to supply before each section in order to prepare them as well as we can for what they need to do.

Note that I have added some bold underlined text at the top called **Instructions**. I have also placed all the text in Bold. This emphasis helps the students realize that the text is not a question and is something that they should pay attention to.

Questions

Now all that remains is to create the five items associated with the **Instructions**. We will create the five True/False questions we need to complete the section.

Remaining sections

For the remaining sections, we will do the same thing as we have done previously: create a Section introduction and the five items to be used in the section.

Adding to the Quiz

Once all the questions have been created and are part of the Question Bank, we will move them to the test. Once we have added all the items to the test, including the **Introductions**, we will go to the bottom of the **Questions in this Quiz** section of the **Editing Quiz** page and we see two options, **Show page breaks** and **Show the reordering tool**. We are going to click on the **Show page breaks** checkbox.

Showing page breaks will give us a visual representation of where each page begins and ends. It will also give us the Up or Down Arrow next to the page break lines, which enables us to move the page breaks to wherever we want. There is also a delete option, the **X**, in case we want to get rid of a page break. We also have the option to add more page breaks by using the **Repaginate with 'X' questions per page**, located at the bottom left-hand side of the page. If we decide that we want to add more pages, or we have deleted some page breaks and want them back, just select the number of items per page you want, click on the **Go** button, and the pages will be added to the quiz depending on the settings you select. This is not the easiest interface to work with, and you have no way to simply add a single page break. If you need to add another page break, you will need to repaginate and get rid of page breaks you don't need. What we have now is shown in the next screenshot:

Questions in this quiz

Order	#	Question name	Type	Grade	Action
↓		General Science Final Exam Introduction	🖼		🔍 ✏ »
		———— Page break ———— ↓ ✕			
↑ ↓		General Science Exam True/False Introduction	🖼		🔍 ✏ »
↑ ↓		T/F One of Saturn's moons is named Ganymede.	••	1	🔍 ✏ »
↑ ↓		T/F The hottest planet in our Solar System is Venus.	••	1	🔍 ✏ »
↑ ↓		T/F The Solar System is about 4.6 billion years old.	••	1	🔍 ✏ »
↑ ↓		T/F The Sun is about 1,000 times bigger than the Earth.	••	1	🔍 ✏ »
↑ ↓		T/F We can see Hally's Comet every 48 years.	••	1	🔍 ✏ »
		———— Page break ———— ↑ ↓ ✕			
↑ ↓		General Science Exam Multiple Choice Introduction	🖼		🔍 ✏ »
↑ ↓		MC What is the name of world's largest desert?	☰	1	🔍 ✏ »
↑ ↓		MC Where are most of the highest mountains located?	☰	1	🔍 ✏ »
↑ ↓		MC Which is the longest river?	☰	1	🔍 ✏ »
↑ ↓		MC Which ocean is the saltiest?	☰	1	🔍 ✏ »
↑		MC Which of the following rocks will float in water?	☰	1	🔍 ✏ »
		———— Page break ———— ↑			

Total: 10
Maximum grade: 10 ⑦

Save changes

As you can see, we have a clear visual representation of how the test will look and how it is organized. If we want to adjust any questions, we can use the **Move** arrows to place them where we want. Once we are happy with the order, we will click on the **Save changes** button.

The second option, **Show the reordering tool**, functions in a similar manner. It places a numerical textbox next to the questions starting with '10' and increasing by multiples of 10 for each item included on the test. The 10 represents the item's place and where it will be shown in the test. The items increase by 10s and you are able to insert items between them by changing the numbers and putting everything in the numerical order you want the questions displayed on the test, for example, 10, 11, 12, 20, 30, 31, and so on .Once you have the numbers in the order you want them to be displayed, click on the **Save changes** button and the new order will be displayed. The ordering numbers will change back to multiples of 10, allowing you to reorder the questions again if needed.

You do not have to use integers and you have the option to use decimal places should you desire. Page breaks are also included in the numbering system. If you have only checked the **Repaginate** button, you will not see the Page Breaks, but you will see missing numbers in the sequence. If you decide to use the **Show the reordering tool**, I would recommend selecting both options for visual clarity.

Previewing the test

Now we will look at the test to see what we have. The first thing we notice is that all the questions are shuffled. This is not what we want. We need to have the descriptions first, to explain to the students what they need to do. We have two options for what to do here.

The first option is simple. We can **Update Quiz** and turn off the **Shuffle** function. If we do this, the questions will be placed exactly as they appear in the **Questions in this quiz** area. This option is easy and is the fastest way to deal with this issue. The drawback is that every student will have the test given in the exact same order, which may increase cheating. On the upside, the responses inside the answers are shuffled, so some variation is still included in the test.

The second option takes extra time, but the effort can we worth it. We will still be turning off the shuffle function, but we'll be settingup additonal categories from which to draw random questions.

Step 1

First, we will turn off the shuffle question order feature in the Quiz setup page. Then, we will go to the **Edit** tab above the Question Bank and click on the **Categories** link directly below the **Edit** tab. Once inside **Edit Categories,** we will see a list of all the categories related to this Quiz that we have so far.

We will scroll down to the bottom and we see the **Add category** area. In the **Parent** drop-down menu, we are going to select **Default** for **General Science Test** because we want the create a subcategory for this quiz. For **Name**, we will enter **General Science ExamTrue/False Introduction**. We will enter the same information for **Category Info**. Once these steps are complete, we will click on the **Add category** button, located below the **Category Info** textbox. The new category will appear as a subcategory in the **Default** for **General Science Test** category. We will do this for each of the other question types we have.

Step 2

Now that we have created our categories, we will add our questions to their appropriate categories. Once the questions have been added to their categories, we need to go to the **Category** drop-down menu just below the Question Bank header and select the category we want to use. We will begin by selecting **T/F Questions about Space**. This will bring us to the questions we just added to the category. Now, we want to add these questions to the exam in a random order. We go to the bottom of the Quiz Bank and we can see **Add 'X' random questions** with an **Add** button on the right-hand side. We select the number of items we want to move, click on the **Add** button, and that number of randomly selected items from the category selected will be placed in the test. We will manually move them to where they need to be and repeat the process for each of the other categories we will be using. When we finish adding the random questions we see this screen in the Quiz:

Questions in this quiz

Order	#	Question name	Type	Grade	Action
↓		General Science Final Exam Introduction	🖼		🔍 ✎ »
		———————— Page break ———————— ↓ ✕			
↑ ↓		General Science Exam True/False Introduction	🖼		🔍 ✎ »
↑ ↓	1	Random Question (T/F Questions about Space)	?	1	✎ »
↑ ↓	2	Random Question (T/F Questions about Space)	?	1	✎ »
↑ ↓	3	Random Question (T/F Questions about Space)	?	1	✎ »
↑ ↓	4	Random Question (T/F Questions about Space)	?	1	✎ »
↑ ↓	5	Random Question (T/F Questions about Space)	?	1	✎ »
		———————— Page break ———————— ↑ ↓ ✕			
↑ ↓		General Science Exam Multiple Choice Introduction	🖼		🔍 ✎ »
↑ ↓	6	Random Question (MC Questions about the Earth)	?	1	✎ »
↑ ↓	7	Random Question (MC Questions about the Earth)	?	1	✎ »
↑ ↓	8	Random Question (MC Questions about the Earth)	?	1	✎ »
↑ ↓	9	Random Question (MC Questions about the Earth)	?	1	✎ »
↑	10	Random Question (MC Questions about the Earth)	?	1	✎ »
		———————— Page break ———————— ↑			Total: 10

What this quiz will do is select five random items from the related category. However, if there are only five items in the category, the items will always be in the same order. You should include at least one additional item to allow for true variation in the questions. While more options for variation are probably better, one thing to consider is the item quality. Are all the items in the category of equal quality or difficulty? In case you are reviewing items and you find some are significantly more or less difficult, you may want to consider removing them to improve the test's validity.

Save

Once you have organized the test and it looks the way you want it to, click on the **Save changes** button. Then click on the **Preview** button and take the test, looking for any errors or issues with format or display, until you are happy with the results. If you made any adjustments, don't forget to save again.

Now all that remains is to make the quiz visible and have the students take it.

Quiz results

So far, we have looked at all the tabs in Quiz except for the **Results** tab. Without useful and well-organized reporting tools, we can't make effective inferences about the abilities or knowledge of the test taker. Moodle Quiz has a variety of built-in ways to review quiz results.

The first thing we need to do is click on the **Results** tab, located between the **Info** and the **Preview** tabs. Once we click on this tab, we will see four options: **Overview**, **Regrade**, **Manual Grading**, and **Item Analysis with Overview** being selected.

Overview

This feature gives us a lot of information about the test and the test taker. The first information we see is the number of attempts that have been made on the test. For our test, we will see two attempts on the test, one from each of the sample students I created. The second piece of information we see is the number of attempts allowed. For our quiz, this shows a message stating, **Only one attempt per user allowed on this quiz.**

Result table

The next information we see here is in the form of a table that includes the student name; when the test was started and finished; the time it took the student to complete the test; the student's grade; which questions were correct or incorrect; the feedback they received based on the score; and, in the case of multiple attempts, information about each. At the bottom of the chart, we are given the **Overall average** score for the test and the average points received for each question, rounded up. Here is an example of how the chart of two students having attempted the test appears:

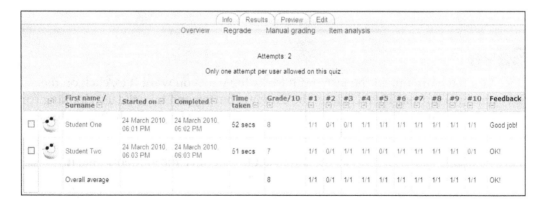

	First name / Surname	Started on	Completed	Time taken	Grade/10	#1	#2	#3	#4	#5	#6	#7	#8	#9	#10	Feedback
	Student One	24 March 2010 06:01 PM	24 March 2010 06:02 PM	52 secs	8	1/1	0/1	0/1	1/1	1/1	1/1	1/1	1/1	1/1	1/1	Good job!
	Student Two	24 March 2010 06:03 PM	24 March 2010 06:03 PM	51 secs	7	1/1	0/1	1/1	1/1	0/1	1/1	1/1	1/1	1/1	0/1	OK!
	Overall average				8	1/1	0/1	1/1	1/1	1/1	1/1	1/1	1/1	1/1	1/1	OK!

The information contained here is very useful to us. We are shown, quite clearly, many of the important details about the student's performance on the test, including final or total grade.

The score under **Grade/10** is a link. If we click on this link, we will be taken to the student's test where we will be able to see all the information detailed in the chart, the correct, partially correct, and incorrect responses, and the **Feedback** for each individual item. In addition, we are given the option to comment or override the grade for each item in the test.

To make a comment or override the grade, we simply need to click on the **Make Comment** or **Override grade** link and we will be shown a pop-up menu. The pop-up menu will have the question name, a comment textbox, a grade textbox, and a **Save** button. To make a comment, simply enter what you want to say into the Comment area and click on Save. Once you have done this, the comment will appear in the related question, just above the correct or partially correct or incorrect message. If you want to alter the grade, simply enter the grade you want in the **Grade** textbox and click on **Save**. This action will change the grade on all pages.

Looking back at the previous chart, we can see that **#2** was the only item that both students got wrong, and this is something we can look at later to decide if we created a question that was misleading, something we didn't fully cover in our course, or something simply too difficult for our students.

Now, if we were using a standard test, with item shuffling turned off, we would know that they both got the same question wrong. But wait, we are using a test with the shuffle feature turned off! Yes, that's true; however, we are using random questions. This means that while they both got the item that was presented second, wrong, chances are they were not the same question. If we click on the **0/1** under **#2** for **Student One**, we will be shown which question they were presented with. In the case of **Student One** , we will be presented with the following screenshot:

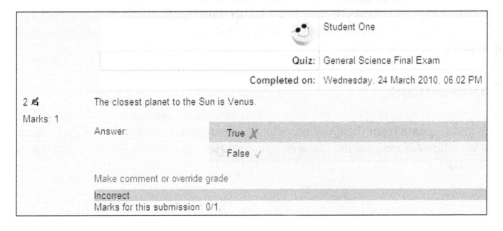

In the case of Student Two, it appears in the same way, except for the True/False statement is not **The closest planet to the Sun is Venus** but **One of Saturn's moons is Ganymede**. If you decide to use the **Shuffle Questions** feature or the **Random Questions**, as we just learned, it is important to remember that, while the numerical order is the same, the items are most likely different.

Deleting attempts

Looking back at the previous chart, you can see a checkbox next to the student names. We can use these checkboxes to delete the student attempt, or multiple attempts if multiple attempts were allowed. For example, if we want to have a student retake the test, we might simply want to delete their original attempt instead of allowing multiple attempts for everyone. There might also have been a problem during the test and you want all the students to retake it. To delete an **Attempt**, simply click on the student or students whose tests you want to delete and click on the **Delete selected attempts** button at the bottom of the chart. There is an option that allows you to **Select/Deselect all**.

Exporting data

To export the student data for printing, further analysis, or file keeping, Moodle Quiz offers three methods: **Download in ODS Format**, **Download in Excel Format**, and **Download to text format**. ODS means Open Document Spreadsheet format and this option will export the files as `.ods`. Excel Format will export the data as `.xls`. Text format will export the data in a plain text format. All files are encoded in UTF-8, which is important to note, especially if you are working in a non-English language.

To export the files, you click the format button of your choice and you will get a message asking how to save or open the file. Make your selection and the file will be placed where you selected. All the data will be set out as it is in the chart, titled and organized in the same manner and order. Note that you can use the backup option and select only the quiz if you want to backup the data. You can then always import it when you need it. Also, the data stored in XML format is quite accessible with the right tools.

Preferences

Below the downloading options, we see the preferences we can set to display the page and the data from the Quiz reports. There are two preferences we can adjust: how we **Show/download** the student data and the report view, as shown in the next screenshot:

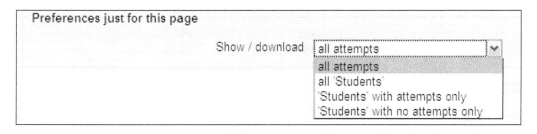

The previous image shows the four options we have for how we will display and download the report. Our options allow us to choose display all the attempts made on the test, all the students enrolled in the course (whether they have attempted the test or not), all the students that have attempted the test, and all the students who have not attempted it. This setting can be extremely useful, although its usefulness depends on your needs and what you intend to do with the data. Another option is to show/download only the attempts that were graded. In the case of multiple attempts, you can also set this option to display the highest grade received.

The second option we have related to preferences is **Your preferences for this report**, as seen in the next screenshot. The two options here are **Page size** and **Show/download marks for each question**. The **Page size** will alter the number of student results seen on the report. If it were set to '1', we would see one student's test results on each page. This option can be useful if you are interested in speaking to students about their grades and showing them their results on screen without them being able to see anyone else's. It can also be useful if you want to focus on individuals instead of groups.

The second option, **Show/download marks from each question** drop-down menu offers a simple **Yes** or **No** option. If you select **Yes**, you will see each item and the score the student received on it. If you select **No**, you will not see the report as shown previously, and a message saying **Nothing to display** will be seen in its place.

Once you have decided how you would like the page displayed or downloaded, press the **Save preferences** button directly below the **Your preferences for this report**.

You also have the option to hide columns in the table by clicking on the minus sign in the column headers. This is particularly useful for users with small screens or Moodle installations with fixed width interfaces, for example, 960px.

Results graph

The only remaining item on the page is the **Bar Graph of Number of Students Achieving Grade Ranges**. This chart gives us a visual representation of how the students performed on the test. We can't manipulate it, but it is a useful tool for a quick overview of how the students scored overall. While it would clearly be more useful if we had more results, here is what it looks like with our two students shown. We can see that one student scored in the **7-8** range and the other student scored in the **8-9** range.

When you have your students grouped and set the **Group mode** to **visible**, the chart will show how many members scored in each band.

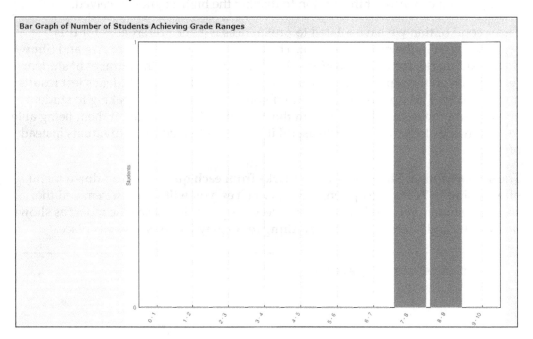

Regrade

Regrade is used if you have decided to alter the grade for a question or test, or if you have changed a question. To use this feature, click on the **Regrade** tab at the top of the screen and the scores will be recalculated. There is nothing else you need to do.

If there has been a change made in any score, a link will be supplied that will bring you to the item that was changed so you can review it. Do not let this function make you think that you don't have to closely review the quiz before using it!

Manual Grading

This feature is used for items that can't be automatically graded by Quiz, such as Essay type questions. If you click on **Manual Grading** and there are no items that require manual grade entry, you will get a message saying that there is nothing to grade. This process is different from regrading or overriding a grade. If you do have an item that requires a manually entered score, you will see the output as shown in the next screenshot:

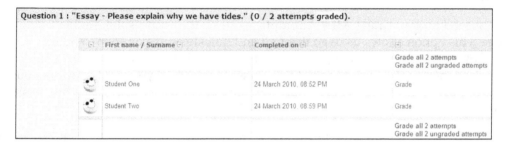

As you can see, I have created an Essay question for our students asking them to explain why there are tides. You can also see that neither of the essays has been graded yet. We have the options to do three things here.

First, we can grade each response individually by clicking on the **Grade** link in the student's row. If we click on this link, we will be brought to a page with the question, the student's response, a comment box for us to give feedback to the student, and a grade box where we will put our score for the item. Once we comment and give a score, we click on the **Save changes** button located in the bottom left-hand side corner of the window. The screenshot is as follows:

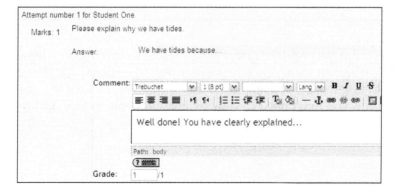

Once we have clicked on the **Save changes** button, the score and comments will be reflected in the test grade and we will see, in the **Manual Grading** link under the **Edit** tab, that the grade has been recorded. The student will be able to see the feedback, depending on which **Review options** you chose to use. Now we can go on to the next student.

This horizontal grading is very convenient, especially when you give the mark scheme as the general question feedback and here only add a comment when you think it is necessary to explain how you applied that mark scheme. You can also paste the mark scheme in the comment and, for instance, make the text of the mark scheme red where the student has missed marks. I find that teachers want to start giving their quizzes in Moodle when I show them how quickly I grade essay questions.

The second option, **Grade All # Attempts** opens all the essays submitted in a single page. This option allows us to go through and quickly read, comment, and score student essays without having to constantly open and close questions. The only drawback here is that should something go wrong, such as your session timing out or dropping your Internet connection, you will lose all your work. Therefore, it is a good idea to save your work occasionally to limit the risks of data loss.

The third option, **Grade All '#' Ungraded Attempts** works in a similar fashion except it opens only those responses that have not been scored.

Item Analysis

This is an extremely useful feature for teachers and researchers. Selecting this feature will open a page containing a list of the questions and how all the students answered each one. An example of what it looks like is shown in the next screenshot:

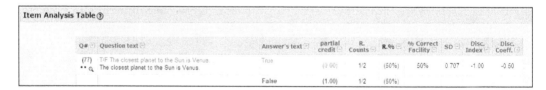

As we can see from the previous screenshot, there is a lot of information available to use here. I've broken them down to make it easy to understand. The screen will become more cluttered when using different question types, so it is a good idea to hide the columns you don't need to view by using the minus sign next to the column headers.

Q#

This narrow column contains several useful pieces of information. First, the number in parentheses is the Question ID number. Clicking on this ID Number will open an **Edit Question** pop-up window, which will allow us to look over the question or make any changes desired.

Below the number, we can see the item type; here it is True/False. Next to the item type, we see the **Preview** icon, which will show us exactly how the question should appear to the students while taking the test.

Clicking on the **Q#** will sort the IDs in ascending order, and clicking on it again will sort them in descending order.

Question text

This column gives us the name of the question and the question text. This option can clutter the screen if you have a long question text.

Answer's text

This column shows us the possible answers. With Essay type questions, this column shows the student answer. The correct answer is highlighted in bold blue text. The incorrect response is in a normal red text.

Partial credit

This section tells us how many points were received for each possible answer.

R. Counts

This column shows how many of the students responded, using the answer in the **Answer's text**. The number here is given as R/S (total number of responses/total number of student attempts).

R.%

This column takes the numbers from the **R. Counts** column and calculates them as a percentage. Basically, it indicates the percentage of students that chose that particular answer.

% Correct Facility

This column is a measure that indicates the difficulty of the question. This difficulty level is calculated by taking the total number of correct responses and dividing by the total possible points. In cases of True/False type questions, the number represented here will be the same as the number of students who answered correctly.

SD

SD stands for Standard Deviation. Standard Deviation is the average distance to the average. This function shows us the numerical spread in responses to the question. If all students respond correctly, the **SD** will be 0.000. The larger the number, the larger the variation in responses.

Disc. Index

Disc. Index stands for Discrimination Index. This feature is used to evaluate the quality of the question itself. To do this, an average of all the scores for the question is taken. Then the group of test takers is divided into thirds: top scores, middle scores, bottom scores. The **Disc. Index** then takes the Top Scores Group and subtracts them from the Bottom Scores Group, then it divides the number by the average. The results will be somewhere in the range of 1.0 to -1.0. 1.0 to 0.0 indicates that the question is 'good'. If the number of the **Disc. Index** goes below 0.0, it indicates that the question was answered correctly more often by the lower-scoring students. This result may indicate a problem with the question and it should be reviewed and altered if necessary.

Disc. Coeff.

Disc.Coeff. stands for Discrimination Coefficient. This calculation is another way to look at the differences between high and low scores and their relationships to the answers of individual students. This function will determine the correlation coefficient between the question being analyzed and the entire test. The only real difference in the **Disc. Coeff.** and the **Disc. Index,** is that in the **Disc. Index** only the top and bottom third of the scores are used, but in the **Disc. Coeff.** all the scores are used.

Analysis options

At the bottom of the page, we see three ways to manipulate the way the data is presented. The **Analysis options** section is seen in the next screenshot:

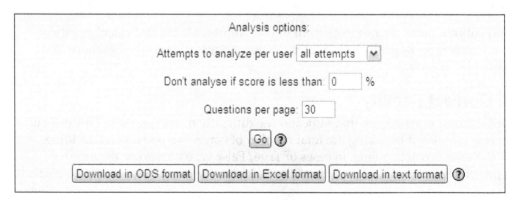

Remember, if any changes are made to the default settings, make sure to click on the **Go** button to save the changes and refresh the review page. The first and second fields also affect what is exported.

Attempts to analyze per user

This drop-down menu offers four options for how we will look at each student's attempts. The first option is **all attempts,** and this will show us all the attempts a student made on the test. The second option is **Highest grade**, which will only display the highest-scored attempt for us to review. The third option is **First attempt**, and this will simply display the student's first try. The final option is **Last attempt**, which will display the student's final effort.

The default setting here is **All**, which will affect the measures. You will probably want to select one of the other options if a quiz has been offered with multiple attempts.

Don't analyze if score is less than 'X'%'

This option will eliminate any test from review if the score is below a certain threshold. This option can be useful under certain conditions. To use this feature, simply enter a number in the textbox and any test that does not exceed the percentage will not be reviewed.

Questions per page

Here, we have the option of setting how many items we want to see displayed on each page. To set the number, simply enter a number in the textbox and that is how many items will be displayed on each review page.

Exporting data

Below the options, we can see there are three exporting options. These options are identical to those described in the **Overview** section. The only difference is what will be displayed. Exporting from here will export the data from the **Item analysis**.

Importing and Exporting Questions

The final aspect we will look at regarding Quiz is the Importing and Exporting of questions. This option is located under the **Edit** tab. We will look at Importing questions first, then move on to Exporting them.

Importing Questions

The Importing Questions function is used if you have already created questions for different programs or systems. Here is what the Import page looks like.

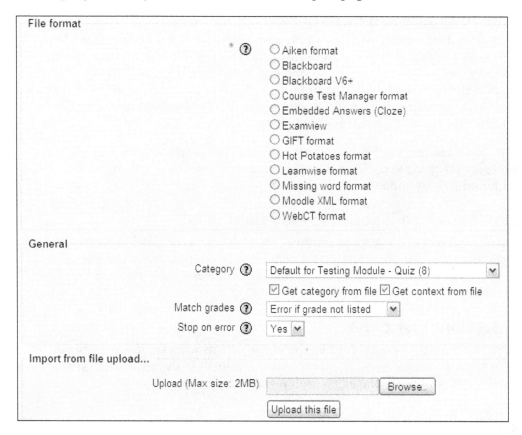

To use Import in Moodle, you must have the files you want imported saved as a text file. Moodle supports a variety of Import formats. The formats the Import function currently supports are listed in the previous image.

First, we need to create some questions to import. Using GIFT is good, because once you make a few items, I feel, it becomes easier to make them. While I don't have the space to explain exactly how to use GIFT, I will show you some sample items and how they look once they are imported. For more detailed information on how to create GIFT questions, see Moodle's documentation at `http://docs.moodle.org/en/GIFT_format`.

Let's say we have four chemistry questions from another test that we want to import to a test we are making: a Matching, a Multiple Choice, a Numerical, and a True/False.

The question will also be presented as the question name. If you would like a different question name, begin the coding with two colons, followed by the question name, followed by two more colons (::question name::). The information between the colons will be displayed as the question name in the Question Bank. After the name, continue the question as normal. The curly brackets {''} indicate the beginning and end of the responses. The = indicates the correct response, except for in True/False, which only requires a {TRUE}/{FALSE}, or {T}/{F}. When creating multiple questions in GIFT, you must separate them with an empty line. The text editor is shown in the next screenshot:

```
Match the elements to their symbols. { =Sodium -> Na =Boron -> B =Gold -> Au =Iron -> Fe }
Which of the following is the correct symbol for Potassium? { =K ~Pt ~Po ~P }
What is the atomic weight of Helium? { =4.0026 =4 = 4.00 =4.002 = 4.003 }
The atomic number of silver is 47. { TRUE }
```

Now that we have our items ready and saved in our text file, we will use the Moodle Import page to import the questions to our test. Looking at the Import Page, we can see four sections: **File format**, **General**, **Import from file upload**, and **Import from file already in course files**.

File format

This option presents is a list of the file types mentioned previously (GIFT, Aiken, and so on) with radio buttons to select the format for the file you are going to import.

General

Here, we have three options to work with: **Category**, **Match grades**, and **Stop on error**.

Category

Here is where we select where the imported files will be sent. There is a drop-down menu with all the categories available to import to. Simply select the location where you want the items to go from the drop-down.

Under the drop-down, there are two checkboxes, **Get category from file** and **Get context from file**. If the **Get category from file** is checked and the category location has been specified in the file being uploaded, the file will be added to whichever category was specified. If the **Get category from context** is checked and if the file was created and exported from Moodle, it might have a category already associated with it. If this is the case, and the **Get category from context** is selected, the file will be added to the associated category. If you do not want this to happen, uncheck the checkbox. If a category doesn't exist when added, it will be created.

Match grades

The grades assigned to imported questions must match the list of acceptable grades in Moodle. These grades are: 100%, 90%, 80%, 75%, 70%, 66.666%, 60%, 50%, 40%, 33.333%, 30%, 25%, 20%, 16.666%, 14.2857%, 12.5%, 11.111%, 10%, 5%, and 0%. Negative percentages are also acceptable.

The **Match grades** drop-down menu has two options, **Error if grade not listed** and **Match to nearest grade**. If the **Error if grade is not listed** is selected and a grade has not been assigned, an error will be generated and the item will not be imported. If the **Match to nearest grade** has been selected, Moodle will assign the item a grade based on the nearest matching grade.

Stop on error

When questions are imported into Moodle, the process happens in two steps. In the first step, the questions are verified. In the second step, the questions are added to the database. If a problem in the verification step is detected, the items will not be added to the database.

Import from file upload

This is where we can select files with questions in them from our computer and upload them to our test. Click on the **Browse** button and locate the file. Once you have located it, click on the **Upload** button and the file will be added to the quiz.

We have selected the file we created and uploaded it to the quiz. The first thing we see is the *parsing* page, where the questions are being verified. All the questions are correct, and we click on the **continue** button. This action will move all the questions to the Question page. The question will be displayed as a long line of text, but don't worry.

Now, we'll click on the **Quiz** link and we will see the Question Bank with our new questions. We will select all the new questions and click on the **Move** button to place all the new questions in the quiz. The questions appear as shown in the next screenshot. We can see the **Question Type** icons are accurate, so they have been imported as the proper type. Now we will preview them all, and make sure they all work. Previewing shows that they are all correct, the format is correct, the responses are correct, and the scoring is working.

Questions in this quiz				
Order # Question name		Type	Grade	Action
↓ 1 Match the elements to their symbols.		⦙⦙⦙	1	🔍 ✏ »
↑ ↓ 2 Which of the following is the correct symbol for Potassium?		⦙≣	1	🔍 ✏ »
↑ ↓ 3 What is the atomic weight of Helium?		▭	1	🔍 ✏ »
↑ 4 The atomic number of silver is 47.		••	1	🔍 ✏ »

This procedure is only one way to import files to Quiz, but it is an extremely useful one, and you may find it faster to create questions using this format. Please take the time to look over the other formats to see if one of the other methods is a better match for you.

Import from File already in course files

If you already have a file in Moodle that you want to transfer from one place to another, all you need to do is click on the **Choose or Upload file** button and the Quiz Files pop-up menu will appear, listing all the possible files you have available. If you see the file you want, you simply need to select it by clicking on the **Choose** link and it will be placed in the **Choose a file** textbox. Once the link is there, click on the **Import from this file**, going through the same procedure as described in the previous section.

Exporting questions

Occasionally, you may want to export your files for some reason, backup data, for example. When exporting, all the items in the category will be exported as text files. Moodle has the capability of exporting files in four formats: GIFT, IMS QTI 2.0, Moodle XML, and XHTML.

The Export page is simple compared to the Import page, with only two sections: **File format** and **General**.

File format

Here, we see the four file formats along with their corresponding radio buttons. We use the radio buttons to select the file format we want our questions exported as.

General

Here, we have four options to work with: **Category**, **Write category to file**, **Write context to file**, and **File name**.

Category

The **Category** drop-down menu allows us to choose from where we will be taking our questions. Any subcategories contained in the category will also be included.

Write category to file

This option, if selected, will include the category in the file, so if it is imported from to another Moodle site, the file has the ability to recreate its **Category**.

Write category to context

This option is similar to the **Write category to file**. However, instead of recreating the category associated with the question, this option will recreate the context it was in (that is, the course). Refer *Chapter 2* for more information on Context.

File name

This is the name the file will be saved as.

The **Export Page** appears, as shown in the next screenshot:

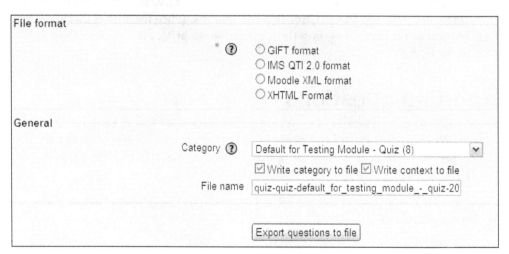

Once you have made your selections, click on the **Export questions to file** button and the questions will be saved to the backup/quiz folder. Here, you also have the option to download the file. This is all you need to do to export question data from Quiz.

Special Characters

Importing to Moodle requires ASCII characters (a, b, c, and others). If any of the text in your file contains any non-ASCII characters such as ä, ç, or ě, the text must be reformatted and saved as UFT-8, or the Import function will not work. Reformatting can be easily done using whichever text editor you use, however, Microsoft Unicode is not the same as UTF-8.

Quiz considerations

As you can see, there is a lot in Quiz, and we could not hope to cover everything in one chapter. For this section's Considerations, I'd like to point out that there are two plug-ins available for Quiz. The built-in data analysis features cover what most users need. However, if you need more detailed Quiz analysis, two useful additions to the core Quiz are Quiz Report Analysis, contributed to Moodle by *Anastasios Pournias*, and Detailed Responses, by *Jean-Michel Vedrine*.

The Quiz Report Analysis adds a graphic interface for students and teachers to review the results. A detailed overview, download link, and installation instructions, are available at http://moodle.org/mod/data/view.php?d=13&rid=2241.

The Detailed Responses plug-in offers an even more detailed way to look at student responses. A full description, discussion, and download details are located at http://moodle.org/mod/data/view.php?d=13&rid=96.

Summary

As we have seen, Quiz provides an effective, fairly easy-to-use way of testing students. Tests created and delivered via Quiz have the added benefit of being easy to create and they can be used over and over again. Quiz also has the ability to do all kinds of things that most instructors need, including: setting test dates and times; altering page length; including a variety of item formats; shuffling items and responses; setting security levels; creating test groups; giving a variety of feedback and results; and even providing basic data analysis tools. Using Quiz, we are able to design and alter tests quickly and easily if required.

While we covered most of the options in Quiz there are a some we weren't able to cover in one short chapter. However, we have given you the tools you need to start making or improving your tests and quizzes using Moodle. Remember, that Moodle. org is a great place to find answers about specific questions related to Quiz and Moodle in General. Answers to advanced questions, or questions relating to different versions of Moodle, should be found there.

5
Using Lesson

Lesson is another module that can be used for testing and assessment in Moodle. It was created to be an adaptive tool that would allow teachers to deliver material to their students in an adaptive and interesting way. The Lesson module contains pages that allow you to add information, data, images, and other information. At the end of the pages, there are questions and, based on the student's response, he or she will be directed to a new or previous page. Using Moodle's Lesson module is something that takes some practice to get comfortable with. However,, once you understand how to use it, Lesson is a valuable tool for self-directed study, teaching, and testing. In this chapter, we will:

- Learn about Lesson options
- Build questions
- Look at branch tables and branches
- Work with clusters
- Create vocabulary drills

What is a Lesson?

So, what is Lesson? Lesson is all about making choices. It was designed to be a self-directed, adaptive module where the students working on the Lesson module are able to move through the material based on the choices they make. Lesson is mainly used by teachers as an adaptive learning activity. However, it also has testing and assessment applications, which is why it is included here. With Lesson, we can create simple vocabulary or flash card tests, or we can create complex tests with multiple item types and paths for students to follow. The paths that students follow lead to one of the following two types of pages: Branching pages and question pages.

What are Branches and Branching pages? These pages are used to help deliver content, images, and navigation options in the Lesson. Each Branch page has a title, some content, and navigation buttons at the bottom of the page, which the students click on to choose their path through the Lesson. These pages also act as an index for the Lesson. These pages are not included in a student's score; they are simply there to provide information on the Lesson and navigation options for the students.

Question pages are exactly what you think they are—pages in the Lesson that contain the information being tested. In Lesson, we do not have access to the full range of questions we saw in Quiz, we only have access to: Multiple Choice, True/False, Short Answer, Numerical, Matching, and Essay.

Lesson was designed to be an adaptive learning activity. However, it also has strong testing applications, and we're going to look at these features next.

Creating a Lesson

Adding a Lesson is similar to creating a Quiz. There are several new field sets and options and, when you first look at the creation page, it can seem daunting. However, we will go through each of the available category features and options to give you a solid understanding of how this module works. So, let's dive in and see what we can do with Lesson!

General

As always, the General section is first and contains the basic parameters. In Lesson, the **General** section contains three pieces of information that we need to enter. The section is shown in the next screenshot:

Name

Here is where we put the name of the Lesson. The previous screenshot is what the students will see on the main course page.

Time limit (minutes)

If we want to limit the amount of time a student can spend on the lesson, we can set the time limit here. To do this, click on the **Enable** checkbox and enter the amount of time (in minutes) here.

Maximum number of answers/branches

This field is where we can set the number of answers that can be used in the Lesson. The numbers range from 2 to 20. So, for example, if you were looking to use Multiple Choice questions with five possible responses, you would want this value set to five. The default setting here is four.

This setting also limits the number of branches that can be created. So, if we set ours to five, we would only be able to create a maximum of five branches.

If at some later date you want to add a question with more answer options than five, you simply need to adjust this setting to however many answers or branches you want.

If you want to create a single question with more possible answers than the setting allows, change the setting to however many answer options you want and create the question. When the question is complete, you may change this number back to its original setting and that question will remain exactly as created.

Grade options

In this section, we are able to determine how the student will be graded. There are six options we can set in this area. The **Grade options** section is shown in the next screenshot:

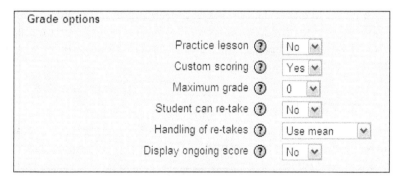

Practice Lesson

This option means just what it says, is this lesson for practice or not? If it is set to **No,** the Lesson is not for practice and the student's results will be entered into the Gradebook. If the drop-down menu is set to **Yes**, the Lesson is for practice, and the student's result will not be recorded.

Custom scoring

This setting is used if you would like to create custom point values for each question.

If this value is set to **No**, the default scoring settings will be used for each item. The default setting for items is 1 for correct responses and 0 for incorrect responses.

If you select **Yes**, you will be able to create your own scores. Negative and fractional point values are accepted.

Maximum grade

This setting allows us to select a number between 0 and 100. This number reflects the maximum grade possible from the lesson. If **0** is selected as the **Maximum grade**, then the Lesson is effectively a practice lesson. A grade of 0 means that the Lesson and results will not be reflected in the student grades.

This number can be changed at any time. For example, if the grade were originally set to 10 and later you want to set it to 20, simply change the number in the drop-down menu and save the changes. Once these changes have been made, all the student scores will be adjusted automatically.

Student can re-take

This setting can be set to either **Yes** or **No**. If the setting is set to **No**, students will only be able to attempt the Lesson tonce. No is the default setting and it is appropriate for giving many tests. If the option is set to **Yes**, students will be able to make as many attempts as they'd like.

Handling of re-takes

If students are allowed more than one attempt with the Lesson, this setting will determine how the final grade is determined. The drop-down menu has two settings, **Use mean** and **Use maximum.**

If the **Use mean** is selected, the final grade will be an average of all the attempts the student made on the Lesson. If **Use maximum** is selected, the student's grade will be the highest score out of all the attempts.

Display ongoing score

This setting has two options, **Yes** and **No**. If the option is set to **No**, the student's score will not be visible until he or she has finished the test. Selecting **Yes** allows the current results to be displayed during the Lesson attempt. This setting can be useful if you want students to see how they are progressing in the Lesson.

The scores are displayed as, You have answered X correctly out of Y attempts. These attempts are attempts at questions. So, for example, with four questions, the screen could state, You have answered 4 correctly out of 6 attempts. This response would mean that one question was answered incorrectly twice times or two questions were answered incorrectly once.

Flow control

This section helps to determine how the test will move forward after responses, and the options available to students when they answer questions. There are a lot of options here, so let's start by looking at the screenshot of the section, then going through each of the options.

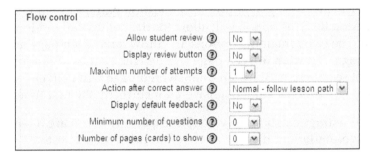

Allow student review

This option is **Yes** or **No**. Selecting **No** will stop students from going back in the Lesson and changing their answers. If **Yes** is selected, students will be able to go back and make changes to their answers.

Display review button

If this option is set to **Yes**, it will display a button to let students know they have answered the question incorrectly, which will allow them to go back and answer the question again. If the drop-down is set to **No**, students will not know whether the question was answered correctly unless the **Display ongoing score** option from the **Grade options** has been set to **Yes** and the student is paying attention to his/her score.

Maximum number of attempts

We have looked at attempts earlier, but this attempt setting determines how many tries a student is allowed to make for each question, regardless of type, in the Lesson. The drop-down menu ranges from 1 to 10, which allows you to offer up to 10 attempts per student per item, if you should desire. However, in most tests, we typically want to allow a single attempt only, so for most testing Lessons, we will want to set this value to **1**.

Action after correct answer

This option allows us to determine how the pages created in Lesson are delivered. There are three settings available in this option.

The first, and most basic pattern, is what a typical Lesson follows: start the lesson, answer a question, move forward to the next question, repeat until you get to the end of the lesson. This sequence is how a normal Lesson would be organized. The default setting for this option is **Normal – follow lesson path** and this creates a Lesson that follows the start-to-finish model.

However, you can also set up a randomized question pattern in Moodle. described as flash cards Moodle. This option will allow for the delivery of randomized pages to the student. The two remaining options are **Show an unseen page** and **Show an unanswered page**. **Show an unseen page** will deliver a series of random pages the student has not seen before. **Show an unanswered page** will deliver pages that are either new or pages that the student answered incorrectly the first time.

These two final settings can both be valuable, especially if you are interested in testing course vocabulary or if you want to offer quick review tests.

Display default feedback

Lesson has default feedback, which can be given after students respond to each question. Leaving this setting at **No** will not display the default feedback. After the student responds to a question, he or she will go to the next page in the Lesson.

Turning this setting to **Yes** will provide two responses to student's answers. If the student answers the item correctly, he/she will receive **That's the correct answer** as feedback. If the item is answered incorrectly, he/she will receive **That's the wrong answer**.

Minimum number of questions

This setting allows you to determine the number of questions that must be answered to get full points in the Lesson. The drop-down menu goes from 0 to 100, signifying the number of questions required. If the setting is set to **0**, the student can answer as many questions as they'd like and they will be scored out of the number of questions they completed. If this value is set any higher, the student must answer that number if he or she wants the chance to receive the highest score possible.

Here is an example of how this process works. Let's say you have 15 items that you put into a test using Lesson, but you want the students to answer only 10 of them, so you set this option to 10 for your test. However, one of your students only answers 7 questions then closes Lesson. It happens that the student answered all 7 questions correctly. Therefore, he or she would get a score of 70 percent (7/10), because he or she got 7 out of the required 10 correct.

It is important to remember that this setting does not make students respond to the minimum number of questions, so you should inform students of this fact and let them know how many questions they are required to answer. A message in the Lesson's instructions is probably the best way to make sure the students understand the minimum requirement. Also, if your Lesson has multiple branches, you might want to provide this message to ensure your students do not simply complete one branch and end the Lesson.

Number of pages (cards) to show

Remember the flash cards described earlier? This setting is used for these types of activities. The drop-down menu, which goes from 0 to 100, will determine how many pages or cards are displayed to the student.

Leaving the setting at **0** will show all the pages or cards in the Lesson. Setting the value to any other number will limit the cards to that amount. If the number is set to something more than the number of cards, all the cards will be shown, then the Lesson will end. Once the Lesson ends, the student will see his/her results.

Lesson formatting

Lesson formatting allows us to determine how the Lesson will be displayed to the students. This dialog box allows us to set the delivery style, menus, and see progress in the as shown in the following screenshot:

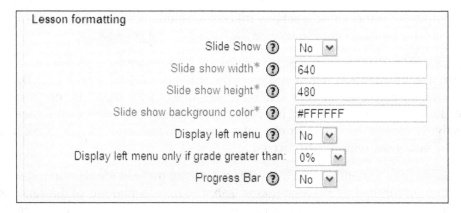

SlideShow

This option is a simple **Yes** or **No** drop-down, which allows us to choose whether or not we want the Lesson presented in a slideshow format. If the setting is left at the default **No**, the Lesson will be delivered normally.

If the setting is changed to **Yes,** the Lesson will turn into a slideshow. If **SlideShow** is selected, the height, width, and background color can be left at the default or adjusted to our needs. If the height or width is larger than the screen, scroll bars will be enabled to allow us to view all the material.

A **Next** and **Back** button will be created for navigation and they will be seen on the right and left of the screen.

Slideshow width and slideshow height

The number entered in these textboxes will determine the number of pixels wide or high the slide will be. The larger the number, the bigger the slide.

Slide background color

This setting allows us to alter the background color of the slides. Setting the color is done by using the HTML Hexadecimal system. As you can see from the previous screenshot, setting the background color scheme using this system requires seven characters. The first thing we must enter is #. The next six characters or hexadigits are numbers or letters, which represent differing colors on the hexadecimal grid. The first two represent the red scale, the second two represent the green scale, and the final two represent the blue scale.

Display left menu

If this option is enabled, a menu containing a list of the branches in the Lesson will be displayed on the left-hand side of the screen.

If you have set a minimum grade value, which we will look at shortly, to display the menu, students will only be able to see the menu if they have achieved that score or higher. This means that they will have to go through the Lesson before they can see the menu. This setting can be useful if we require the students to attain a certain score on the test before they can go back and quickly review the Lesson. If you have left the minimum grade value at zero, the students will be able to see the menu at any time.

As a teacher in the course, you will not be able to see the left menu. If you want to view it, you should log in as a student or use the **Student view** option.

Display left menu only if grade greater than

This is an option where you can determine what score a student needs to achieve to view the left menu. The scores range from 0 percent to 100 percent, with **0%** meaning the left menu will always be displayed.

Progress bar

If this option is set to **Yes**, a bar showing progress in the test will be shown at the bottom of the screen.

This progress bar can help students see where they are in the test and can help them organize their time.

Access control

This section deals with controlling who can enter and attempt the lesson and when he or she can do so. There are four options in this section, as shown in the next screenshot:

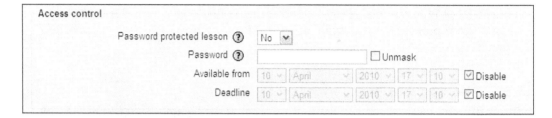

Password protected lesson

As the name implies, setting this option to **Yes** will require a student to enter the Lesson password before he or she can attempt the test. Leaving the option set to **No** will allow anyone with access to the course to attempt the test.

Password

This textbox is where the password is entered. Enter whatever password you desire and the students will need to type in the same thing before they attempt the test. When you enter the password, a series of black dots will appear in place of the characters. If you click on the **Unmask** button, the password will be shown. Passwords are case-sensitive!

If **Password protected lesson** is enabled and the password textbox is left blank, students will not be able to enter the test, so if you enable passwords, make sure to create one!

Available from

By default, this setting is disabled, which allows the Lesson to be attempted anytime. However, if this option is enabled, you can set a date and time when the Lesson will be available.

Deadline

This setting is also disabled by default, allowing students to begin the Lesson anytime after the start date. If you want to limit the number of days or hours the Lesson will be available, enable this function and set the desired closing time for the Lesson. Once the closing time has been reached, no student will be able to enter the Lesson.

Dependent on

This section allows you to set conditions for students to progress in the Lessons. This option can be useful if you are setting up a series of tests and you want the students to take each of the tests in a specific order. There are three options in the **Dependent on** section and they can be used individually or in combination.

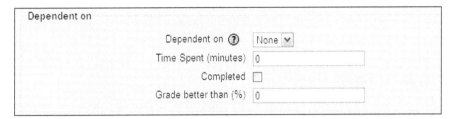

Dependent on

This setting will allow you to select a different Lesson in the same course that the student will be required to take before attempting the current Lesson. This option can be useful if you want to ensure students have completed certain material before moving on.

Time Spent (minutes)

This setting allows you to set the number of minutes that the student will be required to spend on the previous Lesson.

Completed

If this setting is selected, the student must complete the previous lesson in order to attempt the new one.

Grade better than

If this dependent item is chosen, the student will need to have achieved whatever score is entered in the **Dependent on** lesson if they want to attempt the new Lesson.

Pop-Up to file or web page

This section allows you to create a link to a web page or file, which will create a pop-up window for the student to review. The files can be audio, images, or text. The file formats supported in Moodle are: GIF, HTML, JPEG, Media Player, MP3, Text, PNG, QuickTime, and Real media. If a file is not in one of these formats, a download option will be available.

Here is where we select the files we want to use in the Lesson. We can enter the web page address or file location manually, or we can click on the **Choose** or **Upload file** button and select the file that way. The file selection and uploading menu looks like the one we worked with in Quiz.

Show close button

If this option is enabled, a button allowing the pop-up file to be closed will be visible to the students at the bottom of the pop-up.

Window height and width

These two options allow you to set the height and width of the pop-up. The numbers represent the number of pixels, so the larger the number, the larger the pop-up.

Other

I know, Other is a pretty vague title for the section. There are three options available here, and none of them fit neatly into any category, so instead of creating three additional sections, we have an Other section. Here is what it looks like:

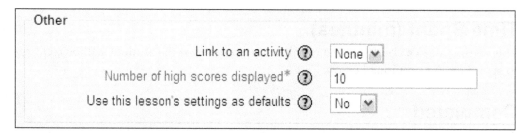

Link to an activity

This option allows you to link to any activity you have already created in the course. In the drop-down menu, you will see a list of all the activities available. If you select one, a link to that activity will be seen at the end of the Lesson. This option can be used as a review tool or preparation for future Lessons, or to give some non-formative assignments.

Number of high scores displayed

This option is a required setting, and the default is set to 10. The number of high scores displayed will be limited to the number entered in the textbox.

In addition, students who achieve the high scores can create custom names for themselves. This feature can be a fun thing for them and a nice reward for doing well, but just to be safe, option provides a profanity filter.

You might not see the High Score tabs due to a slight bug in Moodle. There is a fix for this, which requires accessing the database. The explanation can be found at `http://moodle.org/mod/forum/discuss.php?d=152289`. Once the database Y has been adjusted, you will see the new **High score** tab next to the **Grade essays** tab.

Use this lesson's settings as default

This option can be a very useful feature. If you are designing a series of Lessons for the course with a format you want to use multiple times, changing this setting to **Yes** will use the current settings for the next Lesson you make—a great time-saving tool.

Common module settings

These settings are the common module settings seen in many of the Moodle modules. The options are similar to Quiz, but in Lesson, there are only three available to us. The screenshot is as follows:

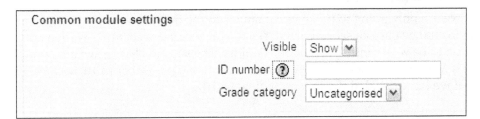

Visible

Here we have the option to **Show** or **Hide** the Lesson.

ID number

Here we can set a number to give the Lesson a unique code for grading. You may have two activities with the same name, but IDs must be unique to allow grading.

Grade category

This setting will allow you to set the category in which the grade will be included.

Setting up Lesson

Now that we have gone over all the settings available in Lesson, it is time for us to make our first Lesson. We are going to be creating a history-based test in Lesson. Our topic is Germany in the 17th century. The test will contain both multiple choice and True/False items and the test will be worth 10 points towards the student's final grade.

The first thing we are going to do is review the settings and make some adjustments.

General

In the General section, we are going to name our Lesson **Germany in the 17th Century**. We also want our students to complete the Lesson within one hour of starting, so we are going to set the **Time limit** to **60**, which will give the students a full hour to complete the Lesson. We are going to be asking our students some True/False and Multiple choice questions, so we want to leave the **Maximum number of answers/branches** at **4**, because we want to have at least four answer options available.

Grade options

Here, we are only going to make two changes to the default settings. First, we are going to change custom scoring from **Yes** to **No**, because we simply want each question to be worth either one or zero points. The second change we are going to make is **Maximum grade**. Here, we want to change the number to **10**, because that is what we have decided the Lesson will be worth.

Flow control

Here, we are going to change two settings. We want to allow our students to go back and change answers if they'd like, so we will set the **Allow student to review** to **Yes**. We also want our students to answer a minimum number of questions. We want them to answer all 10 questions, so we will change the **Minimum number of questions** to **10**, which will force the student to answer every question if he/she wants to finish the Lesson.

Lesson formatting

Here, we are also going to make two changes. First, we want the Lesson to be displayed as a slideshow, so we will set that option to **Yes**, and we are going to leave the **Size** and **Color** at the default for now. The other change we are going to make is to turn **On** the **Progress Bar**, because we want our students to see where they are in the test.

Access control

To control who can take and view the Lesson, we want to create a password for the Lesson. We will turn the **Password protected lesson** setting to **Yes** and, because the test is going to be about German history, we're going to make the password **germany**.

We also want to have the students take the test during class and we don't want them to be able to access it beforehand. We also want to set a time limit for the test, so we will enable the **Available from** and **Deadline**, setting a date and time for both. In the one we are making, the test opens **May 10, 2010** at **10:45am** and closes **May 10, 2010** at **11:45am**.

Dependent on

Since we have no previous Lessons created right now, we can't create any requirements for attempting the test. We will leave this at the default setting of **None**.

Pop-Up to file or web page

We are not going to link this Lesson to any external files or web pages, so we will leave these settings as they are for now.

Other

We are not going to link to any activities and we don't want to have our settings for this Lesson as the default, so we will leave these as they are. However, we only want to have the top five scores shown, so we will change the **Number of high scores displayed** from **10** to **5**.

Common module settings

For the Common module settings, we are going to leave everything at the default settings, except we are going to give the Lesson an ID Number of 1, to make it easy to identify later.

Creating the Lesson content

Now that we have all the settings complete, we save the Lesson settings. Once our options are saved, we are taken to the Lesson **Edit** page where we are able to begin creation of the material and questions inside the Lesson. Part of the page is shown in the next screenshot:

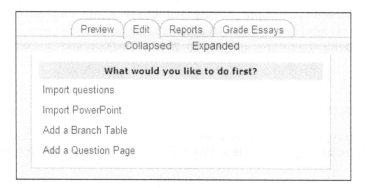

As we saw in the previous screenshot, there are four tabs: **Preview, Edit, Reports**, and **Grade Essays**. Because we have no questions or branches yet, **Preview** does nothing. Also, because there are no attempts on the Lesson yet, there are no reports to see or essays to grade. We will look at each of these sections after we have some material. So, for now, we are left with **Edit**.

Edit

Edit is where we start making the Lesson, and where all the material for the Lesson is created or imported. Here, we can make or import questions, import a PowerPoint, presentation or add a branch.

Previously, I briefly explained what Branches were, and now we are going to make our first one.

Adding a Branch Table

To create a Branch, we need to click on the **Add a Branch Table** link in **Edit**. Once we have clicked on the link, we will see the **Add a Branch Table** creation page. At the top of the creation page, we see textboxes for **Page Title** and **Page Contents**. For **Page Title**, we will enter what we want the page to be called. In the **Page Contents** we are going to explain what the test is about, what material is going to be covered, and what to do in the test.

Directly underneath these sections, we see two checkboxes. The first is **Arrange Branch buttons horizontally**. This option is selected as default, and will place the navigation options horizontally along the bottom of the page. If this option is un-checked, the buttons will be placed vertically.

The second checkbox is **Display in left menu**, which is also already selected by default. If the **Display left menu** option from the **Formatting** section in **Editing Lesson** has been enabled and this option is at the default setting, the Branch Table will be visible to the student in the left menu. If this option is disabled, the menu will not display the Branch Table page.

Under these two options, we start to create the descriptions of the navigation buttons. There are four description textboxes because we entered **4** in the **Maximum number of Answers/Branches**. In each of these textboxes we will enter what we want to be displayed within the button.

Under each of the descriptions, we can see a drop-down menu called **Jump**, which has four options: **This page**, **Next page**, **Previous page**, and **End of Lesson**. Selecting **This page** will move the student back to the top of the current page. Selecting **Next page** will move the student to the next page in the Lesson order. Choosing the **Previous page** option will bring the student to the previous page in the Lesson. Selecting **End of Lesson** will take the student to the end of the lesson. We haven't created any pages to link to yet, so we will select **Next page** for all of our **Jumps** options, and we will change them to the proper pages once the rest of the Lesson is created.

Once we have entered all the information in the appropriate places, we will click on the **Add a Branch Table** button at the bottom of the page and the page will be created. Here is what the page looks like with all the information included before clicking on the **Save** button.

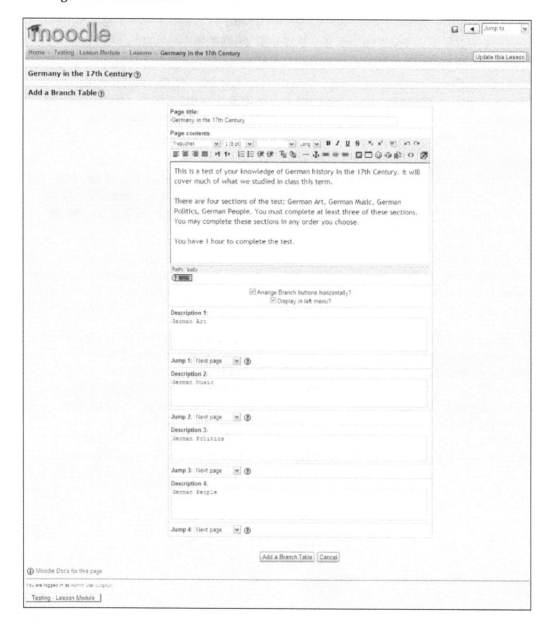

When we click on the **Add a Branch Table** button, the page is created. However, the new page is not what we see when we click on the **Add a Branch Table** button. After clicking on it, we are taken back to the **Edit** tab, where we see our new page details, as shown in the next screenshot:

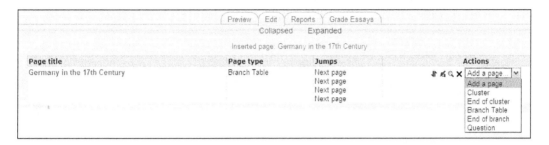

Here, we are shown which page has been added to the Lesson. Under the **Inserted page** line, we can see several headings detailing the pertinent information about the page. We see the title of the page, the page type, number of jumps and where they take us, and an actions drop-down menu. In a vain attempt to stop this run-on sentence... offering options for the creation of new pages.

However, this page is not the only way to view our newly-created page. Notice the **Collapsed** and **Expanded** links just above **Inserted page**? the previous screen shot shows us the Collapsed view – the most basic information about the page. Clicking on the **Expanded** link will give us a much more detailed, and possibly more useful, view of the page. In addition, if you have included any images in the **Branch Table**, they will be displayed here as well, as shown in the next screenshot:

Here, you can see the text of the page, what the jump buttons are titled, as well as all the other information that was contained in the previous **Collapsed** view.

Now that we have created a page and click on the **Preview** button, we will see what the Branch page looks like.

Just to show how an image would be displayed, I have gone back and edited the **Branch Table**. Because we are dealing with 17th Century German history, we will use a painting of the Battle of Nordlingen, a famous military engagement in 1634.

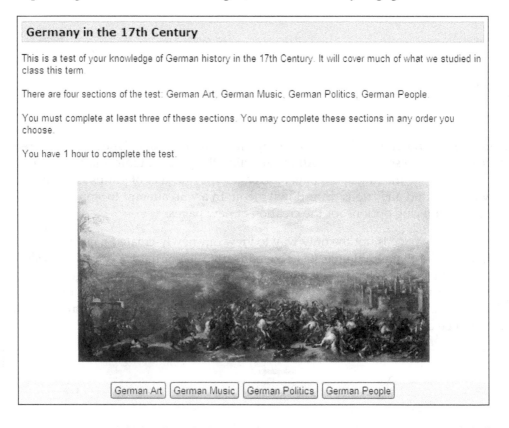

This screen is what our students will see when they begin the test. If you click on any of the buttons, it will simply return you to the same page because there is, so far, only a single page created.

From here, we could create sub-branches, but because of space issues, we will start creating some question pages.

Adding a Question page

As seen from the previous screenshot, we have created a **Branch Table** with four possible paths. We will now create four separate question pages, one for each of the buttons.

To being with, we will click on the **Add a question page here** link in the **Expanded** view page, located just above the page title. Clicking on this link will bring us to the Add a question page. The page is shown in the next screenshot:

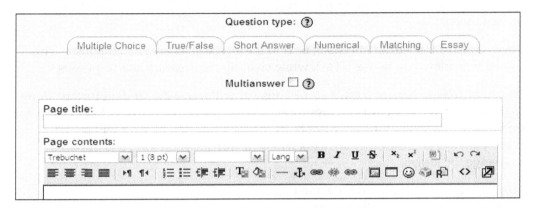

At the top of this new page, we see a series of six tabs showing which question types we can include in the Lesson. The six types of questions available in Lesson are: **Multiple Choice**, **True/False**, **Short Answer**, **Numerical**, **Matching**, and **Essay**. Under the question type tabs, we see a **Multianswer** checkbox, the **Page title**, and **Page contents**.

If the **Multianswer** checkbox is enabled, it allows us to accept multiple responses to the question. The **Page title** will designate the title of the page, which, like in Quiz questions, should be as descriptive as possible. **Page contents** is where we can enter our question, images, and links.

Multiple Choice question

For our first question, we are going to use multiple choice. The question is about German art and includes an image. This question is not a **Multianswer** item, so we will leave the **Multianswer** checkbox blank. Now we create a name for the page. In the contents, we will ask about the image shown. Below the contents we see spaces for Answers and Responses. The Answers and Responses are accompanied by textboxes. Answer is where we put the answer and Response is where we give feedback, if desired.

Note, there is no option to the shuffle response order off or on in Lesson as there is in Quiz; the responses are automatically randomized.

Under the Answer and Response, there is a drop-down menu giving us options of what to do if the student selects that answer. We can send the student to the **Next page**, keep him/her on **This page**, move him/her to the **Previous page**, or send him/her to the **End of the Lesson**.

We will fill in our title, question, include an image, add the Answers and Responses, and send the student back to the Branch Table regardless of his/her response. Once everything has been entered and we have confirmed everything is correct, we click on the **Add a question page here** button and the question will be added to the Lesson.

There is also a **Use editor** checkbox next to the all the answers and responses. This option will allow you to use HTML while creating the answers and responses.

If custom scoring is turned off, a correct answer will move the student further along in the Lesson, while an incorrect response will jump to a page further back or remain on the same page. If jumps have not been changed, the first answer will be the correct answer and the other answers will be incorrect. Therefore, it is important to change the jumps.

Now we can click on the **Preview** tab to see the new question, shown in the next screenshot, but note that the image can be as large or small as you'd like.

Once the student has selected a response, he or so can click on the **Please check one answer** button and receive the feedback for their choice. The student will then click on the **continue** button and will continue on to wherever that response has been directed, in our case, the **Branch Table** we created earlier.

True/False

These questions are very similar to the **Multiple Choice**. The only differences is that there is no **Multianswer** option and there are only two places to enter Answers and Responses.

We will create a simple True/False question related to German Music. After everything has been entered and saved, the preview shows us something that looks like a Quiz True/False item.

Short Answer

In Lesson's Short Answer questions, we have two types to work with: **Simple Analysis** and **Regular Expressions Analysis**.

Simple Analysis is similar to the Short Answer items in the Quiz module. We enter a question, enter acceptable answers, use any wildcards we want, and create a final wildcard in the final answer slot to catch anything that falls outside of what is acceptable.

Asterisk review

The asterisk says that the character directly preceding can be used or not and also allows any number of characters to be used between the character preceding the asterisk and the character immediately following it. J*Tolkien would accept JTolkien, J Tolkien, JR Tolkien, J R R Tolkien, John Ronald Reuel Tolkien, or anything else, as long as the expression began with J and ended with 'Tolkien.

If you ever need to use an asterisk in your actual answer, the asterisk must be preceded by a backslash. Here is how it needs to be entered: *.

The **Regular Expressions Analysis** is our second option in **Short Answer**, which is enabled by clicking on the **Regular Expression** checkbox. While offering a lot of power and flexibility, this option requires a little practice to master the basics, and a lot of practice to become an advanced user. Regular expressions work by placing special characters inside the answer string, which allow the computer to recognize an acceptable response. Let's look at how this works. We are only looking at a few basic examples here, so if you want more information about these expressions, you can start by checking out the following websites:

`http://gnosis.cx/publish/programming/regular_expressions.html` and `http://www.zytrax.com/tech/web/regex.htm#intro`.

 If your expressions don't seem to be working, before you panic, make sure you have checked the checkbox!

Asterisk

The asterisk functions a little differently in Regular Expressions. While it means that there is any number of characters preceding it, it must be preceded by a period, because the period means any characters in this position. So, using the J*Tolkein example again, we would enter J.*Tolkein to enable the system to accept any of the previous combinations.

Plus sign

The plus sign functions in the same way as the asterisk, except that the plus sign requires that the preceding character be a part of the final answer. So, using the previous example, **J+Tolkien** would accept JR Tolkien, JRRTolkien, J R R Tolkien or anything else that began with **J+one letter or more** and ended with **Tolkien**.

Vertical bar '|'

This symbol, when used to separate two words, tells the computer to accept one of the two as correct. For example, **center|centre**, would accept either **center** or **centre** as a correct response.

Parentheses

The parentheses indicates what we are working with. This can be a phrase, word, or even part of a word. For example, placing the parentheses as they are seen here, **Cent(er|re)** would accept either **center** or **centre** as correct.

Question mark

Using the question mark in an answer will allow the previous character to either be entered or not, and accept the response. For example, **media?eval** would accept **medieval** or **mediaeval**.

Square brackets

Using brackets will allow any letters inside the bracket to be acceptable as an answer. If [bce]ar is entered as the answer, bar, car, and ear, will all receive full points and a correct response feedback.

/i

The Regular Expressions are case-sensitive. If you do not want the response to be case-sensitive, you must include a **/i** at the end of the answer. It is from **Italy/i** would not require any capital letters.

Missing Information

In order to use Regular Expressions to determine if something is missing from the correct response, you need to include two minus signs **--** at the beginning of the answer. For example, **--.*socks.*** will tell the system that the word **socks** is missing from the answer. The student would then see the feedback you entered, and be directed to the page you selected.

Incorrect Information

As shown previously, to enable the system to detect incorrect information, we need to include two addition signs **++** at the beginning of the sentence. For example, if the answer should be **dogs and cats**, we might enter, **++(birds | snakes | fish | rabbits)**. So, if a student entered **dogs and fish**, fish would be identified as incorrect. From here, in the response, you would enter some appropriate feedback and link the student to where you want him/her to go.

Combinations

These symbols can also be used in combination. For example, **(| I am) working at the Colour Theater | Theatre/i** .would allow for a variety of responses, such as I am working at the Color Theater, working at the colour theatre, I am working at The Colour theatre, Working at the color theatre, and many more.

As you can see, Regular Expressions can be a very powerful tool. I have only covered the basics here. Refer to the Moodle documentation at `http://docs.moodle.org/en/Lesson_question_types#Short_answer` for more information.

Now we are going to continue and make a Short Answer question about German politics. We are going to use the Regular Expression option and we will enter our question title, question text, answers, and responses. It is important to note that, unlike Quiz, we are limited in the number of possible answers we can accept. We have set our **Maximum number of answers/branches** to four, so we only have four possible response options. We have two options to change this. We can either edit the Lesson settings and increase the number of answer options, or we need to make sure that the question is framed so that the possible response options are limited. We are going to stick with our four Answer/Branches and try to create a question that will limit the response possibilities.

The question we are asking is, **What happened on May, 15, 1648?** The response we are looking for is something about the signing of the Treaty of Westphalia. To try and cover as many possibilities as we can with as few entries as possible, we have created two answers and two responses. We have also redirected the student to the branch table regardless of their response. This is what was entered, as shown in the next screenshot:

```
Answer 1:
.*Treaty of Westphalia.*/i


Response 1: [Use editor: ☐ ⑦ ]
Correct.
Answer 2:
--.*Treaty of Westphalia.*/i


Response 2: [Use editor: ☐ ⑦ ]
Sorry, the answer was the Treaty of Westphalia was signed.
```

We can see that the **Answer 1** will accept any answer as long as **Treaty of Westphalia** is included, we have also added the **/i**, which eliminates case sensitivity. In **Answer 2**, we can see that any answer that does not include **Treaty of Westphalia** will be considered incorrect, again with case being ignored.

The student will see the question and be given an empty textbox to write in his/her answer. The output is shown in the next screenshot:

```
What happened on May 15, 1648?



                          Your answer: [                          ]

                          [ Please enter your answer in the box ]
```

Short answer questions can be complex, and they require practice, but these question types are a great addition to any test you are designing. It is also important to remember that answers to Short Answer question are viewed in the order entered, so it is always best to have the most correct answer first, following a descending pattern to the final, incorrect response.

Numerical

These items are set up like Short Answer, but require a number as the answer. Numerical questions are similar to Numerical questions in Quiz, but the options available and the way they are set up are different.

To use Numerical questions, we write a question that will elicit a numerical response. Then we enter the correct answer, or answers in the Answer textboxes available. If we are willing to accept a variation in the numerical response, for example, 150-200, we can use a colon between the numbers, 150:200, and this will tell the system to accept any number within that range. Unfortunately, there is no wildcard available in Lesson Numerical questions.

To deal with incorrect answers, and to provide feedback, we need to create a range of acceptable and unacceptable answers. For example, in the question we have on German people, we are going to ask about population in the 1650s. The correct answer is that (about) 10,000,000 people were living in the region at the time. So, in the first answer space, we enter 10000000. Note, there are no commas. If you enter a comma, the system will interpret the first comma it comes to as a stop marker, and the answer will only include the answer up to the first comma. Now, we have the correct answer, and that is the only response we want. Because there is no wildcard in this question type, we need to give a range of incorrect responses: 0:9999999 for **Answer 2** and 10000001:99999999999999999 or so for **Answer 3**. Now, if the student responds with 10000000, he or she will receive the correct answer feedback. For any other answer, the incorrect feedback will be given instead., they will receive the incorrect feedback.

The final numerical product is shown in the next screenshot. Note that I added a message telling the students exactly how to enter their answers, just in case they are unfamiliar with Lesson or the Numerical format.

What was the approximate population of the Germany (in its present borders) during the 1650s?

Only enter numeric characters. If you enter anything other than numeric characters, the system will mark your answer incorrect. For example 10000000 not 10,000,000 or 100,00

Your answer: _____

[Please enter your answer in the box]

Alternative Numerical Item

If you want to allow words and numeric characters in a single response, you might consider using Essay. This alternative will allow both any character to be entered, but the drawback is that you will have to manually grade the essays.

Matching

Matching questions in Lesson are very similar to how they are set up in Quiz. There is a series of pairs titled Answers and Matches With. Depending on how the students match the items, they are directed to the appropriate page.

It is important to note here that the Answers in Matching in Lesson are not shuffled. The items will be presented exactly the same each time; however, the Matches With are shuffled. Here is our example of German artists and their art forms.

Essay

Essay is extremely easy to set up. Once the Essay is opened, we simply need to enter a title and a prompt for the students to respond to. Once that is done, we choose where we want them to go once they have finished with their response, then we click on **Save page**.

When the students open the Essay page, they are presented with the prompt and a textbox to enter their response. When they have finished, they click on **Please enter your answer in the box** button, and are directed to the page determined during the item creation. The question is shown in the next screenshot:

We have seen all the question types available in Lesson and showed how to create them. We have looked at the Branch Table and the Question Pages, but now we need to look at the other Lesson pages, the first of which is called **Clusters**.

Clusters

Clusters are groups of questions inside the Lesson, typically focusing on some sub-aspect of the main material or a quiz inside the Lesson. Clusters are also the way to enter variations into the Lesson. For example, if, in the German Art section, we wanted to have our students look at some art and tell us if *Flegel* had painted it or not, we could either create questions within the Branch Table and place them in the order we wanted, or we could start a Cluster, create the questions we wanted, and allow the computer to decide the order. All we would need to do is create a Cluster including the items we want included and then create an end of the Cluster. Let's do one now.

First, I have gone back and added several more True/False questions to the German Art branch. All the questions are True/False, showing an image and asking the same question, **Is this one of Flegel's paintings?**

Now that I created have all the questions I want to include, I go to any drop-down menu and click on **Cluster**, which will add a new Cluster to the Lesson. Once the cluster is there, I need to move it to an appropriate place.

I have titled the new Cluster **Cluster - German Art – Flegel? – T/F w/ Images**. This title tells us that it is the beginning of a Cluster, is related to German Art, the questions in the Cluster are going to be related to *Flegel*, and they are all T/F questions with images.

In the Cluster, I have included a brief introduction (the students will not see this, but it helps to organize Lessons more effectively) and in the **Jumps** drop-down, I have set the link to **Unseen question within a cluster**, so, regardless of the students responses, they are directed to a random question in the Cluster. This action forces the students to work through every example in the Cluster until they have seen them all, then they will automatically be sent to the **End of Cluster**.

Now, we need to create the **End of Cluster**, which lets the system know that the Cluster has been completed and it is time to move on to another part of the Lesson. To create the **End of Cluster**, click on the **Edit** tab, select the **End of Cluster** link from any drop-down menu, and click on **End of Cluster**, which moves to the end of the questions in the cluster.

Next is the **Collapsed** view of how the Cluster is organized. You can see that the **German Art – Flegel – MC w/ Image** link? leads to the Cluster. Once the Cluster starts, there are five T/F questions in the cluster, which will be presented to the student in a random order. This random order is done by directing all five questions back to the start of the Cluster. The system recognizes which questions have already been presented, so each item will only be seen once. Once all the items have been attempted, the system directs the student to the **End of Cluster**, which will bring them to the Next Page in the sequence, in this case, **German Art – Artists and Their Art Forms – Matching**.

Germany in the 17th Century ⑦			
Preview Edit Reports Grade Essays			
Collapsed Expanded			
Page title	**Page type**	**Jumps**	**Actions**
Germany in the 17th Century	Branch Table	German Art - Flegel - MC w/ Image German Music - Michael Praetorius - T/F German Politics - Treaty of Westphalia - SA German People - Population - Numerical End of lesson	⬍ ✎ ⚲ ✗ Add a page ▾
German Art - Flegel - MC w/ Image	Multiple Choice	Cluster - German Art - Flegel? - T/F w/ Images Cluster - German Art - Flegel? - T/F w/ Images Cluster - German Art - Flegel? - T/F w/ Images Cluster - German Art - Flegel? - T/F w/ Images	⬍ ✎ ⚲ ✗ Add a page... ▾
Cluster - German Art - Flegel? - T/F w/ Images	Cluster	Unseen question within a cluster	⬍ ✎ ⚲ ✗ Add a page.. ▾
German Art - Flegel? 1 - T/F w/ Image	True/False	Cluster - German Art - Flegel? - T/F w/ Images Cluster - German Art - Flegel? - T/F w/ Images	⬍ ✎ ⚲ ✗ Add a page ▾
German Art - Flegel? 2 - T/F w/ Image	True/False	Cluster - German Art - Flegel? - T/F w/ Images Cluster - German Art - Flegel? - T/F w/ Images	⬍ ✎ ⚲ ✗ Add a page ▾
German Art - Flegel? 3 - T/F w/ Image	True/False	Cluster - German Art - Flegel? - T/F w/ Images Cluster - German Art - Flegel? - T/F w/ Images	⬍ ✎ ⚲ ✗ Add a page ▾
German Art - Flegel? 4 - T/F w/ Image	True/False	Cluster - German Art - Flegel? - T/F w/ Images Cluster - German Art - Flegel? - T/F w/ Images	⬍ ✎ ⚲ ✗ Add a page ▾
German Art - Flegel? 5 - T/F w/ Image	True/False	Cluster - German Art - Flegel? - T/F w/ Images Cluster - German Art - Flegel? - T/F w/ Images	⬍ ✎ ⚲ ✗ Add a page ▾
End of Cluster - German Art	End of cluster	Next page	⬍ ✎ ⚲ ✗ Add a page ▾
German Art - Artists and Their Art Forms - Matching	Matching	Next page Next page	⬍ ✎ ⚲ ✗ Add a page ▾
End of branch	End of branch	Germany in the 17th Century	⬍ ✎ ⚲ ✗ Add a page ▾

This sequence is how most clusters work. There are a few other ways to organize them, but for now, this example will get you started. If you want to get some additional information on Clusters, check out Moodle's site. Also, remember that Clusters are not included in the progress bar or standard grading, so when you are checking the Lesson and you see that the progress bar is not moving or the grade is not correct, don't worry.

Clusters can be a tricky at first, but once you try a few, they get to be pretty easy. Just remember that you need to put all the cluster questions somewhere between the start and end cluster. Also, all the items should, if you want the items displayed in a random order, be redirected to the Cluster start page.

End of branch

End of branch functions like End of Cluster. It signifies the end of a particular branch and directs the user back to the Branch Table. End of Branches are created just like end of cluster pages. Simply go to the **End of branch** link or any of the drop-down menus in the **Edit** tab and click on **End of branch**. Place the newly-created **End of branch** at the appropriate place in the Lesson sequence and make its **Jumps** link take the user to the **Branch Table**.

End of Lesson

As of now, if a student entered the Lesson and answered all the questions, he or she would not be able to complete the Lesson, because we have not added any way to end it. Unless the Lesson was timed and the student sat and waited for the time to run out, he or she would receive an **Uncompleted** message. We don't want this. We want the students to finish and then begin working on something else. What we need to do now is create an End of Lesson Page.

End of Lesson is created in a Branch Table. Using one of the **Jumps** drop-down menus from the **Edit** page, you can see an **End of Lesson** option. Clicking on this will create the **End of Lesson** Jump, which will bring students to the final page of the Lesson congratulating them on finishing, and showing them their results. You must write, some text, for example, **End of Lesson**, in the **Description** textbox.

Now the students have a way to end the Lesson when they are ready.

Import questions

Importing questions to Lesson is a simplified version of importing to Quiz. To import questions to Lesson, we are given a drop-down menu with all the Moodle-acceptable formats. We choose the file format type when we enter the filename we want to upload in the **Upload** textbox. Once this step is done, we click on the **Upload this file** button. The **Import questions** page is shown in the next screenshot:

Once you have selected and clicked on the **Upload this file**, you will see a page showing the number of questions being imported at the top of the page and a list of the questions. At the bottom you will see a **continue** button. Click on it to complete the upload of the file. Once this action is done, the files will be added to the Lesson and are ready to be used.

Import PowerPoint

Import PowerPoint allows you to take a PowerPoint presentation and have it added to a new Lesson as a Branch Table. The menu to do this looks just like **Importing Questions**; however, there are a few steps that need to be taken before we import the file.

First, we need to open our PowerPoint presentation and save it as a web page. Once it is saved as a web page, you will see an `.htm` file and a folder containing all the presentation data. Do nothing with the `.htm` file but zip the folder. Once the folder has been zipped, go the new Lesson and click on the Import PowerPoint link. You will see the Import menu. Find the zipped folder and upload it to the course. You will see a **continue** button. Click on it and the upload will be completed. You do not need to upload the `.htm` file.

The PowerPoint presentation will be now be displayed as a Branch Table and will have **Next** and **Previous** buttons for navigation between slides. From here, you can click on the **Edit** button and begin to enter clusters, branches, or question pages.

Reports

Now that we have a way to complete the test, we need to be able to see how the students did. When a student completes the Lesson, he or she will see a page similar to this.

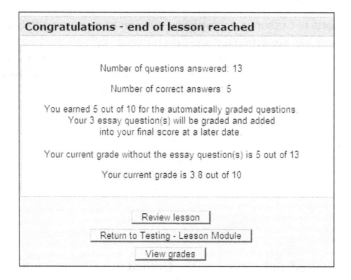

The data presented shows the student the number of questions answered, the number they got correct, their current grade without the essay points, and the overall current grade.

The students are also presented with three buttons linking them to a review of the Lesson, which, if enabled, will allow students to attempt the test again. The second button links the student back to the course homepage, seen in the previous screenshot as **Return to Testing – Lesson Module**. The final button leads them to their grades.

The instructor's report page is very different. Instructors are offered an overview and a detailed statistics view. The overview gives detailed information about individual students and also gives the class high, low, and average of scores and time. The teacher report view is shown in the next screenshot:

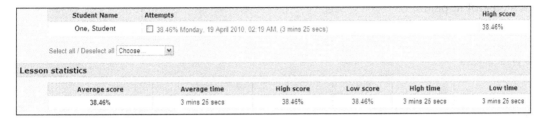

Careful!

The drop-down next to the **Select all / Deselect all** only has a single option, **Delete selected**. If you click on this option, you will not get a second chance to confirm the deletion, and the student results that were in the report a moment ago will be lost forever! If you have accidentally selected the **Delete** option, but not yet released the mouse button, the *Esc* key can save you!

The detailed statistics view offers instructors the class response statistics of each of the items. This report can be useful for evaluation of question difficulty or other possible question issues or research. The detailed view of a question, in this case a matching question, is shown in the next screenshot:

Grade Essays

Clicking on this tab, located next to the **Reports** tab, will link us to a page where we will be able to review each student's essay and comment on it. In addition, we can e-mail our comments and grades to them. When we click on the tab, the next screenshot appears:

By clicking on any of the essay links, we will be shown a page that has the essay prompt, the student response, a place for us to make our comments, and a drop-down for us to give the grade. The available grades range from No Credit to the point value assigned to the lesson. We can see the German music essay opened and ready for our comments in the next screenshot:

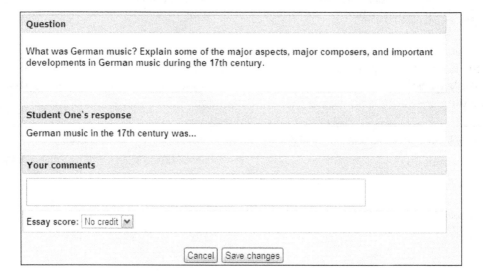

Vocabulary drills

As mentioned in the introduction, Lesson can give vocabulary, or flash card quizzes and drills as well. If you have a vocabulary list you are interested in quizzing your students on or having them review, here is how you can do it using Lesson.

First, we need to create a new Lesson. Go through the normal steps to create a Lesson and in the **Flow control** section of the Lesson settings page, adjust the settings depending on what you want to do with the test. The only setting we really have to work with here is the **Action after correct answer** drop-down. The functions available from this menu were described earlier in the **Flow control** section. You can set the minimum number of items the student will need to complete, as well as the **Number of Pages (Cards) to show**. If the **Number of Pages (Cards) to show** is left at **0**, all the vocabulary in the Lesson will be displayed. If you set a number greater than zero, that number of cards will be displayed.

After getting the **Flow control** and the rest of the Lesson set to our liking and saved, we begin to add the vocabulary items to the Lesson. Multiple Choice and True/ False provide quick vocabulary reviews or tests and they are also easy to design and create, but you could use any question style you wish. Once all the questions have been created, reviewed, and saved, it is time to move on to the preview of the test.

As you go through the vocabulary test, see if there are any problems with the setup or items. Once you have confirmed that the vocabulary test is working properly, you're ready to give it to your students.

Summary

Lesson is a complex and somewhat quirky tool that can be useful for a variety of reasons. The Lesson module takes a lot of time to get used to, but once you start using it, and if it works for your situation, it can become an exceptional tool for teaching and learning. While its applications for testing are solid, there are issues, such as limited question types and features available from Quiz-based items that are missing in Lesson-based ones.

The ability to create simple or complex multi-branched Lessons, questions, and clusters for students to work through, is the key function of Lesson. These features are what sets Lesson apart from other applications, and, while Quiz, is a more robust testing option, Lesson certainly has its own strong points. We have only looked at using Lesson for testing here, but it was mainly created as a self-guided learning tool.

Finally, it is important to start using Lesson on a small scale, for example, starting with a limited number of branches, and slowly building up your skills and knowledge until you are confident that your Lesson-based tests or activities are well-designed and clear, and what you want for your students. The more you practice using Lesson, the better you will get at putting together more useful and advanced paths for your students to follow.

In the next chapter, we will be looking at another module called Workshop, which is good for self-assessment and group assessment.

6
Using Workshop

Workshop is an important part of our look at testing and assessing with Moodle. So far, we have only looked at tests and questions with pre-determined responses or those that were only assessed by the teacher. Here, we will look at Workshop, which offers a way to interact and assess students through their submitted work as well as offering the option of self-assessment, peer assessment, and teacher assessment.

Workshop was one of the first contributed modules in Moodle, and it is one of the more complex modules available due to the sheer number of options available. It was intended to be a module where students would be able to upload assignments and their classmates and teacher would review then assess the submitted work. It has many settings and functions, and requires several steps to be completed before it can be used in class, but once it is finished, it will be one more way you can assess your students.

In this chapter, we will:

- Explore Workshop's features
- Create a sample Workshop
- Look at self-assessment, peer assessment, and teacher assessment options in Workshop

Why use Workshop

Before you decide to use Workshop, you need to come up with an idea of how and why you are going to use it. Are you going to use it to have your students simply upload files and assess them yourself? Will you have them peer-assess the work? Are you going to have the students do any self-assessment? Will you give them a sample assignment to practice how to effectively assess work? If so, how many? How long will they have to submit their work? These are all things you will need to think about before you begin to use Workshop. Once you have decided on how you want to use it, you need to locate it.

Finding Workshop

Everything we have worked with so far, has been initially available as part of Moodle and we have not installed or enabled anything. However, in a new site, some of the modules, including Workshop, are not available from the start. As a teacher, you will not be able to access these hidden or installable modules yourself, unless you also have administrator access. The first thing you will need to do is contact your site admin and have them 'Show' the Workbook module. Once it is visible, we can begin working with it.

If you are the admin, you can go to the homepage and click on **Modules | Activities | Manage activities**, which will show a list of modules available. Workshop is one of them, and to make it visible, click on the closed-eye icon. Once this is done, Workshop will be available for use by going to the **Activities** drop-down menu on your course page and selecting it.

Workshop features

Before we begin to create our Workshop, we will look at the options Workshop has available and talk about their functions. Workshop is different from Quiz and Lesson, in that there are no sections used to divide fields into categories. We will be looking at all the options in the order they are presented, so we know exactly what we can do in Workshop.

Submission Title

This is where we name our Workshop and enter what the link in the course will be labelled. There is no difference between **Submission Title** and the Title we have seen in Lesson and Quiz.

Description

Enter the description of the Workshop's aim and what the students are expected to do here. All students entering the Workshop will see this, so it is important to include here a detailed outline of what they are to do, including assignment requirements or anything else that is expected of the students.

Since this is just like the Description in Quiz and Lesson, you can do the same things including: adding images, tables, text files, and so on. In fact, you can do the same things anywhere you encounter the rich text editor.

Grade for Assessments

This is a score between 0 and 100, which reflects the total points the student or peer can assign the work submitted to the Workshop. In the previous image, we have ours set to **50**. Instructors are only involved in assessing this section if the Workshop uses a strategy we will talk about shortly called **Accumulative**.

However, this is only part of the total score. This score is added to the **Grade for Submission** to calculate the total score for the Workshop assignment.

Grade for Submission

This is a score between 0 and 100, which reflects the maximum points the teacher can assign the work submitted to the Workshop. Once the teacher has assessed the work and added their score, the score from **Grade for Assessments** is added to it for the final grade.

For example, our **Grade for Submission** is set to **50** and let's say we assign Student One 45. If the score given in **Grade for Assessments** was 42, Workshop would add the two scores together to get the final grade, which would work out to be 42 + 45 = 87.

Grading Strategy

The **Grading Strategy** offers five 'strategies' for using the grades. They are as follows: **Not Graded, Accumulative, Error Banded, Criterion, Rubric.**

Not Graded

This means that there will be no grades given for the Workshop. Instead of grades, the students and their peers are able to give comments on the submitted work. The instructor can then grade the comments. If there is no grade given by the teacher, this is only a self-assessment or peer assessment and will not be used in the calculation of their course grade.

When creating Not Graded assignments you will see an Element textbox with no grading options; you will see this page when the **Save changes** button—at the bottom of the Editing page—is clicked. You should enter a statement or instructions about what you want the reviewers to comment on in the Element textbox. Here is what it looks like. When you finish, click on the **Save changes** button at the bottom of the page and the comments will be displayed to the student.

Accumulative

This is the default setting for Workshop's grading strategy. If this is used, the assignment is graded based upon a series of what Moodle terms *assessment elements*. These *assessment elements* will look at the submitted work using either one of these 'elements' for a very simple evaluation, or from two to twenty for more complex and detailed submissions.

When creating elements, there are three things that need to be decided on and entered into the Element editing page; they are: Description, Scale, and Weight. The Editing Assessment Elements page is shown in the next screenshot:

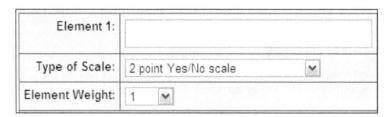

Description

In the **Element 1** textbox, we enter the description of what we want the student assessing the Workshop to do with this element. For example, if we have given a writing assignment, we may want the student to review their classmate's work and determine if they used effective support for their topic or if they had a strong conclusion. So, in the description we would want to enter a message telling the student exactly what to look for, and how to grade based on what they read.

Type of Scale

In the **Type of Scale** section, we determine how points are awarded. There are ten scales in the drop-down ranging from a **2 Point Yes/No scale** to a **5 Point Excellent/ Poor Scale** to a **Score out of 100**.

Depending on the assignment type, some of the scales might be easier to justify than others. For example, using a 2 Point Yes/No Scale to determine whether or not the writing assignment submitted has the required minimum of four paragraphs might make more sense than a 5 Point Excellent/Poor Scale, or a score out of 100. Selecting an appropriate and useful scale for the students to use while assessing peers, and for the assessed student to understand, is an important aspect of creating effective Workshops.

The final thing to note about **Type of Scale** is that whichever scale you decide to use, they are all equivalent in grading as long as the **Element Weight** is set the same.

You can also create custom scales. To do this, look in the Gradebook chapter for more information on how to do this.

Element Weight

This setting sets the weight of the Element. By default all of the Elements in the Workshop are set equally to one. If you wish to give more importance to a particular Element, go to the drop-down menu and adjust it. The scale for weights goes from +4 down to -4.

It is important to note that the weight given to the Elements, regardless of changes made, does not affect the total possible points a student can receive from the assignment.

Error Banded Grading

Using this setting the teacher will create a series of Yes/No questions, which the student reviewing the Workshop will respond to. This is a good way to create criteria-based assessments. For example, if you created a writing assignment you might want to ensure that there were the requisite number of paragraphs, ten new vocabulary items used, a title, and so on. This is an easy way to do it, and it is also an easy method for students to begin working with self-reviews and peer reviews.

The Element editing page looks slightly different from the previous Grading Strategies. Here is what you will see if this option is selected:

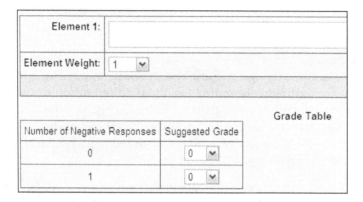

As you can see from the previous screenshot, there is the usual **Element** and **Element Weight**. These are completed as normal. Underneath you see **Grade Table**. In the **Grade Table** there are two columns: **Number of Negative Responses** and **Suggested Grade**.

The **Number of Negative Responses** show how many 'No' responses the student receives. The **Suggested Grade** drop-down menus allow you to set the number of points the student should receive depending on the number of 'No' responses they get. For example, if you had an assignment with 5 criteria and a Grade for Submission of 25, you would probably choose to set zero negative response to 25 points and five negative responses (meaning they were all incorrect) to 0 points. You can adjust the scores as you see fit.

Criterion

In Criterion rating, the instructor creates a series of statements about the assignment as well as a score associated with each statement. The reviewers go through the work and then choose the statement that best fits the assignment they worked with. The setup for Criterion is fairly simple, and a single Criterion is shown in the next screenshot:

Criterion 1:	
Suggested Grade:	0 ▾

The statements entered should include a clear description of the level of work required and/or specific information or material that needs to be included to achieve the rank being assigned to the statement.

Using the Criterion rating, while a useful way for assigning scores, isn't something that students new to peer or self-reviews should probably start with. Using statements often leaves open too many possibilities for those new at assessing and can lead to inaccurate scoring and interpretations, unless the statements are very precise and detailed.

The scoring goes from 0 to 100, so there are many possible criterion statements that can be created, although, creating too many can be counterproductive since it requires the students to look through many options and they can get bored or begin skimming just to find something that looks about right.

Rubric Grading

The **Rubric Grading** option is how Moodle integrates a rubric into the Workshop. Each 'element' or aspect of the assignment that needs to be evaluated by the reviewer is entered into an Element textbox. Variations in the quality of the 'element' are assigned to the respective Grade. Workshop uses a 5-point scale with a **Grade 0** giving no points and a **Grade 4** the maximum points. The Rubric Grading scale is shown in the next screenshot:

Element 1:	
Element Weight:	1 ▾
Grade 0:	
Grade 1:	
Grade 2:	
Grade 3:	
Grade 4:	

Using the Rubric Grading system is another useful way to introduce students to self-reviews and peer reviews. By creating clearly outlined ranks, students will be able to make more effective and useful evaluations of assignments. In addition, creating a series of rubrics for students to use for assessment is useful to the students themselves, since it enables them to know exactly what they need to do to achieve a specific level or score on the assignment.

The five grading strategies we have just looked at all have their uses. When creating Workshops, you need to make sure that the method selected for grading is appropriate to the assignment and the students and that the reviewer's task is clearly described.

Now let's move on and look at the next three items in the Workshop creation page as shown in the next screenshot:

Number of Comments, Assessment Elements...

This feature determines how many Elements will be used to assess the assignment being reviewed. The setting has a drop-down with a number from 0 to 20 used to determine how many grading Elements can be used.

It is also important to note that while we can change many of the settings at any time, this number may not be altered once an assignment has been submitted. This means that if you find you have too few or many set here, you will either need to create a new Workshop and have students submit their work to the new one or delete the submitted work, change the setting, and have the students resubmit their assignments to the same Workshop. Either way, it is a hassle, so it is best to take your time and think through exactly what you want from the assignment when creating the Workshop.

Number of Comments—Not Graded grade strategy

The number entered in the drop-down will determine the number of comments the reviewer can make on an assignment. For example, if you set the drop-down to 3, there will be three Elements available for comments plus a General Comment textbox.

If the drop-down is set to 0, there will still be a single, General Comment textbox available to the reviewer.

Assessment Elements—Accumulative grade strategy

The number in the drop-down menu will determine the number of statements that can be made. The more statements you create, the more precise you are able to be with the way the work is reviewed, but too many and you run the risk of overwhelming the reviewer with detail.

Grade Bands—Error Banded grade strategy

The number selected in the drop-down menu determines how many of the Error Banded Yes/No statements can be made. In contrast to Assessment Elements, a large number of simple Yes/No statements, which are easily answered, can be a good way to give clear and effective feedback to the author of the assignment. These are also a good way to give students just beginning to work with self-reviews and peer reviews a good introduction to the practice.

Criterion Statements—Criterion grade strategy

The option to create up to 20 criterion statements should give you ample space to create very precise and specific criterion statements; however, creating too many can be counterproductive since it requires the students to look through too many options. It is important to strike a balance, and if you are not able to create exactly what you are looking for using this option, you may want to look to Rubric Grading.

Categories in a Rubric—Rubric Grading

Here, we can create the number of categories that will be included in the rubric. The higher the number here, the more detailed rubrics we can create. I would, once again, like to caution against using too many. Not only do you need to create the Elements and the details for each Grade in the Element, you need to make sure that the reviewers have time and clearly understand what is expected of them. Most rubrics I have seen use something between 5 and 10, depending on the level of detail necessary for the assignment's evaluation.

Number of Attachments expected on Submissions

This feature sets the number of upload boxes available to students when they submit their work. The numbers go from zero to five, with zero being the default, meaning that students are not expected to have any attachments and the only assessed work is submitted by posting in the Submit Assignment Form. However, if this were set to two, there would be two separate attachment boxes available for attachments.

It is important to note that this does not require or limit the number of attachments a student can make. If the setting was two, a student could upload no attachments or one attachment, or if they had already attached two files and decided to edit their submission, they could add an additional of two files, and so on. If additional files are added, the previous files do not get overwritten.

Allow Resubmissions

This is a simple **Yes** or **No** drop-down menu. The default setting is **No**, which means students are only able to submit one assignment.

If the **Yes** option is enabled, students are able to submit multiple copies of the assignment. This can be useful if you are interested in having students look at the feedback or grades they received and rework their assignment to incorporate that information into a better piece of work. Also, if this setting is used, the highest graded submission will be used to calculate the student's grade.

Number of Assessments of Examples from Teacher:	0 ⌄ ⑦
Comparison of Assessments:	Fair ⌄ ⑦
Number of Assessments of Student Submissions:	0 ⌄ ⑦
Weight for Teacher Assessments:	1 ⌄ ⑦

Number of Assessments of Examples from Teacher

This setting, ranging from 0 to 20, allows the instructor to create sample assignments for students to practice assessing. If this is set to **0**, students are not required to assess anything before submitting their work. If it is set to any other number, then the students are required to work through that number of sample assignments before they are able to submit their work. This can be very useful to students with little experience in assessment or before using a new assessment technique.

Comparison of Assessments

This feature is used to determine how closely the student's assessment of the assignment matches the instructor's. The scores are calculated based on the differences between the score the instructor gave and the score the student gave.

There are five options available here: **Very Lax**, **Lax**, **Fair**, **Strict**, **Very Strict**. A **Very Lax** setting causes low percentage changes in score when the student and instructor scores are different, while **Fair** causes moderate changes, and **Very Strict** the greatest changes.

Number of Assessments of Student Submissions

This setting determines the number of assessments the student will make on their classmates. The numbers in the drop-down go from 0 to 20. A **0** will not give any work to the students for assessment. Any other number will give the students involved in the Workshop that number of assignments to review.

If you are giving teacher example assessments or self-assessment, you need to add those numbers to the total number of assessments you want the student to make on their classmates.

Weightage for Teacher Assessments

This function sets the value of the instructor's assessment versus the value of the student or students' assessments. The default setting here is **1**, which means that student and instructor assessments are of equal value. A zero setting will make the instructor's grade worth nothing as part of the grade. Any value over one will cause the instructor's score to be weighted more heavily than a student's.

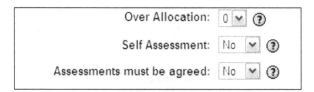

Over Allocation

This feature sets the number of times an assignment will be allocated, made available, for assessment. The drop-down offers three options: 0, 1, 2. The default setting is **0**, which means that each assignment will be allocated an equal number of times. This is the ideal situation, however, this is not always possible.

Unless all work is uploaded by the submission deadline, some students will need to wait until they can finish their peer reviews because the correct allocation can't happen until all work has been submitted. Changing the **Over Allocation** setting to one will cause some of the assignments to be allocated an additional time, which will, most likely, help those students unable to complete their work due to someone else's incomplete assignment. Changing the setting to two will do the same thing as one, except it will allow some works to be assessed an additional two times, which in most cases, will alleviate any issues with students being forced to wait to complete their assignments.

Self Assessment

This is a simple **Yes** or **No** drop-down menu, which handles self-assessment in Workshop. The default setting is **No**, which means that however many assignments the students are allocated to peer review, they will not see their own work.

If this is set to **Yes**, students will assess their own work in addition to the number of assignments set for peer review. So, if **Number of Assessments of Student Assignments** was set to 10, and **Self Assessment** was turned to **Yes**, students would evaluate a total of 11 assignments.

To create a self-assessed assignment, you need to set the **Number of Assessments of Student Submissions** to **0** and the **Self Assessment** should be set to **Yes**. This will give the student only their own work to review and grade.

Assessments must be agreed

This feature is a very useful part of Workshop, one that provides a method for assessment negotiation. The option itself is a simple **Yes** or **No** drop-down, which is by default set to **No**. The **No** option allows the student to see the assessments made by those who reviewed their work.

The **Yes** option is very different. Selecting **Yes** gives the student who submitted the work a chance to agree or disagree with their reviewer, and it offers a method for students to negotiate the assessment. If a student agrees with the reviewer, the assessment is considered valid and will be used in the grade calculation. However, if a student disagrees with a reviewer, and they send them a feedback, this may cause a reconsideration of the assessment. This can continue until a solution to the dilemma is found or the Workshop is closed. If no solution has been reached by the closing of the Workshop, the assessment will not be used to calculate the student's grade.

Hide Grades before Agreement:	No
League Table of Submitted Work:	0
Hide Names from Students:	No

Hide Grades before Agreement

If the **Assessments must be Agreed** has been set to **Yes**, this feature can be used. The default setting is **No**, and this will allow the students to see their current Workshop grade even before an agreement is met between the student and their reviewer.

If this is set to **Yes**, the grades will not be shown until an agreement has been met. Once the agreement is met, the grade will be made visible to the student.

League Table of Submitted Work

This setting is basically the High Score board. The drop-down menu ranges from 0 to 20, with two additional numbers 50 and 100. Setting this to zero will not show any scores. If the number is set to any number above zero, the League Table will be shown with the number of top scores selected. For example, if five was selected, the top scoring five submissions would be shown.

It is important to note that the students may be able to identify their classmate's work by the title of the assignment. This could cause issues in the class or between classmates, and should this be a concern, setting this to zero will eliminate this possibility.

Hide Names from Students

This is another **Yes** or **No** setting, which has the capability of adding a level of anonymity to the assessment process by hiding the names and profile images of the students.

If **No** is selected, the person reviewing the assignment will see the name and profile image of the person they are assessing, and the person being assessed will see who reviewed their work. This can cause scoring bias.

If **Yes** is selected, the peer reviewer does not see the name of the student they are reviewing, they only see the file they are working with; however, the file name itself can also lead to bias in scoring if the reviewer recognizes the peer through the assignment name. In addition, the student doing the grading will have the same anonymity.

Regardless of whether or not this setting is enabled, the instructor's grade will always be visible to student being assessed.

Use Password

This feature allows the instructor to set up a password to enter the Workshop. The default, **No**, will not require a password to enter the Workshop. Changing the setting to **Yes** will require students to enter a password before they can begin the Workshop.

Password

If the **Use Password** option is selected, this is where the password is entered. The password can be letters, numbers, or a combination of the two. The length of the password can be up to a maximum of ten characters and they are case-sensitive.

Maximum Size

This setting determines the maximum file size that students will able to upload to the Workshop. Depending on the setup of your course and site the maximum size can vary. As an instructor in the course, you may have the ability to increase the maximum upload size in your course settings. Go to **Edit Course Settings** and find the **Maximum Upload Size** menu. If you are able to increase the upload limit, you will have the option here. If you are already at the maximum size, speak with the site administrator and ask them to increase the site upload limit.

Start of submissions

This setting determines when students may begin to submit their work in the Workshop.

Start of assessments

This setting determines when students may begin to assess their classmates' work.

End of submissions

This setting determines when submissions to the Workshop will no longer be accepted.

End of assessments

This setting determines when Workshop assessments will stop.

Release Teacher Grades

This setting determines when the students will be able to see their instructor's assessment of the assignment. The default is set to have the grade seen immediately, but there may be instances when the instructor would not grade until later, for example, after the close of the Workshop. Changing this setting will allow for other examples of this nature.

Group mode

This functions the same way as in other modules. The drop-down has the same three options: **No groups**, **Separate Groups**, and **Visible Groups**. **No Groups** means that there are no groups and the whole class is able to work together. **Separate Groups** places the students into smaller groups, and only allows them to peer-assess with others in their group. **Visible Groups** shows all the groups and students in the group, and it allows the students to interact among the groups.

Visible

This function is a drop-down with two options: **Show** and **Hide**. **Show** is used to allow the students to see the **Workshop** link. **Hide** will make the link invisible to the students.

Whew! Now that we have looked through the options available when creating a Workshop, let's get to work making one!

Making a Workshop

The first thing we need to do is name the Workshop and give it a description. We will call ours Paragraph Writing Workshop. In the description, we will write a brief summary of what is expected. We are going to test our students on their ability to write a paragraph on a topic of their choosing, with the requirements being that they have a main idea, supporting sentences, and a conclusion.

Now, we need to choose our settings. For our first Workshop, we're going to leave most of the settings at the default. The first settings we are going to change are the **Grade for Submission** and **Grade for Assessments**. We want our Workshop to be worth 100 points, with each aspect, the teacher and peer assessment, of the Workshop making up half the grade, 50 percent and 50 percent respectively. The other setting we're going to change is **Number of Comments**, **Assessment Elements**, **Grade Bands**, which we will move from one to three. We are moving it to three because our paragraph has three elements we are going to evaluate: main idea, support, and conclusion. Once we've made that change in the Workshop, we will save it.

The first thing we see after saving the Workshop is **Editing Assessment Elements**, since we decided to stay with the default Accumulative grading technique. We have three Elements to complete here, and for Element 1 we are going to enter 'Has a main idea.' For Element 2 we are going to enter 'Has supporting sentences.' For Element 3 we are going to enter 'Has a conclusion.' For each **Type of Scale** menu, we are going to leave it set to the two point **Yes** or **No** scale, since we are simply going to be checking whether or not the paragraph has met the requirements set. We are also going to leave the **Element Weight** set at **1**, since we want each Element to be equal. Once we have entered everything and confirmed the spelling, we click on **Save changes**.

Once the page has been saved, we are taken to the Paragraph Writing Workshop page.

Workshop page—Teacher's view

This page has all the information you need regarding the Workshop. It has three sections, which give us all the details about the Workshop. The top section is shown in the next screenshot:

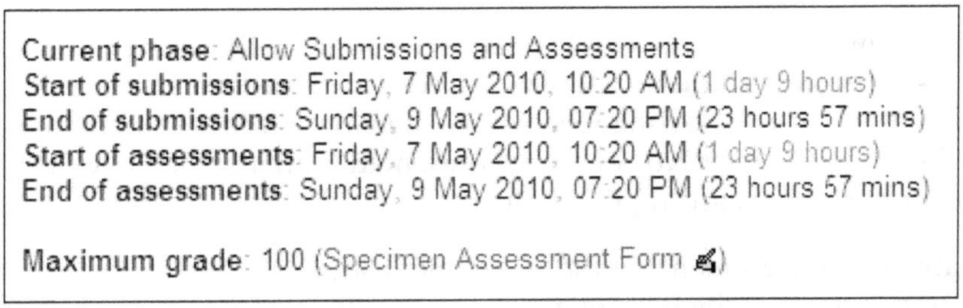

```
Current phase: Allow Submissions and Assessments
Start of submissions: Friday, 7 May 2010, 10:20 AM (1 day 9 hours)
End of submissions: Sunday, 9 May 2010, 07:20 PM (23 hours 57 mins)
Start of assessments: Friday, 7 May 2010, 10:20 AM (1 day 9 hours)
End of assessments: Sunday, 9 May 2010, 07:20 PM (23 hours 57 mins)

Maximum grade: 100 (Specimen Assessment Form ✎)
```

Here, we have the information about the phase the Workshop is in. The phases are **Set up Assignment**, **Allow Submissions**, **Allow Submissions and Assessments**, **Allow Assessments**, **Calculation of Final Grades**, and **Show Final Grades**. The phases let us know where we are in the Workshop. As you can see, we are in the **Allow Submissions and Assessments** phase. We also see the start and end of submissions and assessments.

The final information contained in this section is the **Maximum grade**. Here, we see that our maximum grade is **100**. This is because we changed the settings from default and the **Grade for Assessments** and **Grade for Submission** were both set to **50**. Next to the **Maximum grade**, we see the **Specimen Assessment Form** link. Clicking on this link will bring us to a sample of the Assessment Sheet we created. This is shown in the next screenshot:

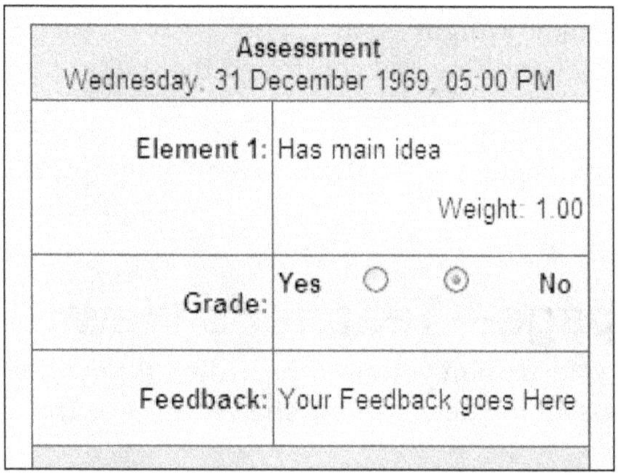

I have only shown the first Element here, and the others follow the same pattern. At the top we see the date and time. Under that, we see the criterion we are assessing in the submitted work. Following this, we see the **Grade**. We have chosen to use a simple 2 Point Scale, **Yes** or **No**, so we are presented with just that. Under this we see an area for comments regarding **Element 1**.

Underneath all of the Elements of the Assessment sheet, there is a box for general feedback or comments, which is not graded.

At the very bottom of the page, you will see a **continue** button. Clicking on this will bring you back to the Workshop page.

The final thing to mention here is that next to the **Specimen Assessment Form** link, there is an **Edit** icon. This can come in handy if you missed something or want to change something in one of the Elements.

The second section of the Workshop page is shown here:

Show Workshop Description				
First name / Surname ↓	Submission Title	Date	Teacher Assessment	Total Grade
	() Assessment by Student; [] Assessment by Teacher; <> Assessment Dropped; () Automatic grade for assessment; [] Teacher grade for assessment. Grades for Submissions are out of 100. Grades for Assessments are out of 100			

In the previous screenshot, we see the **Show Workshop Description** link. Clicking on this link will show the description entered when the Workshop was created. Once review of the Workshop description is done, click on the **continue** button to return to the Workshop page.

Under this, we see information about submitted assignments. There are five columns, **First Name / Surname**, **Submission Title**, **Date**, **Teacher Assessment**, and **Total Grade**. Under this, in the small letters, we see information about how to interpret the grades as well as the total possible points. Each of these columns will display the appropriate information, and we will look at this again once we submit an assignment.

The final section we see on the Workshop page is called Grading Grade Analysis and is shown in the next screenshot:

Grading Grade Analysis				
Count	Mean	Standard Deviation	Maximum	Minimum
0	0.0	0.0	0.0	0.0

We can see the **Count**, **Mean**, **Standard Deviation**, **Maximum**, and **Minimum** in the previous screenshot. Again, we have not submitted any work or assessed anything yet, so there is nothing here. However, once scores are entered into the Workshop, these numbers will be automatically calculated and updated.

Now, all we need to do is have our students log into Moodle and they will see the Workshop and they will be able to enter and begin using it.

Workshop page—Student's view

When the students enter the Workshop, they will see a page that looks a bit different than the one we have just looked at. This is shown in the next screenshot:

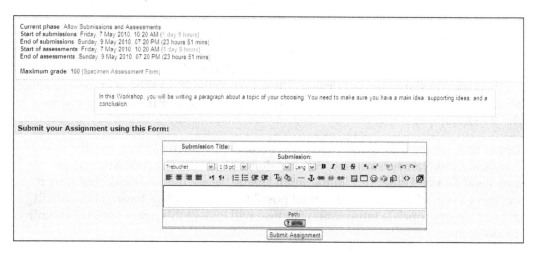

As you can see, at the top of the page, they see the same thing as the instructor. The student can see the **Current phase**, which has now moved to the third phase, **Allow Submissions and Assessments**. It moved to the third Phase because we set the opening for Submissions and Assessments at the same time. We would have seen the second Phase if we had set the Submission and Assessment times to be different.

Students will also see the Workshop submission's and assessment's open and close dates and the **Maximum grade** possible for the Workshop. They are also able to preview the **Assessment Form** that will be used. This preview is identical to the one the instructor sees.

Under this, the students will see the description of the Workshop with the instructions on how they should complete it.

Under the Workshop description, we see the Assignment Submission Form. Here is where the students enter their work. There are three things that are done with this form. First, the student will need to create a title in the **Submission Title** box.

Submission Titles

Since Workshop is mostly about peer assessments, you may want to control the way titles are handled. While we can hide the student's name from the peer assessor, the title will always be visible. You may want to have students to use an anonymous system, numbers or some other form of code, so that there is no bias in grading.

The second thing the students will do is enter their work in the **Submission** rich text editor. If there were any attachments included as part of the assignment, they would be seen directly below the textbox.

When the students have finished with their submission, they click on the **Submit Assignment** button and the work will be uploaded to a new area called **Your Submissions**. What a student sees after clicking on the **Submit Assignment** button is shown in the next screenshot:

Your Submissions			
Submission Title	**Action**	**Submitted**	**Assessments**
Funding Education	Edit	Delete	Saturday, 8 May 2010 07:31 PM	0

This newly created section has four pieces of information for the student to see. The first is the **Submission Title**. Clicking on the title link will bring the student to a new page where they can view their work.

The second section is the **Action** link. If the student is not satisfied with their work, they have the option to either edit or delete it. Clicking on the **Edit** link will bring the student to the submission screen where they can change whatever they would like, including uploading additional files, should this feature be enabled. The **Delete** link will permanently erase the file, but as a safeguard, Workshop will offer the student one chance to change their mind before completely erasing the file.

The third is the column that shows the date the assignment was submitted. If the assignment is edited, the time of the editing will be reflected in the **Submitted** column. This can cause a problem for instructors if the deadline for submissions is not set properly. For example, say a student submits the work on time and as they are reviewing the work later in the week, they notice a misspelling, which they edit. The submitted time will be changed to reflect the last edit completed.

The final column is **Assessments**. This is where the student can see how many times they have been assessed. We have no assessments yet, but we do now have a newly submitted piece of work, so we will switch back to our Teacher profile and look at the changes that have taken place.

Teacher assessments of submitted work

The view that we saw before has changed. The view we have now with a student's work included is shown in the next screenshot:

Show Workshop Description				
First name / Surname ↓	Submission Title	Date	Teacher Assessment	Total Grade
Student One	Funding Education ✎ ✗	8/05/10 18:02	Assess	0.0

Now that we have a submission, all the assignment information is available. We see the student name, the title of the assignment, and the date it was submitted. Under the heading **Teacher Assessment**, we now see a link called **Assess**. This link will bring us to the **Assessment Form** we saw earlier. We are going to click on this link now and assess the students work.

Once we click on the **Assess** link, we are brought to a split-screen page, with scrolling options in both areas. The top half of the page has the **Assessment Form** and the bottom part has the student's name and work. It is shown in the next screenshot:

As you can see, at the top we are shown the title of the assignment we are assessing. Under this, we see the Assessment Form with our name, **Teacher One**, and the date we began the assessment. Under this we see the requirements for the assessment, the grade we will give, and any feedback we want to give. There is also a button called **Add Comment**.

The **Add Comment** button allows you to make as many comments as you like during your assessment and save them, so you don't need to retype them each time you want to use them. Once you add a comment, you will see it displayed next to the **Add Comment** button with a delete mark next to it. The word or phrase itself is a link, and if clicked will add the phrase to the Feedback textbox it is associated with. If you want to get rid of the comment, press the **Delete** link and it will be erased. So, once you finish with your current assessment and begin the next one, you will see the comment you added there earlier, and you will be able to use it again if you want.

If you decide to use the **Add Comment** function, and you also want to add feedback in the **Feedback** textbox, you can. One thing to note is that the comments added via the 'comment bank' will be added to the bottom of whatever was entered in the **Feedback** textbox. Here is the completed **Element 1** with an **Add Comment**.

Assessment by Teacher One Saturday, 8 May 2010, 07:35 PM	
The Grade is : 33.33 (Maximum grade 50)	
Element 1:	Has main idea
	Weight: 1.00
Grade:	Yes ◉ ○ No
Feedback:	Good job!
Add Comment ⑦	<<Good job!>> <--Delete

As you can see under the date, we have already graded this assignment. You can see that the student received a **33.33** score. To give our scores, we simply go through each of the Elements and at the bottom of the page, you can see a button called **Save My Assessment**. Click on this button and you will see the final score you gave and you will be brought back to the Workshop main page.

On this main page you will see that all the information is the same except under the Teacher Assessment column, where you will see the grade you gave. The total grade will still be 0, since only half of the scoring has been completed. Now, we will need to have a student assess their classmate's work.

Student Assessments

Now that we have seen how the teacher view looks, let's see how a submitted assignment looks to the reviewer.

The first thing that needs to be done is that the students must go through the Specimen Assessment Form and look over the options available and their assessment task. When finished, they click on the **continue** button and return to the Workshop page.

Once they have work to assess, the screen will change and they will see something like the next screenshot:

Please assess these Student Submissions			
Submission Title		**Action**	**Comment**
Green Energy		Assess	
Your assessments of work by your peers			
No Assessments Done			
Your Submissions			
Submission Title	**Action**	**Submitted**	**Assessments**
Funding Education	Edit | Delete	Saturday, 8 May 2010, 07:31 PM	0

At the top, Student One is being given a list of the work they are supposed to assess. Under this, the student will be able to see their assessments of their classmates. Finally, they see their own submission information.

Student One is now going to click on the **Assess** link to begin their assessment of the Green Energy submission. They will go through the same process as the instructor, giving a score and any feedback related to the Elements being assessed. When they complete their work, they will click on the **Save My Assessment** button and they will return to the previous page.

In order to show a complete view, we have created a third student who has submitted a new piece of work. Look at the following screenshot. This shows a student with one piece of work to assess, the student's assessment for a peer, a peer's assessment of the student, and finally, the student's submission, the time and date it was submitted, and how many times it has been assessed. The full view is shown in the next screenshot:

Submission Title			**Action**	**Comment**
Environmental Protection			Assess	
Your assessments of work by your peers				
Submission Title		**Action**	**Comment**	
Green Energy		View	Assessed on Saturday, 8 May 2010, 08:00 PM	
Assessments by Students				
Submission Title	**Action**	**Comment**		
Funding Education	View	Assessed on Saturday, 8 May 2010, 08:04 PM, Grade for Submission: 50.0 / 50		
Your Submissions				
Submission Title		**Action**	**Submitted**	**Assessments**
Funding Education			Saturday, 8 May 2010, 07:31 PM	2

As you can see from the previous screenshot, there is a lot of information on this page, information your students will want access to.

Teacher Administration page

Once the students have begun to make assessments, you might want to see how they are progressing, and if necessary, step in to make adjustments. There is a link at the top left-hand side of the screen called **Administration**. Clicking on this link will open a new page that will show four sections, two of which are new. At the top you will see the current phase, deadlines, and so on. The second section, and the first of the new sections, is **Student Assessments**.

Student Assessments shows a box with three columns: **Name**, **Submission Title**, and **Action**. The **Name** column, as you might expect, lists the names of the students in the Workshop. The second column lists the titles of all the assignments they have assessed for this Workshop. Note the **{50 (50)}**; here the first number indicates that the student has achieved a score of 50 and the second shows the total possible points, 50. The third column, **Action**, has a link to a page with the student's Assessment Forms containing the grades, comments, and feedback they gave. This is shown in the next screenshot:

Name	Submission Title	Action
Student One	Green Energy {50 (50)} Environmental Protection {50 ((50))}	List Student's Assessments (2)
Student Two	Funding Education {50 (50)}	List Student's Assessments (1)

{} Assessment by Student; [] Assessment by Teacher; <> Assessment Dropped;
() Automatic grade for assessment; (( )) Teacher grade for assessment
Grades for Submissions are out of 50; Grades for Assessments are out of 50

The third section is the **Grading Grade Analysis** section, which appears as shown in the previous screenshot, except it now has a new link titled **Re-grading Student Assessments**. This link is not used often, as the calculations are automatic. However, if you were to change any settings or change the weighting of any items, clicking on this button will recalculate all the grades.

The fourth and final section is the second new one. It is called **Student Submissions**. Here, we have a four-columned box containing: **Submitted by**, **Submission Title**, **Submitted**, and **Action**. **Submitted by** and **Submission Title** are the author's name and the title of the submitted work respectively, with the **Submitted** column showing the date it was added to the Workshop. The **Action** column has a few special options. The whole section is shown in the next screenshot:

Submitted by	Submission Title	Submitted	Action
Student One	Funding Education (Grade: 50.0 [33] ✎ ✗ {50 (50)})	Saturday, 8 May 2010, 07:31 PM	Amend Title | Re-assess | List Assessments (2) | Delete
Student Three	Environmental Protection (Grade: 0.0 [33] ✎ ✗)	Saturday, 8 May 2010, 08:10 PM	Amend Title | Re-assess | List Assessments (2) | Delete
Student Two	Green Energy (Grade: 50.0 [50] ✎ ✗ {50 (50)})	Saturday, 8 May 2010, 07:14 PM	Amend Title | Re-assess | List Assessments (2) | Delete

As you can see, **Action** has four links: **Amend Title**, **Re-assess**, **List Assessments (2)**, and **Delete**. **Delete** will erase the student's work completely. The **List Assessments** link will show all assessments that have been done on the student's work, including the teacher's grading. **Re-assess** will allow the instructor to change their marks for the Workshop and **Amend Title** will allow the instructor to change the student's **Submission Title** to whatever they choose.

Summary

In Workshop, there are so many options that it is not practical or possible for me to cover them all here. In this chapter, we have seen the basic functionality in Workshop and worked through setting up a single, basic Workshop. We have looked at the different forms for assessment and seen both the student and teacher views. We have looked at the way grades are seen and how the Assessment Form works.

We have looked at the important features of grading and assessing, but one thing that we did not do is create a sample assignment for students to practice on. This is something that you may want to consider for each and every Workshop you create. Making a sample for the students to work through will not only be a useful exercise for them, but it will also give them practice using the Assessment Form, so when they begin assessing their peers, they have already been exposed to its style and functionality.

Time is another factor that we didn't cover, but it is something that needs to be carefully considered. Your students will need to learn about the assignment, create their submission, and then do their assessing. It is vital that students are given an appropriate amount of time; if they aren't, the quality of the assessment will be reduced.

Another important thing to remember is the group of students you are working with, their experience in self and peer assessments, and how comfortable you are with your students assessing others for a grade. Remember to start them off slowly, with simple tasks, such as the 2 point **Yes** or **No** scale before working up to more complex assessments.

Remember that self-assessments and peer assessments can cause problems. Some students may not take it seriously. You will have some students who may give very high scores to poor submissions and poor scores to great ones. As the instructor, you can always override the students' scores; however, the best tactic is to teach your students the value of honest assessments and how they help. Workshop may not work for all of your classes, but hopefully, it will work for most.

There is even more you can do and we could talk about, but we simply don't have the space here to get into any more detailed creations or settings. However, what we have done here is given you the tools you need to get started with Workshop and help you understand what many of the options are, and using Workshop is really the best way to learn what works best for you and your students.

In our next chapter, we will begin looking at skill-based activities for testing. We will be starting with listening tests and look at several ideas for listening test development.

7
Listening Tests

So far, we have looked at options for creating tests in Moodle. What we have not looked at yet are skill-specific tests, but we will now. The first skill we will be looking at will be listening. Testing listening is an integral part of many tests, especially in language courses. Listening tests are typically used to check comprehension of lectures, discussions, dialogs, speeches, and so on; to test for the ability to listen for details such as dates, time, names, or sounds, and so on; to test things like prediction; and so on. When we make listening tests in Moodle, these are the kinds of things we will be trying to do.

In this chapter, we will work through several aspects of setting up listening files and listening tasks and show you how to integrate them into the tests you are creating. We will look at:

- Downloading and setting up a recorder
- Uploading audio files
- Making the MP3 links
- Adding listening tasks to quiz
- Using forums with audio
- Multiple vs. single-play files

Using audio files

To create listening tests, we need audio. There are millions of places to get audio files. You can make them yourself, download them, link to them, or buy them. The first things we will look at in this chapter are how and where to get the audio you want to use in your site.

Creating audio files

Creating your own audio files can be fun and rewarding. By creating your own files, you can make the content exactly what you want and you can build up a library of audio files, which can be used in later tests or for review. In addition, students listening to their instructor's voice can make the listening tasks easier since students should be used to the sound of your voice, which can help them focus on the listening task itself. However, you don't have to limit your audio recordings to yourself. You can use your students, your co-workers, friends, family, or anyone else.

Creating audio files in Moodle is easy. There is a variety of software packages out there that can be used to record audio. The one we will look at is Audacity, the recorder I use. It is free, it's open source, but best of all, it is very easy to use. First, you need to go to the Audacity website and download it. Go to `http://audacity.sourceforge.net/` and download the latest version of Audacity. Once it is downloaded and installed, open it and you will see the next screenshot:

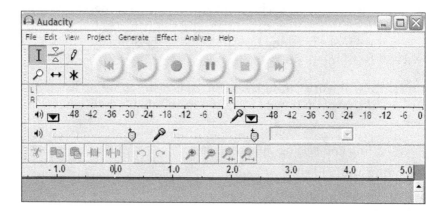

What we will be looking at now are six round buttons in roughly the center of the screenshot. The button with the circle in it is the **Record** button. When you have your microphone set up and you are ready to record, click on the button and begin speaking. When you have finished recording, click on the **Stop** button. To listen to your recording, click on the **Play** button and you will hear what you just recorded. If you don't like it, go to **File | New** to open a new recorder and try again.

When you have a file you like, then we need to save it. Go to **File | Save Project As**, then give the project a name and it will be saved. It is important to save your audio this way because it will allow you to go back and make changes to the recording later, should you need to.

Now that we have saved the audio file, we want to import it into our course. Unfortunately, as good as Audacity is, it can't do this alone. We need to download an MP3 encoder. Audacity uses the LAME MP3 Encoder, which can be downloaded for free via a link in Audacity's site or directly from `http://lame.buanzo.com.ar/`. Find the version you need based on your system and follow the instructions to install the LAME MP3 Encoder.

Once the LAME MP3 Encoder is installed, you will go to **File | Export as MP3**. This will open a Tag Box, which allows you to name and categorize the file. When you finish entering the information related to the file, click on the **OK** button and the file will be saved as an MP3 file. Once we have the MP3 file, we can then import it into Moodle. The first time you do import into Moodle, you will need to make the LAME MP3 Encoder work with Audacity. This is very easy to do and the instructions on how to do it are located at `http://audacity.sourceforge.net/help/faq?s=install&item=lame-mp3`.

The Tag Box

The Tag Box is a good way to organize your sound files. By creating specific Album Titles and adding descriptive Comments, such as Aboriginal Art Listening Task, you can easily pick out the files you want to use.

There are many other things you can do with Audacity. A few things you can do are alter the sound quality, add background music, and quickly edit tracks. As you can see, there is a lot to learn about this software package, but it is easy and fun to use. The more you play with it, the easier it will get to use. I'll leave you to explore all the options Audacity offers on your own.

Importing audio files

Moodle has a built-in MP3 player, which is very simple, and easy to use. That is what we are going to work with. First, make sure the multimedia plugin filters are turned on. This is done in the **Admin | Modules | Filters** page. In the **Settings** page, make sure to enable the MP3 filter.

Now that we have a recording saved as an MP3 file, we want to import it. First, go to the course you want to import to. In the course, we will need an activity or resource to place the recording in. You can use several of Moodle's modules to do this in. A basic one we can use is **Compose a Webpage** in the **Add a Resource** drop-down menu.

First, you need to click on the **Turn editing on** button. Once this is done, go to the **Add a Resource** drop-down menu and click on **Compose a web page**. In the **Name** textbox, enter the name for the page. In the **General** section, enter some kind of description. Once this is done, move down to the **Compose a web page** section.

This is where we are going to put the MP3 player. In this section, we can enter any text we want. What we have so far is shown in the next screenshot:

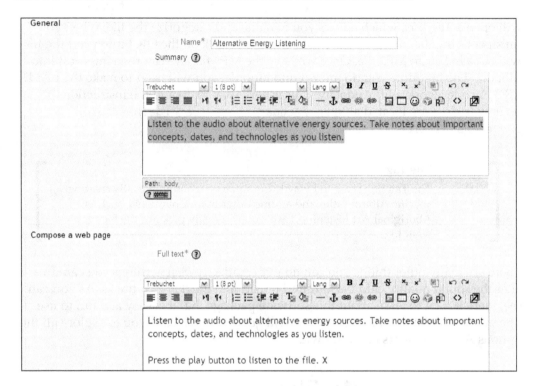

As you can see, we have given a clear title to the listening. This is important when students are on the site and searching for the assignment. In the **General** section we have given a clear description of the activity. In the **Compose a web page** section, we have copied the **General** section text and underneath that, we have placed an extra line with an 'X' at the end. This is where we are going to put our MP3 player.

The first thing we need to do is create a link. You probably remember how to do this, but if you don't, no problem. First, we need to highlight the text we want to use for the link. Notice the 'X' we entered after the final sentence? We will select this text and then go to **Create a web link** icon, the chain icon located to the left of the anchor in the formatting area.

Once we click on the **Create a web link** button, a menu will appear asking for a **URL**, **Title**, **Target**, and **Anchors**. The menu with the link and title included is shown in the next screenshot:

If you know the **URL**, type it in. If you don't, click on the **Browse** button and you will see a new menu, also titled **Insert Link**. At the bottom of the screenshot below, you can see another **Browse** button. If you click on this **Browse** button, you will see your computer's files. Locate and select the appropriate file, then click on **Open**. This will cause the file's location to be placed in the textbox next to the **Browse** button.

Once the file location is there, click on the **Upload** button and the file will be added to the course. Here is what it looks like after a file has been uploaded.

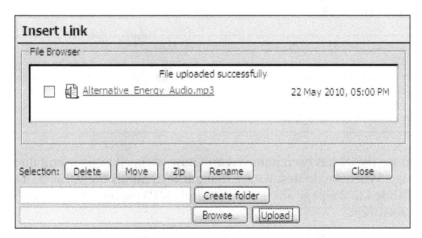

Now that the file is in place, we can add it to our web page. Simply click on the link in the **File Browser** area and the menu with the file will disappear and you will again see the original **Insert Link** menu with the **URL** added. We will need to add a title, and we can see that **Alternative Energy** is what we entered for ours.

You can also see the **Target** and **Anchors** drop-down menus. We will not worry about these now, so just leave them as they are. Click on the **OK** button and the link will be added to the 'X' at the end of the final line of the **Compose a web page** textbox.

Now, we need to do a little modification in the HTML to make this look correct. Click on the **Toggle HTML Source** button located in the formatting menu; it looks like this: **< >**. Clicking on this button will show the code. We need to remove the 'X' we linked to in the code. This will get rid of the 'X' in the textbox and leave only the MP3 player.

First we need to find the 'X' in the HTML. It is located between the **<a>** and **</a>** commands. Simply delete the 'X' leaving everything else as it is. Here are two screenshots showing the before and after shots.

```
You are in TEXT MODE. Use the [<>] button to go back to WYSIWYG MODE.

 Listen to the audio about alternative energy sources. Take notes about
important concepts, dates, and technologies as you listen.<br /><br
/>Press the play button to listen to the file. <a title="Alternative
Energy" target="_blank" href="http://www.language-testing.org/moodle
/file.php/6/Alternative_Energy_Audio.mp3"> X </a>
```

The **X** is located at the end of the of the text, just before the **</a>**. What we are going to do is remove it. Just select it and click on **Delete**. After we have finished, we see the following screenshot:

```
You are in TEXT MODE. Use the [<>] button to go back to WYSIWYG MODE.

 Listen to the audio about alternative energy sources. Take notes about
important concepts, dates, and technologies as you listen.<br /><br
/>Press the play button to listen to the file. <a title="Alternative
Energy" target="_blank" href="http://www.language-testing.org/moodle
/file.php/6/Alternative_Energy_Audio.mp3"></a>
```

As you can see the 'X' has been removed and now we need to **Save and display** the new page. When we do this, we see that our text, minus the 'X', and audio file have been added to the page along with a simple MP3 player. The result is shown in the next screenshot:

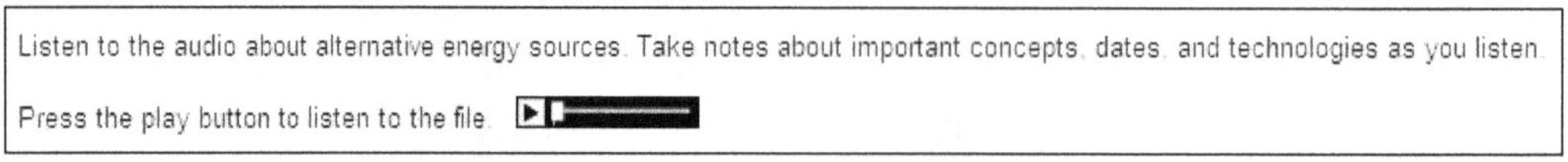

```
Listen to the audio about alternative energy sources. Take notes about important concepts, dates, and technologies as you listen.

Press the play button to listen to the file.  ▶▮▬▬▬▬▬▬
```

Clicking on the play button will let anyone viewing the page listen to the recording. This recording can be listened to as many times as the listener desires.

So, this is how to create an MP3 player in Moodle. There are other players you can use, but this is the one we will use for now. So, now that we are able to make our own recordings, import them, and create a player, let's start testing our students' listening skills.

Listening questions in Quiz

Now, we will revisit our first few chapters and head back to Quiz. There are often times when we want to incorporate listening questions into Quiz and other tests. Whether we want to have students listen for details, gist, main ideas, or anything else, Quiz is a good place for adding listening them to tests because there are so many ways you can include them.

The first thing that we need to do is create test to use. The topic we are going to cover is Shakespeare's Plays. We'll create a title, a short description, and follow all the other steps needed to make a Quiz in Moodle.

Once the Quiz is created, we're ready to start with the question creation.

True/False with audio

The first thing we need to do is decide on our question type. The first question we will make is going to be a simple True/False item.

We will now go through the steps to create the True/False question. First we will add a name and text for the question.

Multiple Question Formats

If you decide to include multiple skill-based (for example, Listening, Reading) questions in your tests, it is a good idea to title the questions with something like 'Skill – Question Title – Question Type'. By following this type of naming procedure, you will place all the skills together in the Question Bank. You will also be able to quickly determine which skills you are working with and where to place them in the test.

Now that we have the text in the question, we will add an additional character marking where the player will be located. Anything is fine, but I always use an X. You also have the option of simply using a word, like player, but whatever you do, you need a place to make a link.

Now we repeat the process that was explained earlier. Select the **X** and click on the **Insert a web link** button. Browse to locate the file, and then upload it. Click on the link and enter a title in the **Title** textbox, then click on **OK**.

Once you have followed these steps, you click on the Toggle HTML Source button and remove the 'X' from between the <a> and </a>. Then click again on the Toggle HTML Source button to turn off the HTML view.

Once this is done, I will select the correct answer, in this case False, and add feedback for each answer.

Finally, we go to the bottom of the screenshot and click on the **Save** button. This will create the item. We will see the item is now placed in the Question Bank and when we click on the **Preview** button, this is what we see:

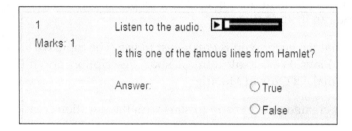

Now, when a student sees this item, they will be able to click on the item as many times as they want to listen to the audio. Once they have finished listening they choose their answer and click on the **Submit all and finish** button and their response will be saved.

That's all there is to creating a listening item in True/False.

Multiple Choice with audio

This is set up in a very similar fashion. The only difference between a True/False item and a Multiple Choice is the number of options available for the answer.

Here is an example of a Multiple Choice item with a listening component.

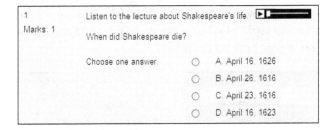

As you can see, it is very similar and just as easy to produce.

Images and audio

Let's say that you do not want to write the question for students to see. Maybe you want the students to look at a picture and respond to some questions about it or identify something in the image based on the audio.

Notice the text next to the player in the following image. These types of instructions can easily be recorded and added to the audio file, requiring the student to do even more listening.

The Moodle MP3 player has settings that will allow you to force the audio to be played immediately upon loading the page, once the full audio has downloaded, or after a set amount of time. To adjust the player to perform these functions, you can check the Moodle docs at `http://docs.moodle.org/en/index.php?title=MP3_player&oldid=60361`. These docs give you the information you need to find the player settings and tell you what you need to do to make this work. The section you need to look for is **MP3 Playback Options**.

To add an image and audio to a question, we simply need to insert the audio and image as we have done before. Using the **Insert Image** button will allow us to place an image in the question and using the **Insert a Web Link button** will enable us to add the audio.

Let's say that we want to test our Spanish class on prepositions of location. We take an image of a room and record ourselves making a statement about the location of something. For example, we might say, in Spanish, 'It is on the table, next to the television.' Here is an example of what a Multiple Choice Quiz question containing an audio file with an image and text can look like:

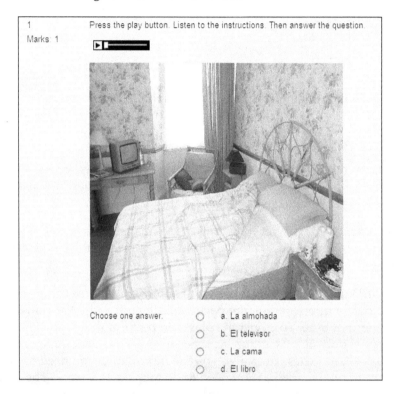

Other question forms with audio

It is possible to add audio to all the other question forms as well. You would follow the same procedure as shown in the previous screenshot to add the audio to the description.

Some things you can do are create audio prompts for essays or create short answer or calculated items where students are required to enter the appropriate response. There are many possibilities for listening questions in Quiz, and you will, I'm sure, have more ideas than I can think of. The sky's the limit, so enjoy playing with the options you have available and be creative.

Multiple audio in questions

As seen in the previous screenshot, we added audio to the question. What I'd like to show you now is how to add more than one. This is not going to be used by everyone, but there will be occasions when it will be useful to know how to do it.

Let's use another multiple choice item for our example. In our class, let's say we have been studying the plays of Shakespeare and we have reviewed several of the major scenes in several major plays. We want to determine whether or not students are able to identify the play with the 'Tomorrow, and Tomorrow, and Tomorrow' soliloquy.

We go through and set up our question as normal. The question text will read, **Which of the following soliloquies was in Macbeth?** Once we have finished with this, we need to create the audio files.

We have a few options here. The first, and simplest, is for us to record the soliloquies ourselves using Audacity. If this does not work for you, or you are shy about your own voice being used, we can use Audacity to record directly from streaming audio files. Basically, it will record whatever is coming out of your speakers. So, you can go online, find one of the many sources of free audio files, stream the audio, record it, and then edit it down to the parts you want. The instructions for doing this are on the Audacity site and vary based on your system and set up. Once the audio is ready for use, we go to the question text and begin to enter our audio responses.

We are going to include four audio files in this question. First, we set up the link to each audio file and then turn on the **HTML Source** button. Once we have done this, we see something like the following screenshot:

```
You are in TEXT MODE. Use the [<>] button to go back to WYSIWYG MODE.
Which of the following soliloquies was in Macbeth?<br /><br />1. <a
href="http://www.language-testing.org/moodle/file.php/6/hamlet1.mp3"
title="To be or not to be">X</a><br /><br />2. <a
href="http://www.language-testing.org/moodle/file.php/6/romeo1.mp3"
title="Oh romeo romeo wherefore">X</a><br /><br />3. <a
href="http://www.language-testing.org/moodle/file.php/6/macbeth1.mp3"
title="Tomorrow and tomorrow">X</a><br /><br />4. <a
href="http://www.language-testing.org/moodle/file.php/6/othello1.mp3"
title="Thus do I make my fool my purse">X</a><br />
```

We can see here that we have titled each of the audio files with a quote from the play instead of the name of the play so when the students scroll over the player, they will not see Macbeth, or the like. Now, we will go back and delete each of the X's from the lines.

Once that is done, we will go to the **Response** section and enter a number corresponding with the numbers in the Question Text. I would recommend turning off numbering and turning off the shuffle function for these types of questions. They will only serve to confuse students and there may be errors made from a mistake in choice selection instead of in lack of knowledge due to the shuffled responses.

Once everything is completed and we save the question, we see the next screenshot:

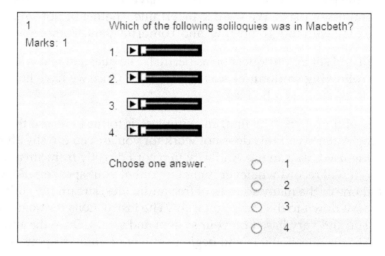

Unfortunately, it is not currently possible to add audio to the answers, so we can't make a question like that in Quiz. However, we will look at some other options in a few minutes.

Using video

Video can be an extremely useful tool for listening tests. Conversations between characters, monologues, and lectures can all be used for listening comprehension and listening for details testing. There are a few ways to add video to your listening tests. We can embed videos, link to them, or upload them to our course.

The biggest sites today, sites like YouTube, Dailymotion, and Hulu, offer a variety of videos and categories that can be used for classes and testing purposes. Since YouTube is the biggest and offers the largest variety of videos, in multiple languages, we will use it as our main source for video.

Linking video

The first option for adding video is using a link. First, we will look at simply copying and pasting a link into the question text. Then, we will look at adding a link to a video by using the same method we used for adding a link to the MP3 files we just saw.

The first thing we need to do is decide what the listening task will be. We have decided that we want our students to be able to identify a play by watching and listening to a famous soliloquy. We will use the 'Tomorrow, and tomorrow, and tomorrow' one once again.

Our next step is to find a video we want to use. We want to have a large selection available to choose from, so we will use YouTube. We do a simple search in YouTube and we quickly locate several videos that look useful. After watching several, we select the one we want to use and now we need to create our question.

We will be using a Short Answer question format in Quiz, so I open the Question bank in the Quiz I am working with and select **Short Answer** under **Add a New Question**. I enter in the text of the question, enter the answer, and feedback.

Next, we copy and paste the link from the YouTube address bar and paste it in the textbox. This will directly link the question to the video from the site and students will see what they are supposed to view in the question.

Following these instructions we see something like the next screenshot:

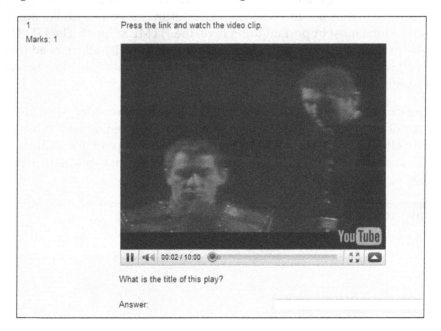

The same effect can be accomplished by using the **Insert a Web Link** button. We need to have some text to create the link. So we can either, as I usually do, insert an 'X' or some other text, then highlight it and click on the **Insert a Web Link** button, which will bring up the **Insert Web Link** menu. Since we have already copied the address for the video we want to view, we simply paste the address from the YouTube site into the **URL** textbox. This will give us the same question format as the previous image, but instead of a link to the video as the **Title**, we have the option to title it whatever we'd like. This can be useful especially if the site name gives students information about the video they should not have, for example, if the site we used for the video was titled Shakespeare-Macbeth.org or something similar.

Embedding video

Embedding video is a little more complex but still easy to do. It is like linking, but the user will access the video from inside Moodle. This time we will use a simple True/False item to show how this works.

Assuming that we already have a question we want to use, the first thing that we need to do is find a video we want to use. We will use the same Macbeth video as we used for the linking explanation.

Looking at the video's page on YouTube, we can see directly under the video a button called **<Embed>**. Clicking on this button will open a window below with several options including colors, borders, and size. We will not worry about these now, but feel free to play around with the video settings if you want. We are only going to look at the most important thing here, the HTML snippet. The HTML snippet, which should already be highlighted for you, is really all we need from here. We will simply copy the snippet and go back to the question. Now we can embed the video in the question.

In the question, we are going to ask the students to watch the video, then identify whether or not the scene is from Macbeth. We write our question text. When this is finished, we click on the **Toggle HTML Source** button and paste the address where we want it. The before and after screenshots that show the changes made when embedding the video are as follows:

```
You are in TEXT MODE. Use the [<>] button to go back to WYSIWYG MODE.
Watch the video.<br /><br />Is this scene from Macbeth?<br />
```

```
You are in TEXT MODE. Use the [<>] button to go back to WYSIWYG MODE.
Watch the video.<br /><object width="480" height="385"><param
name="movie" value="http://www.youtube.com/v/4e8avPkjRL4&hl=en_US&
fs=1&rel=0"></param><param name="allowFullScreen" value="true"></param>
<param name="allowscriptaccess" value="always"></param><embed
src="http://www.youtube.com/v/4e8avPkjRL4&hl=en_US&fs=1&rel=0"
type="application/x-shockwave-flash" allowscriptaccess="always"
allowfullscreen="true" width="480" height="385"></embed></object><br />Is
this scene from Macbeth?<br />
```

This will produce a question that looks identical to the linked videos described previously, except it will be embedded and not a link. When finished, click on the **Save** button at the bottom of the page.

Listening tasks

Now that we know how to add audio and video files, let's look at some ways to test listening. When testing listening, we design questions around specific listening skills. We can test for listening comprehension, listening for details, listening for gist, listening for specific sounds, and several other listening skills. We also have pre- and post-listening tasks we can ask our students to complete. Here we will show some possible listening test ideas.

Listening for sounds

One of the simplest ways to check listening skills and have students listen for sounds is using the Quiz Module and setting up audio files with the sound you want the student to be able to hear.

For example, say we are teaching English as a Second Language students and we want to determine whether or not they are able to differentiate between *ship* and *sheep*. We can simply record the single word or sound we want the students to be able to identify into an audio file and create a two answer question. The question text could be something like, **Listen to the audio. Which word do you hear?** We add the audio and in Answer 1 we enter **ship** and in Answer 2 we enter **sheep**. An example of what it would look like is shown in the next screenshot:

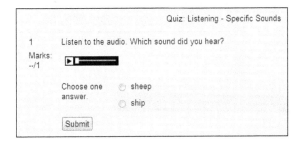

Grading this type of item is automatic, so all you need to do is assign a point value appropriate to the task and difficulty of the item.

Listening for vocabulary (Cloze Listening)

Another commonly used listening activity is what is known as Cloze Listening. Typical Cloze Listening activities have a set number of words then a blank space. In Moodle, we can do this in one of the following two ways. We can use Embedded Answers (Cloze), which will create a drop-down menu for each missing word and the students will have to choose what they hear. The second option, one which is much more difficult for students, is creating Short Answer items. We will look at both as well as one question containing both.

Embedded Answers (Cloze) Listening

The first option we will look at is a simple audio file with a Cloze activity. Depending on the source of the material, chances are you will either have text that needs to be recorded or you will have located an audio file and need the text. If you have the text, all you need to do is record it. If we have an audio file we want to use, but no text, this takes a bit more work. The first thing we need to do is get the audio transcribed into text.

To transcribe text, we have a few options. If the audio is from a famous source, a book, movie, song, and so on, chances are you will be able to find the text online. If the audio is something less well-known you will either need to spend the time listening and typing out the text yourself or using a speech-to-text converter. There are a several commercial products available for this.

Once we have the text available, we want to create an embedded question using the text. We will decide which words need to be identified and set up the question accordingly. For our text, we will use a famous soliloquy from Shakespeare and make our Cloze listening question from it.

To set up the question, I simply go to the Quiz Module and find the quiz I want to use or I create a new one. Once in the Quiz, I need to create an Embedded (Cloze) question. Here is what our Embedded Answer (Cloze) question looks like after we have created the item and included the audio as shown in the next screenshot:

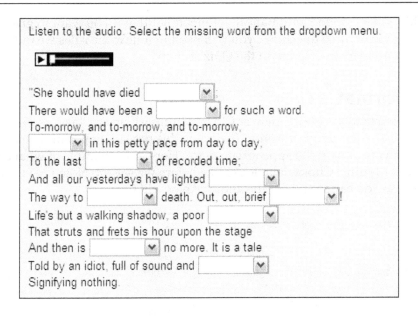

Grading this is done automatically; however, you need to determine the point value for the question. This question, as it was created, was worth 10 points but it is a fairly simple task. With items like this you may want to limit the entire question to 5 points or something else. Regardless of what you decide to do, make sure you are assigning a fair value in points-to-difficulty when creating multiple responses in a single item.

Short Answer

We can do the same thing with Short Answer. These items are more difficult because they require students to type in the correct response. Using the same text and audio used previously, we can see what this would look like:

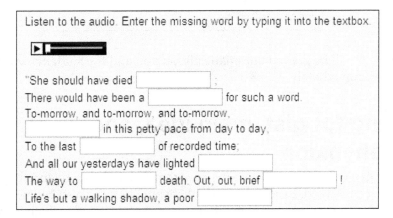

Again, this will be graded automatically. Remember that if you want to give feedback to one of these questions, you will need to follow the rules we outlined in the Short Answer description in the Quiz section.

Mixed format

It is also possible to use Short Answer Cloze, Multiple Choice Cloze, and even Numerical Cloze in a single question. To create this type of item, simply insert the type of item you want in the appropriate place. Here is an example of what a Short Answer and Multiple Choice item looks like before we save it. Note I have left the 'x' link visible so you can see where the audio player will be.

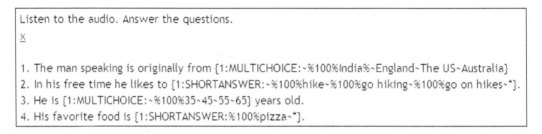

Now that we have everything in place, we are going to place the MP3 player in the question and then save the item. Once we have done this, we see the following:

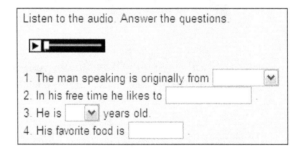

Again, this item will be graded automatically, so you and the students will be able to see the grades immediately.

Listening for gist, main idea, and comprehension

Listening for gist or main idea is making sure the students understand the core message being presented. Listening comprehension tasks can also be used in a similar fashion. You can use a variety of means to do this, one of which is by using the Essay question in Quiz.

Let's say we are teaching about a current event. We take audio from a source and we want to make sure our students are able to listen and understand what the main idea of the report is. To set up this kind of activity we are going to use Essay.

The first thing we need to do is find our audio. There are many sites out there with free audio samples and reports. Where you should look really depends on what you are teaching.

Let's say that our class has been working on *The Prince* by *Machiavelli*. We want the students to listen to a part of a chapter and let us know the gist of what *Machiavelli* was taking about. Again, we have a few options about how we will do this. The first is we can sit down and read the parts we want. This technique allows the students to be immediately comfortable with the reader since they are already used to your voice. This also has the advantage of allowing you to read only the sections you want.

Another option is using an audiobook. Now, there are copyright issues, so make sure you aren't doing anything illegal! There is a way around this, at least for 'the classics'. You can go to several free audiobook sites and find free MP3 files to use. One site is LibriVox (`http://librivox.org`), a site with a vast library of books in the public domain read by regular people with a variety of styles and accents. Librivox has a nice bonus as well, the page with the listening files for the book you have chosen also holds a link to the entire text of the reading. This is very useful should you want to use the text later for some type of comprehension task. If you decide to use this site, it is simple and you will quickly figure out how it works. There are many other sites offering similar things, so feel free to search and find the one you like. Regardless of the site you choose, you will need to make sure that your students' computers are all set up to play the files.

Now, our options here are directly linking to the page, directly linking to the file, or we can use our Audacity recorder to record what we hear directly from the site and then upload the recording to Moodle and use the Moodle MP3 player.

If you decide to link to the page, make sure the students know exactly which file to select and listen to. An image of the file to select and/or specific instructions on where to go are usually sufficient. In the **Insert Link** menu, in the **Target** area, you have the option to choose to have the page open in a new window. This is the option you should choose, since the student will be able to go back and forth between the page and the question.

If you decide to link to the file, the student will simply need to click on the link on the page and the file will begin playing. If the file you are linking to is an MP3, the Moodle player will be shown. In this case, you will want to adjust your question text accordingly.

If you want to upload the file and use the Moodle MP3 player, you can. There are several ways to do this. First you can save the file, and most of the time this will be an option. Occasionally, you won't be able to. In this case, you can use Audacity to record the file and upload it yourself. To do this you need to open **Audacity**, click on the **Record** button, and then open the file you want to record. Audacity will record what you are hearing through the computer. Once you have finished, you can edit the file down and cut out the space at the beginning and end if necessary. Once this has been done, you add the file just like we did with the True/False and Multiple Choice items. An example of what this looks like with the audio recorded by Audacity and uploaded as an MP3 file is shown in the next screenshot:

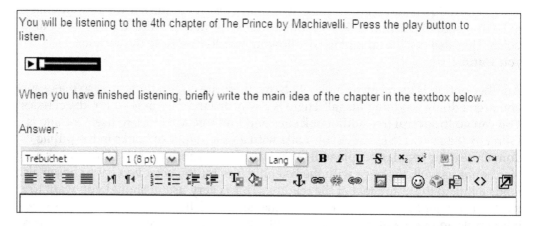

Grading these types of questions is not automatic, so you will need to go through each student's response individually. This can be time consuming, but it will give you a clear idea of what each student took away from the listening and this type of test question can really help identify students with strong and weak listening comprehension skills.

Using forums for listening tests

Forums are another place where we can deliver listening material to students. They are one of the core components of Moodle and one that we haven't looked at before. Forums have a lot going for them: they are great places for students and teachers to interact, they allow us to see posts and replies, and the instructor can to create several different types.

There are a few settings in Forum that we have not looked at, and we will not look over all of them. There are a few that are important to be aware of however.

Forum Type

Directly under the **Forum Name**, at the top of the page, there is the **Forum Type** drop-down menu. This menu has four settings.

A single, simple discussion

This is the most basic forum. It is a single discussion based on a given topic. The posts are all seen in a nested form. They can be useful in many ways, particularly for class or group discussions and assignments.

Standard forum for general use

This is a Forum where anyone is able to start as many discussion topics as they would like. This forum offers the most flexibility and is the default setting.

Each person posts one discussion

This type of Forum allows each member of the course to post a single new thread. The thread can then be viewed by other members of the course and they will be able to reply. This is a good way to set up Forums for self- and peer-review work.

Q & A Forum

For testing purposes, this is probably the one you want to use. This Forum requires each student to submit their work before they are able to see anyone else's submission. This will stop students from viewing another student's work before their own is completed, thus reducing copying or cheating.

For the assignment we are going to create, we will use the **Q & A Forum** because we do not want students to see what their classmates think will happen next.

Grading

The second setting we want to look at is how to grade a Forum. There is a **Grading** drop-down menu, which contains several ways to give final scores:

Average of ratings

This takes the score of all the Forum posts, adds them together, and divides by the number of posts. It is the simplest way to determine scores in Forum and it is also the default setting.

Count of ratings

This method of giving a score is based on the number of posts made. This is one that is not used as much as others, but it can be useful if you require a certain number of posts, say over the term or year.

Maximum rating

Using this setting will take the highest graded post and use that as the final grade. This is very useful for self- and peer-review assignments.

Minimum rating

Using this setting takes the lowest rated post and gives that as the final grade. This setting can force students to make carefully constructed posts at all times because any poor quality post will cost them points.

Sum

This Forum setting takes every post made and adds them all together to give a grade. This can be useful if you want to give a number of points for each post or if you want to have the student work in stages. The total score will never go over the maximum grade allowed for the Forum.

For example, let's say we are working on predicting and we want our students to watch or listen to a brief clip of something and then to predict what will happen next. We can find the audio or video and embed or link it to our Forum. In the forum, we ask our students to listen and then predict what will happen next. We can also have the Forum divided into several parts. For example, we can set up a pre-listening activity, a listening activity, and a post-listening activity.

Another benefit to using forums is that you can discuss issues with your students and keep a record of revisions and shifts in thought or understanding. Here is an example of a Forum set up with an audio component.

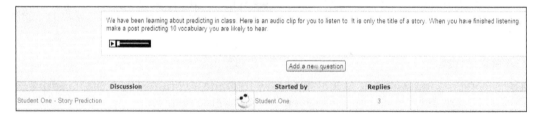

Now, look at the replies. You can see I have already gone ahead and replied and assessed the student. Here you can see what they look like. The replies are seen in a flat, nested form.

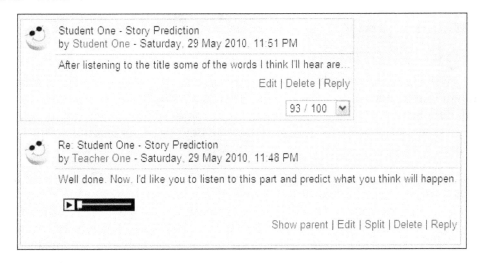

As you can see, the teacher can see the student's response and can use the drop-down menu in the lower right-hand corner of the student's post to assign a grade. The teacher can then add a new post, with a new recording, and continue the thread. These kinds of extended tasks can be very useful to observe student growth over the course of the term.

Obviously, predicting is not the only way to test listening in Forums. We can test comprehension, gist, or even ask opinions based on audio or visual clips. In addition, these forums are great places to set up self- and peer-reviews. Setting up forums where students work alone to revise their work or where classmates can see what other students are working on can be a good way to assess students.

Podcasts

Using podcasts is another way to test students' listening skills. One way to do this is to locate useful podcasts for the course you are teaching and asking students to listen, then testing them on the material either using Quiz, Forums, or some other activity that fulfils the skill you want to test.

The second option is creating your own podcasts. In Moodle, there is a podcast module that you will need to enable. To do this, you will need the Administrator to install the Ipodcast module. The instructions and files are located at `http://docs.moodle.org/en/Ipodcast_module`. This can be an effective method of testing listening comprehension because you are able to focus on the area being discussed and the student will find it easier listening to your voice as opposed to someone else's. You can set up a variety of essay and comprehension questions based around podcasts.

Multiple playing of audio files versus single attempts

When giving listening tests, it is usually important to control the number of times a student is able to listen to a track or file. This enables us to put all students on an equal footing in regards to the test and helps conserve time. While there may be times when this is not true, nearly all tests do limit listening tasks to one or two times.

Unfortunately, there is no way of setting up the built-in Moodle MP3 player so that it plays a single time. There is, however, a way around this. We have the option of installing a different player. One player that has been developed specifically for testing in Moodle is *Matt Bury's* Moodle MP3 Player for Tests. It can be downloaded from `http://code.google.com/p/moodle-mp3-player-for-tests/` and an explanation of how it is used is found at `http://code.google.com/p/moodle-mp3-player-for-tests/wiki/HowToUse`. It is a simple-looking player, much like the Moodle MP3 player, but with a bit more functionality. The next image is an image of the player taken from the site hosting the download:

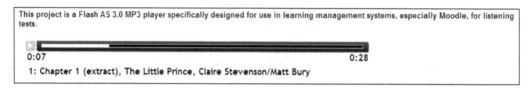

This player allows many options in the audio setup, including the key ability to play files automatically and limiting the number of times a student is able to listen to the file. In many tests this type of setting is necessary or desirable. The setup takes a bit of work, and it is not too difficult for those with a bit of HTML skill, but it could be a bit overwhelming for those without any coding experience. Most likely your institution's system admin will be able to help you get it working.

Summary

Listening is an important skill for many fields and positions, and tests usually contain a listening component. In this chapter, we have gone over some of the ways you can add listening items to your Moodle-based tests, but we have by no means gone through all of them. We have looked at how to upload audio, insert a player, and gone through how to create a variety of question types in a variety of activities. All these things can be extremely useful when testing. However, we really have only scratched the surface.

There are so many plugins and additional hacks and players and resources that we simply don't have the space to get into here, although the Moodle MP3 Player for Tests mentioned earlier is something you will probably want to set up on your site.

What we have done in this chapter is given you the basic tools you need to get started with testing listening. When you come to something you want to try out that wasn't covered here, you should have the building blocks to learn more yourself. If you want to learn more or ask questions about how to do something, the forum `http://moodle.org/mod/forum/view.php?id=1301` in the Moodle Language Teaching area focuses on using listening. While it is not the most active of forums, there are many members and they are almost certainly able and willing to help with issues you come across.

One final note, many of the activities described in this chapter will take up a lot of space. Your system administrator may not be happy with large files being uploaded to Moodle. Before you begin uploading a lot of video or audio files, you might want to check with the system administrator to let them know what you want to do and make sure there aren't any problems or space issues. They will appreciate it!

Now that we have looked at listening tests, we will move on and look at some reading test options in Moodle.

8
Testing Reading

Testing reading is another major skill area tested in every field. Reading tests are similar to listening tests and typically have things like vocabulary questions, reading comprehension, reading for details, gist, inference, and identifying main ideas, support, and conclusions.

Moodle has several aspects that make it a good place to test your students' reading skills, and in fact, any test a student takes that contains text tests their reading skills. Simply by having students read and interpret the instructions we are testing reading comprehension. We will begin with looking at vocabulary testing and move on to reading tests. We will look at several methods available for each testing area, looking at two in detail. In this chapter, we will:

- Make Flash Cards for vocabulary testing
- Create timed readings
- Develop a QuizPort test

Testing vocabulary

Vocabulary assessment is important for many reasons. Students need to understand the words and terminology used in the subject being studied. If we are talking about art history, then your students would need a solid grasp of the terminology used to talk about paintings, sculptures, and anything else related to the topic. We will start our reading tests by looking at some ideas for testing vocabulary.

Quiz

The first and most basic idea for checking student vocabulary knowledge is by using the Quiz module. We have gone over this module extensively, and you should be able to create any type of item using it by this point.

Quiz offers a variety of question styles that allow for vocabulary assessment, from Short Answer to Multiple Choice.

Flash Cards

We have already seen a method to create a Flash Card-type test using Quiz, but we will now look at a module called Flash Card Set. This module is one way for students to test themselves with the course vocabulary, images, or audio they should know. The current version is available at: `http://download.moodle.org/plugins19/mod/Flash Card.zip` and the documentation for the module is available at: `http://docs.moodle.org/en/Flash Card_module`.

What this module does is allow you to create decks of vocabulary for students to work through and practice with. It can be used for a variety of reasons, but self-assessment and review is where it works best. The set-up page appears as shown in the next screenshot:

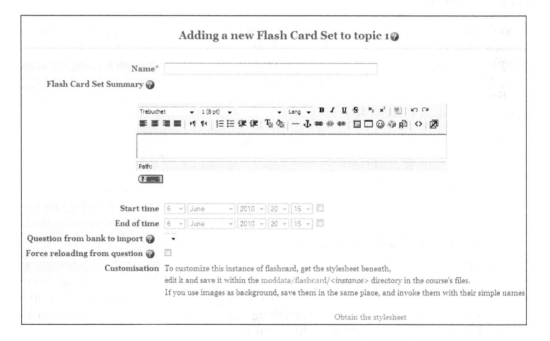

Name and Flash Card Set Summary

Enter the **Name** of the Flash Card Set and a description of the vocabulary to be covered here.

Start Time and End of Time

By default these are disabled, allowing students to use the Flash Cards whenever they desire. If you want to enable the cards only for a certain period of time, enable these features by clicking on the checkboxes next to the dates and set the times and dates accordingly.

Questions from bank to import

This is a very useful function if you are using Quiz. Flash Card allows the direct importing of Matching questions from Quiz. Any Matching items available in Quiz will be available to import to the Flash Card module via the drop-down menu. The drop-down menu will list the question name, so all you need to do is select the one you want.

It is important to note that if you do this to an already existing set of cards, the previous cards will be deleted. If you do not want this to happen, make a new Flash Card Set for the words you want to import.

Force reloading from question

If you choose a Matching item to import to the Quiz, it will require the page to reload. Checking this box will automatically reload the page. It will also reset all old user data related to the Flash Cards and student results.

Customization

By going to the stylesheet, you will be able to make changes to the way the cards are displayed. This requires a bit of CSS knowledge and is something that you may or may not want to learn how to adjust.

If you are interested in learning about how to work with CSS, check out `http://www.cssbasics.com/`, which has a good overview of CSS and is fairly easy to understand and work with.

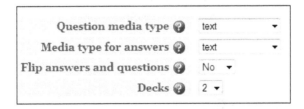

Question media type

Do you want to create image or text cards, text or text cards, or something else? This drop-down setting allows you to choose the type of media that will be used by the question Flash Cards. The types of media available here are **text** (the default setting), **image**, **sound**, and **image and sound**.

Media type for answers

This setting is used to determine the type of media that will be used for the answer Flash Cards. The options are identical to the **Question media type** choices.

By adjusting these settings, you are able to create a variety of Flash Card activities for students. You can create image-based questions with text-based responses, audio-based cards with image-based responses, or any other combination.

Flip answers and questions

This setting allows a Jeopardy-type Flash Card activity. The default setting here is **No**, which will present Flash Cards with the Question on the front-side and the Answer on the back-side of the card. If you change this setting to **Yes**, the order will be reversed showing the Answer on the front-side and placing the Question on the back-side of the card.

Decks

This setting determines the number of decks that will be displayed. The default is **2**, but you have the option to include up to four decks in the activity.

Using two decks is best for reviewing small sets of material, with 20 or so items as the top end of the scale. Three decks is better for larger sets, with about 50 or so as the recommended max. Four decks is used for very large sets, things like end of term reviews and the like.

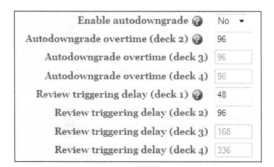

Enable autodowngrade

This setting enables the moving of cards from one stack of cards to another, more difficult stack. The default setting here is **No**, which means that the cards will always be a part of the original stack. If the setting is changed to **Yes**, cards will move from the basic stack to a stack with less reviewed cards after a time. The items are moved to these less reviewed stacks if students do not spend time working with the cards on a regular basis.

Autodowngrade overtime

This setting is used to determine how long after review the cards are moved from the basic deck to a less reviewed deck. The number written in the textbox shows the number of hours from the last review that the card will be moved to the less reviewed deck.

If you are using more than two decks, you have the option of setting different timeframes to move cards for each of the additional decks.

Review triggering delay

This setting allows you to set a timeframe, in hours, of how long the student has to review the cards until the Autodowngrade begins its countdown. For example, if you set this to 24, then 24 hours later the Autodowngrade will begin its countdown if the student has not done a review.

Setting up a Flash Card review

We will now create a Flash Card activity. Since we are talking about art history and painting, we will set up Questions with images and Answers with text. The idea is to help students review famous paintings and have them name the painter.

First, we will make sure we have the images we want to use for our cards. I have already added five images to our site for use with the cards. I have also noted the dates they were made and the artist credited with the work, which we will use for the answers.

Next, we will add the new activity called Flash Card Set. In the Name and Description area we will enter **Art History - Paintings - 1500-1650**, which will make it easy to identify later.

In our set up, we are going to use only two sets of cards, so we will leave **Decks** set to **2**. We will set the **Question media type** to **image** and the **Media type for answers** to **text**. Click on the **Save and display** button. You will see a message telling you there are **No Cards Defined**. You will see a **continue** button below the message. Click on it and on the next page you will see three buttons, **Add a new question**, **Add three new questions**, and **Import**. Click on the **Add three new questions** and the following screenshot appears:

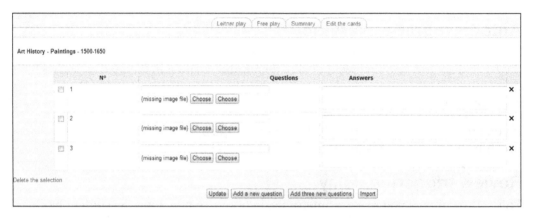

Click on the **Choose** button to find the images you have uploaded, or to upload images you want to use. You may click on either of the **Choose** buttons. If you decide to use image and sound, then you will use both.

Once you have the image selected and added to the Question on the left-hand side, you will enter the Answer text on the right-hand side.

Image Sizing

Make sure the image you select is an appropriate size for the card. If you select an image that is too big, it can cover a large part of the page, forcing the student to scroll to completely view it. Complex and detailed images may need to be too large for inclusion with Flash Cards.

Once we have all the images and text entered, we click on the **Update** button and we can see the cards with the images and the Answers. Above the images, we also see four tabs. The tabs are **Leitner play**, **Free play**, **Summary**, and **Edit the cards**, which is where we have been working. It is shown in the next screenshot:

Now, we will click on the **Leitner play** tab and we will be presented with two stacks of cards. The first stack is labeled **Hard Set** and the second stack is labelled **Easy Set**. Our cards will all be in the **Hard Set** since we have not gone through them yet.

Clicking on the top card in the **Hard Set** will start the Flash Card activity and we will see one of the images we uploaded presented. On the right-hand side, we will see three buttons, **I got it!**, **I missed !**, and **Reset cardset**.

We now make our guess regarding the image and click on it. Once we click on it, we will see the Answer. If we got the item correct, we click on the **I got it !** button. If incorrect, we click on the **I missed !** button. Click on **Reset cardset** to restart the game.

Once you have gone through the set, the cards you got correct will be moved to the **Easy Set**. The cards you missed will remain in the **Hard Set**. The **Lietner play** game is shown in the next screenshot:

Lietner play

This game is what we have been describing, and is a typical Flash Card-type activity. Students look at the card, make a guess, click on the card, and then see the answer. Once this is done, they select the appropriate button. All cards begin in the **Hard Set** and move to the **Easy Set** once they have been correctly answered.

Free play

This is another version of Flash Card play style. Here, all cards are presented in a random order and the student can flip through the cards as many times as they like. The can move forwards or backwards through the deck and when they are confident that they understand the card, they can remove it from the play. This can be a very useful tool for students working through lists of course vocabulary or Q&A-type items.

Summary

The teacher's view page shows what the students have done with the Flash Cards. It is shown in the next screenshot:

Under the **Username** you will see the names of all the students enrolled in the course.

In the **Decks state** column, we see two separate columns. On the left-hand side, we see a stack of cards with two clocks next to it. There is move-like mark in the centre pointing to the right-hand side. On the right-hand side, we see another stack of cards with four clocks.

The deck of cards on the left-hand side of the clocks shows the number of cards remaining in the set, with the left-hand side set being the **Hard Set** and the right-hand side set being the **Easy Set**. Move your pointer over the card stack to see the number remaining in the stack.

The clocks show how much time remains for the students to complete the review. Again, scrolling over the clocks will show the remaining time for the review. Normally the clocks are gray, but they can change to red, which means a student is late in completing the assignment.

The **Reset** button is also available here. Clicking on this button will erase all of the student's progress, so be careful. This can't be undone.

The **Counters** column shows the card usage statistics. It shows less and more viewed ticks, which show the number of times a card is viewed, the **Mean ticks per card**, which gives the mean views of the cards, and finally the **Total viewed cards**, which is arguably the most important, since it shows the total number of cards reviewed in the activity. This number can give you an idea of how much work the student put into their review by seeing how many cards they went through.

Glossary

Glossary is another method Moodle has that can be useful for reviewing and testing vocabulary. It allows the user to create and review lists of vocabulary and matching definitions. We simply don't have the space here, but if you are interested in working with Glossary, check out `http://docs.moodle.org/en/Glossaries` for additional information and details on how to use it.

JCross

JCross is a Hot Potatoes activity that creates crossword puzzles. Students are given clues and they attempt to fill in the spaces accordingly. Many students enjoy these types of activities, and they are fairly simple to create and they are scored automatically. We will look at Hot Potatoes more closely soon. Note that this is an extension and it is not installed by default.

Testing reading

As with testing anything, there are many ways to test reading skills. In this section, we will look at how to create a timed reading and how to set up a QuizPort.

Creating timed reading tests with Quiz

One of the basic issues with reading tests is often time, or more specifically time limits. Students are given a set amount of time to read some material and answer the questions related to the passage or article. Unfortunately, right now, there is no module in place to specifically do this. However, it is possible to set up a Quiz that does time students.

The first thing that needs to be done is to set up a Quiz. In the Quiz creation page, you need to set the time limit to however long you intend the test to be. Once this is done, make sure the number of questions per page is set to unlimited. The method being described here uses a question at the beginning of the Quiz to hold the reading passage, so make sure the item shuffling is turned off or the students won't see the reading in the proper place.

Once the settings are finalized, save the Quiz and go to the Question Bank page. Here, make a Description question to hold the reading passage. This will be the first question on the page. After this item, include all questions you want relating to the reading.

When you have added all the questions you want, you will have a timed, reading test with the passage at the top and all the related questions below. An example is shown in the next screenshot:

Time Remaining 0:30:50	assage Quiz - Attempt 1

Bosch was born about 1450 and was an early Netherlandish painter of great skill. He is well-known for his...

1

Marks: 1

Which of the following works is Bosch most famous for?

Choose one answer.

- ○ Saint Jermone
- ○ The Magician
- ○ The Merchant and His Wife
- ○ The Garden of Earthly Delights

As seen in the previous screenshot, the passage is at the top and the questions follow. The timer is visible in the upper-left corner of the screen showing how much time remains. This method of creating a timed reading test is very useful and something that you will find very easy to put together.

If you don't want a timed reading, simply leave the time limit disabled.

QuizPort

Hot Potatoes is probably one of the best-known activity creation programs used with Moodle. Hot Potatoes is a Quiz-type module that offers some additional question formats like JCloze, mentioned earlier. However, Hot Potatoes looks like it is going to be replaced by Gordon Bateson's QuizPort in upcoming Moodle versions from 2.1. QuizPort, which will be renamed TaskChain, is also available for use in pre-2.0 versions.

QuizPort allows you to create a set of activities that are viewed as a single entity and are given a single grade. The design of QuizPort, which is similar to HotPot, allows you to use several different item creation tools. You can use Qedoc, Hot Potatoes, and HTML to make quizzes. We will work with Hot Potatoes activities, since so many people use it. To start with, we will look at the options available in QuizPort, but first, we need to install it.

To install QuizPort, you need to first download it. To download it, go to Moodle's Downloads and Plugins page at `http://download.moodle.org/`. Once there, go to the **Download** tab and select **Modules and Plugins**. Once you are on this page, click on the **Search** tab and in the **Name** textbox, enter **QuizPort**. Click on the link and you will be taken to the download page. The file you download will be a ZIP file titled **quizport-module.0.9.x**. Click on this file and add it to your `mods` folder and unzip it there. Once it is added, the site admin needs to log in and click on the **Notifications** link on the site admin page. Once this link is clicked, the module will begin installation. Once it is installed, go to your course and in the **Add an activity** drop-down, select **QuizPort**. This will open the module and you will see the QuizPort editing page. The first part is titled **General**.

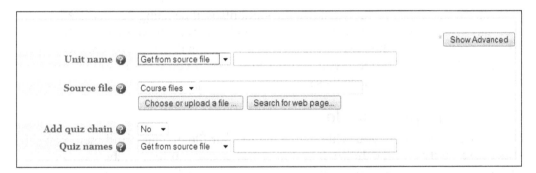

General

Here, we make decisions about the naming and the activities to include in the QuizPort.

Unit name

QuizPort offers several ways to name the activity. The drop-down menu lists four options for naming.

Get from Source file

This option will get the name of the QuizPort from the source file.

Use Source file name

Using this option will name the QuizPort activity the same thing as the name of the file being used.

Use Source File Path

If this option is used, QuizPort will use the file path to create a name for the activity. Any backslashes in the path will be replaced with spaces.

Specific text

Specific text functions just like all other naming procedures we have looked at. Here, you simply enter the name you want the activity to have.

Source file

This setting determines which activity the students will be using in the QuizPort. For example, you can use a Hot Potatoes activity, a Qedoc activity, or even a URL. There are two ways to select the files you want to use. As an instructor, you only have the option to choose files from your course; however, if you have administrative authority, you can also choose files site-wide.

Choose or upload a file

If you select this button, you will be directed to your file manager and there you can select the activity of your choice. If you have not already uploaded the file you will simply follow the same patterns as we have looked at earlier to find and upload the file to the file manager.

Search for a webpage

This button will open a browser, which will allow you to find the webpage you want to use, which you then copy and paste into the textbox.

Configuration file

This is an optional feature and is only seen if the **Show Advanced** feature is selected. This setting is used to format QuizPort settings to mimic another activity's settings. For example, if you had another QuizPort set up in a way you wanted to use again, this would be a way to easily do that.

The configuration depends on the activity and the settings used in the configuration files, and will override the source file settings. Here, you have the option of locating the file by uploading and choosing a file or by locating an HTML file.

Add a Quiz chain

This is where we decide whether we want to create a single quiz or if we want to create a chain of them.

No

If **No** is selected, only one quiz will be included in the QuizPort.

Yes

If **Yes** is selected, you can begin to create the chain of quizzes that the students will work through. Depending on the activity to be added, different things will happen.

Folder

If a folder is selected, all the activities in the folder that can be utilized as quizzes will be added to the QuizPort chain of activities, all of which having the same settings.

Unit file

If a Unit file is selected, all the quizzes associated with the unit will be added and made part of the chain of activities. All the activities will have the same settings.

Quiz file

If a single quiz-type file is selected, it will start the chain. All files added after this file will have the same settings.

Quiz names

Quiz names gives names to the quizzes in the QuizPort. It functions like Unit Name mentioned previously, offering the same methods for automatic or teacher-determined naming.

Display

This section is where we can determine how the QuizPort will look, whether or not it will have an **Entry page** or an **Exit page**, and what the next activity in the chain will be.

The view seen previously is the **Basic View**, with only the options you need to create a QuizPort. However, clicking on the **Show Advanced** options button, reveals many more useful options.

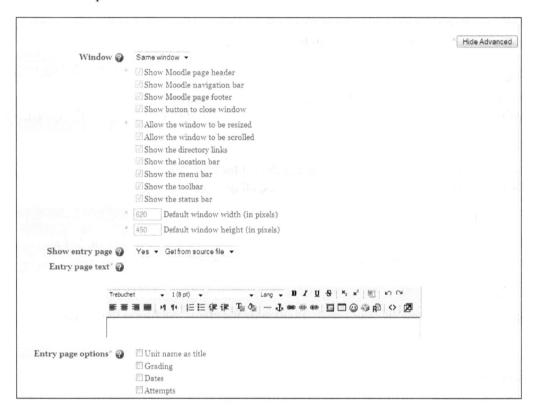

Window

This option shows how the QuizPort will be delivered. If you leave the setting at the default, the QuizPort will be completed in the same window that is already open.

If you change the setting to **New window**, the QuizPort will create a new window with the activity. If **New window** is selected, there are many options you can apply, all of which are listed here. You have the option to allow the page to be resized, get rid of navigation tools, show the toolbar, and other options seen in the previous screenshot.

Show entry page

This Yes/No drop-down determines whether or not the QuizPort shows an Entry page to the student. If **No** is selected, then there will be no Entry page and the student will begin the test immediately.

If **Yes** is selected, an Entry page will be shown to the student before the quiz begins. The **Entry page text** and the contents are determined based on your selections in the **Entry page options** located under the **Entry page text**.

Entry page text

The text, images, or audio files entered here will be seen by the students on the Entry page. This is a good place to give instructions, background, or any other pertinent information the students will need to know before going on with the QuizPort.

Entry page options

Each of the four options listed here will display the associated information to students on the Entry page. To use any of the options, simply click on the box to activate it.

Unit name as title

If this option is selected, the name of the unit will be given as the title of the page.

Grading

If this option is selected, the method used for grading will be shown.

Dates

If this option is selected, the QuizPort opening and closing dates will be shown.

Attempts

If this option is selected, all previous attempts will be shown to the student. If there are any attempts that can be continued, a button to do so will be visible.

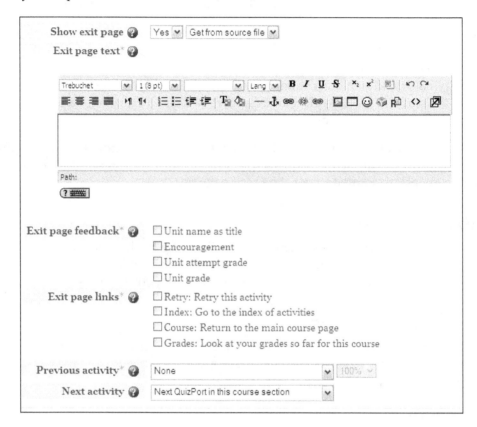

Show exit page

This is another Yes/No drop-down menu. If **No** is selected, there will be no exit page and the student will return to the course page or move on to the next activity.

If **Yes** is selected, there will be an Exit page with settings determined by the options selected.

The drop-down menu next to the Yes/No determines where the name of the Exit page is taken from.

Exit page text

The text, images, or audio files entered here will be seen by the students when they complete their final activity and move on to this page. This is a good place to give instructions on what to do next, offer comments on the assignment, or to give any additional information to your students.

Exit page feedback

Here, you make decisions about what information—in addition to your text—will be displayed on the Exit page.

Unit name as title

Here, as in the Entry page, if you select this option, the name of the unit will act as the title of the page.

Encouragement

If you would like to offer some feedback based on the student's performance, you can offer it here in a general sort of way. The feedback is determined by the score the student achieved. Greater than 90 percent will receive "Excellent!" Greater than 60 percent will receive "Well Done". Greater than 0 percent will see "Good Try", and a student receiving 0 percent will see "Are you okay?"

Unit attempt grade

If this option is selected, the student will be shown their score for the activity that was just completed.

Unit grade

This will show the student the final grade for the unit. Also, if the **Highest grade** was selected as the scoring method, this will let the student know whether the current score was higher than or equal to a previous score.

Exit page links

The options available here are used by students to continue on after they have finished with the QuizPort activity.

Retry

If you have allowed multiple attempts on the QuizPort, then the students will see an option to retake the QuizPort. If a student has already used up their allotment of attempts they will not have this option.

Index

If this option is used, students who reach the Exit page will see a list of links to activities in the QuizPort.

Course

If this option is selected, students will see a link to the course page.

Grades

If this option is chosen, students will be shown a link to the Gradebook.

Previous activity

This drop-down allows you to set requirements for attempting the QuizPort. Using this setting will allow you to select which activity the student must have completed before attempting the QuizPort. You are able to select a specific activity or you can use one of the preset options: **Previous activity in this course**, **Previous activity in this section**, **Previous QuizPort in this course**, and **Previous QuizPort in this section**.

If you decide to use this setting, there is a second drop-down with percentage scores to the right of the activity menu. You are able to set the percentage the student must have achieved in the activity selected before they are able to move on to the QuizPort.

Next activity

This acts in a similar fashion to the **Previous activity** described earlier. Here, you are able to set what activity the student will need to complete next in the QuizPort. You have the option to move students on to a specific activity, or you can use one of the four preset options: **Next activity in this course**, **Next activity in this section**, **Next QuizPort in this course**, and **Next QuizPort in this section**.

Access control

This section deals with how and when students can attempt the QuizPort, and contains several features that will help control the access to the test.

Available from and Available until

These two settings are the same as we have seen before. They allow you to set the date and time the test will be made available as well as when it will stop being accessible to students.

Time limit

Enabling this setting will limit the time a student has to complete the test. This time limit applies to a single attempt.

Delay 1

If you have allowed multiple attempts on the test, this setting will allow you to create a delay between the first and second attempts.

Delay 2

This functions just like **Delay 1**, except this setting deals with every attempt following the second one.

Attempts allowed

This drop-down menu offers eleven options for setting the number of attempts. You can either set the number of attempts from one to ten or you can allow unlimited attempts.

Allow resume

This setting determines how attempts that are incomplete are handled. There are three options here: **No**, **Yes**, and **Force**.

No

If this setting is selected, the student will not be able to return to any previous attempt.

Yes

Choosing **Yes** will give the student two options. The first option allows the student to continue to work on their previous attempt. The second option allows them to make a new attempt.

Force

This setting will force a student to continue to work through a previous, incomplete attempt.

Require password

This will require students to enter the password specified in order to make an attempt on the quiz.

Require network address

This option will only allow those with specific network addresses to make an attempt on the test. This is useful if you want to ensure that only the students working in your lab or classroom are able to access the test.

Limiting access to the test is a critical part of testing. Only those who are intended to use it and those delivering it should have access, and only those delivering it should see it before it is given. This is something that can be less or more important depending on the type of testing you're working with, but is something that should be kept in mind. Using this setting can go a long way in improving test security.

There are several ways to set this up:

- Full IP Address: 123.456.78.9 — Limits the access to a single computer
- Partial IP Address: 123.456 — Limits access to any computer with those numbers at the beginning of its IP address
- IP Address Range: 123.456.78.9-15 — Limits access to any computers running IP addresses in the range, in our case 123.456.78.9 to 123.456.78.15
- Classless Inter-Domain Routing (CIDR): 123.456.78.9/10 — Limits access by only allowing certain IP subsets access

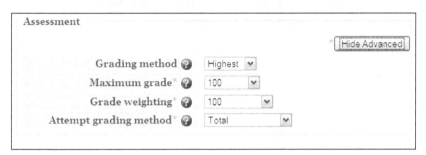

Assessment

In this section, the scoring of the assignment is determined. It contains four categories: **Grading method**, **Maximum grade**, **Grade weighting**, and **Attempt grading method**.

Grading method

This setting determines how the final grade for the test will be decided. The drop-down has four options: **Highest**, **Average**, **First**, and **Last**.

- Highest — This will use the highest score out of all attempts to determine the grade.
- Average — This will take all the attempts and average them to determine the final grade.
- First — This will use only the first attempt to determine the final grade.
- Last — This will use the last test taken to determine the final grade.

Maximum grade

This allows you to set the maximum score possible. The scores range from 0 to 100. The score you select will be included in the Gradebook.

Grade weighting

This setting allows you to set the weight of this assignment in Gradebook.

Attempt grading method

This setting is used to let you determine how the grade from a single unit attempt will be calculated. There are several settings available.

- Total—This will use the total of the weighted quiz scores.
- Highest—This will use the highest weighted quiz score.
- Last—This will use the last test's weighted quiz score.
- Last (Completed)—This will use the last completed quiz's weighted score.
- Last (Timed-out)—This will use the last timed-out or the last completed quiz's weighted score.
- Last (Abandoned)—This will use the last timed-out, completed, or abandoned quiz's weighted score. It will not use any test that is 'In Progress'.

Common module settings

This section contains the common module settings: **Visible**, **ID setting**, and **Grade category**. We have looked at these before, so there is no need to cover them again here.

Hot Potato activities

Now that we have seen all the options available in QuizPort, we are going to create one. First, we will need to create some activities to insert into the test. We will use Hot Potatoes to create the test activities for our QuizPort.

If you are unfamiliar with Hot Potatoes, go to their website at `http://hotpot.uvic.ca/` where you will be able to read through the information related to the software and download the newest version. Hot Potatoes is now freeware and the current version is 6.3. This is likely to be the last version since they are no longer developing or supporting Hot Potatoes and it is not open source. Once you have it installed and opened the package, you will see an image of a pile of potatoes on one side and one big potato about to get squished on the other. Each of the potatoes offers a different activity type to work with. The five quiz types available in HotPot are JCloze, JCross, JMatch, JMix, and JQuiz.

- JCloze—This item type allows you to create gap-fill activities.
- JCross—This option allows for the creation of crossword puzzles.
- JMatch—This allows you to create matching items.
- JMix—This item allows the creation of jumbled word or sentence items. It has two settings, drag-and-drop and standard.
- JQuiz—This item type allows you to create Multiple Choice, Short Answer, Multi-Select, and Hybrid Items.

There is one additional feature called The Masher. To use The Masher, you need to click on the large potato on the right. The Masher is how you take all the items and mash them together into a unit.

There is a lot you can do with Hot Potatoes, so I recommend you get it and start to play around with it and see how you feel using it. There is a discussion forum in Moodle related to QuizPort and Hot Potatoes. It is found at `http://moodle.org/mod/forum/view.php?id=1599`.

For our QuizPort, we will create one JCloze, one JMatching, and one JQuiz.

Making a QuizPort test

Now, we are going to make our own QuizPort reading test. Our test will have two vocabulary tests and one reading test. We will have an Entrance page, a series of three tests, and an Exit page.

On the Entrance page, we will give our students a description of the activities and explain the test structure and content. Since we are making a reading and vocabulary test, we will also include our reading passage here. However, if you use QuizPort for some other type of test, you may want to adjust how you set up the Entrance page.

After the Entrance page, we will have three HotPot activities, a JCloze, a JMatch, and a JQuiz.

After the final activity, the students will be directed to the Exit page with a closing message from us.

For our QuizPort settings, we will do the following:

1. Using the **Specific text** setting, we will name the QuizPort Dutch Masters Test. We will leave the rest of the first section alone for now.

2. We will click on the **Show Advanced** in the **Display** section to display the options for the Entry and Exit pages.

3. We need to set both **Entry page** and **Exit page** to **Yes**, since we want to use both of them.

4. In the Entry and Exit page options, we will select each of the boxes, which will give students additional information about the test.

5. In **Access control** we will set the **number of Attempts allowed** to **1** and we will change the **Allow to resume setting** to **Force**, since we want our students to finish everything.

6. Finally we will confirm our QuizPort by clicking on **Save and display**.

Once you click on **Save and display**, you will be taken to the **Preview** page. Right now it is empty, but at the top we see four tabs: **Info, Results, Preview**, and **Edit quizzes**. The first thing we are going to do is click on the **Edit quizzes** button, which will bring us here:

As you can see, there is a message telling us no quizzes have been added to the QuizPort. We will go to the available actions area and click on **Add more quizzes**. Once the button is selected, you will see a box with **End of unit** in it. It is the only option at this point, but leave it alone and click on the **Go** button towards the bottom of the page.

We are now taken to the Add a Quiz page. For **Quiz name** we will select **Use source file name**. In **Source file**, we will click on the **Choose or upload a file** button and select our first activity, the **HotPot JCloze**. We now go to the bottom of the page and click on the **Save changes** button. Once we do this, we will be returned to the previous page, but we will see the activity we just added at the top of the page. We will repeat this process twice more to add the JMatch and the JQuiz. You will note that when we click on the **Add a quiz** button this time, there are three options: **Start of unit**, **End of unit**, and **After Quiz** with a drop-down menu listing the currently available activities we have. You can place them wherever you'd like, but we will use **After Quiz** and set the drop-down to the JCloze already added. This will cause the new activity to appear after the first. We will repeat the process for the third as well, changing the drop-down menu to the appropriate activity, in this case the JMatch. When we finish, the tab will look like the next screenshot:

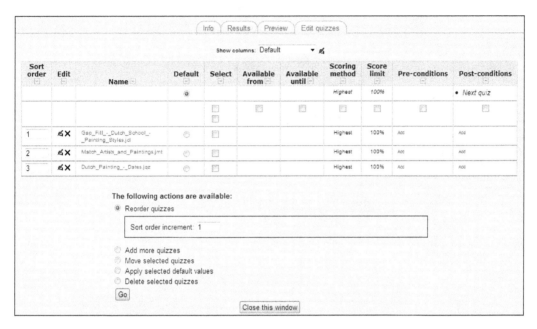

Note the **Show columns** drop-down menu. This drop-down will allow you to look at different aspects of the QuizPort setup in detail. The options are basically the same as the Edit QuizPort page: **Default**, **General**, **Display**, **Access control**, **Assessment**, **Conditions**, and **All**.

If a student went to the QuizPort now, they would be able to take any of the quizzes in any order. However, we want the students to take them in the order we placed them in the QuizPort, so we need to go to the **Pre-conditions** column and click on the **Add** button. This will allow us to force students to complete the activities in a specific order.

We want our students to complete the **Gap Fill** first, **Matching** second, and **Dutch Painting** third. To do this, we need to do two things. First we need to go to the **Reorder quizzes** radio button, seen in the previous image. Click on it and you will see a message reading **Sort order increment**. Now, go to the **Sort order** column and number the items in the order you want them displayed. Once this is done click on the **Go** button and the items will be reordered. Now that we have the items in order, we need to go to the Matching row and under the **Pre-conditions**, click on the **Add** button. This will bring up a menu as shown in the next screenshot:

As you can see here, there are several pre-conditions we can set. In the **Condition quiz**, we see **Previous quiz** in the drop-down. This is the default setting and the one we will use. However, if you click on the drop-down, you will see a list of all activities in the QuizPort, which you can choose from as a pre-condition for taking the quiz. You also have the option to set the minimum score required, the number of attempts, and so on. We will only use the **Previous quiz** for now. All we need to do is click on the **Save changes** button. We will do this for Dutch Painting as well.

Now that we have our **Pre-conditions** set up, we also want to have our **Post-conditions** organized. In the **Post-conditions** column, click on the **Add** button in the **Gap Fill** row. This will bring up a similar menu, but instead of **Condition quiz** as we see in the **Pre-conditions**, we will see a drop-down titled **Next quiz**. We will select **Next quiz** from the drop-down for the first two. For the final quiz, Dutch Artists, we will select the **End of unit** option, which will bring us to the Exit page.

Here is what the page looks like with the **Pre-conditions** and **Post-conditions** added:

Sort order ⊟	Edit ⊟	Name ⊟	Default ⊟	Select ⊟	Available from ⊟	Available until ⊟	Scoring method ⊟	Score limit ⊟	Pre-conditions ⊟	Post-conditions ⊟
			◉				Highest	100%		
				▭ ▭	▭	▭	▭	▭	▭	▭
1	✎ ✖	Gap Fill - Dutch School - PaintingStyles	◌	▭			Highest	100%	Add	• Next quiz ✎ ✖ Add
2	✎ ✖	Matching Artists and Paintings	◌	▭			Highest	100%	• Previous quiz ✎ ✖ Add	• Next quiz ✎ ✖ Add
3	✎ ✖	Dutch Painting - Dates	◌	▭			Highest	100%	• Previous quiz ✎ ✖ Add	• End of unit ✎ ✖ Add

As you can see, students will begin with the first item, and after the first item is completed, they will be moved to the next item, and so on.

Now that we have set the parameters of the test, we will move on to **Preview** to see what we have. Once we click on the **Preview** tab, we will see the Entrance page. On the Entrance page we see the text we entered. Click on the **Preview now** button and we will immediately begin the first test. Once it is completed, we will be shown our score and moved to the next test. This will continue until we finish all the tests in the QuizPort and reach the **End of unit**. At the **End of unit**, we are shown the Exit page with our score, feedback, and the text we entered.

Now a student will see things a bit differently. For starters, they will not have access to the tabs along the top, and for them to start the test they will need to click on the **Start new unit attempt** button to begin the test. Once they finish, they will see the same thing as the teacher's preview, their final score, feedback, and the Exit page text entered. Students can also get more detailed information about their performance by pressing on the breadcrumb titled QuizPort, which will open the student results page.

⊟	Name ⊟	Unit grade ⊟	Unit status ⊟	Unit date ⊟	Unit duration ⊟	Unit attempt ⊟	Attempt grade ⊟	Attempt status ⊟	Attempt date ⊟	Attempt duration ⊟
👤	Student One	88%	Completed	16 Jun, 21:11	35 secs	1	88%	Completed	16 Jun, 21:11	35 secs

This data is useful to students who want to follow their progress or to confirm they have completed all required work. If the student attempts to enter the QuizPort again, after their number of attempts has expired, they will receive a message stating that they have no remaining attempts available.

The final thing we'll look at in QuizPort is the **Results**. Going back to the Teacher's View, if we click on **Results**, we are shown all the student attempts on the QuizPort, their scores, the status of the test, the time it took to complete the test and the last time they attempted the test. This is shown in the next screenshot:

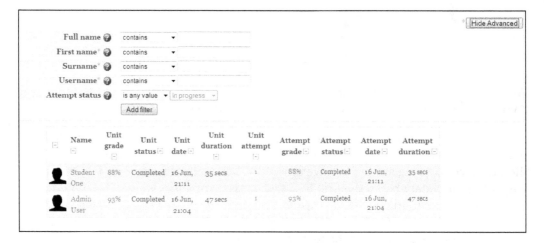

As you can see, the results are identical to the view the students receive. However, you are able to use the new filter section above the results to look through the data.

QuizPort offers some great possibilities for testing vocabulary and reading. In addition, the grades from the QuizPort will be exported to the Gradebook and added to the student's grade without any extra steps.

Forums

There are, of course, multiple methods of using Forums for reading activities. You can set up links directing students to online readings, you can include short readings and discussions based on the readings, or have students interact with each other over classroom readings. Forums are a useful feature for reading and discussion, and can make an ideal place to test students' reading skills.

Summary

There is so much more that can be done with reading in Moodle. There are many activities available, some are contributed and some are core modules used in inventive ways. Regardless, whatever you are doing in Moodle, there will be text, and this is something that will help develop and test a student's reading skills.

While we have looked at a few modules here, we have really only touched the surface of what can be done. The Flash Cards offer a good way of helping students review and gives you a way to track their progress. QuizPort offers a lot of possibilities for reading and other tests, since it is really limited only by the way you design the activities inside it. Timed readings, vocabulary testing, and reading comprehension are just a few activities that can be done in Moodle. For additional activities related to reading, you might want to check out Moodle's site and look into the Teaching Strategies and Moodle for Language Teaching – Reading forums or look at some other books published on teaching with Moodle that list many other methods for creating reading activities.

Testing Speaking

Testing speaking online can be tricky and many don't even attempt it. One of the reasons testing speaking on computers is tricky is because you have to deal with synchronous versus asynchronous testing methods. Testing someone's speaking skills requires that there is output or production from the student, something not seen directly in listening or reading tests. To test speaking in Moodle, we need to be creative and willing to try new things. We can set up Skype for real-time speaking activities (synchronous) or we can set up a variety of other recording modules to review and/or respond to later. What we will look at here are ways to test speaking using both concepts and some of the modules available to do this.

One of the things we will look at in this chapter is NanoGong, a simple recording device where conversations over time can be had. Another thing we will look at is a new module called Voiceshadow and its partner Voiceboard. This is a great resource for students studying languages, but can be modified to work for speaking tests.

In this chapter, we will:

- Work with NanoGong
- Introduce VoiceBoard and Voiceshadow
- Discuss Audio in Forums
- Look at the Skype module

Using NanoGong

NanoGong is a simple audio recorder and player that can be used to complete speaking activities with students online. This process can be set up to be like a conversation, but it is a conversation that can be engaged in over a long period of time. You are able to score the NanoGong activity and comment using it.

The first thing you will need to do is have your site admin get NanoGong set up for use in your course, or you can set up your own Moodle installation and use it there. Once you have access to NanoGong, the actual setup is fairly easy.

You are also able to insert NanoGong into Forums. Placing NanoGong activities in Forums allows for running commentary as well as tracking the conversation through text. A Forum-based NanoGong could test both listening or reading and speaking skills. The listening skills could be assessed by forcing the students to listen to your comments or another students' comments and transcribe them or respond to them. Once this is done, you can have the student orally respond to the comment or question. We will discuss how to set this up in a Forum later.

NanoGong Description

The newest version of NanoGong that has been released supports all versions of Moodle, pre-2.0. This version offers several new features and upgrades from the previous versions, one of the big ones being that you are now able to set the length of a student's recording instead of being limited by the software to two minutes or less The setup page of a NanoGong activity is shown in the next screenshot:

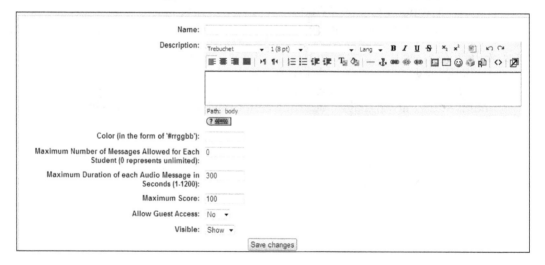

Name

Type in the name of the NanoGong activity in the **Name** textbox.

Description

Enter the instructions for the NanoGong here. Be clear and, if necessary, explain how it works and how it will be scored. You may add images and audio files in the description.

Color (In the form of '#rrggbb')

This is the Hexadecimal or HTML color system we looked at earlier. One quick reference page is located at `http://html-color-codes.info/`. You can alter the color of the player by entering a color scheme in this box.

Maximum Number of Messages Allowed...

This setting determines the number of messages a student is able to record. You can enter the number of recordings you want to allow each student to make. Entering a **0** will allow unlimited recording sessions.

Maximum Duration of Each Audio Message...

This setting allows you to set a time limit for each recording. The time can be set anywhere from 1 second to 1200 seconds (20 minutes). This can be useful for saving space or for forcing students to consider their thoughts and prepare themselves before speaking.

Maximum Score

This setting is used to determine the highest score a student can receive for the NanoGong activity. The students will see their results along with their recording and comments once the teacher has reviewed and marked the recording.

Allow Guest Access and Visible

These are two of the **Common module settings**. **Allow Guest Access** will let people who are not members of your course enter the activity. **Visible** will show the activity.

Setting up your NanoGong

So, let's say we are teaching a Turkish language class and we are interested in testing our students' ability to make descriptive statements about places in Turkish. We will be asking our students to listen to an audio file and then they will need to record their response, using complete sentences.

The first thing we need to do is record our audio file. Our question is going to be very simple, "Please look at the image. I want you to tell me about five things you see in the image. Please use complete sentences and descriptive words. When you are ready to record, click on the **Record** button and start speaking. When you are finished, click on **Stop**" We can use a number of recording methods; however, I'm going to use Audacity like we did before.

Once the audio file is set, I'm going to get a picture to use. I'm going to go to one of the free photo sites online and choose an image that will be a good challenge for my students. I have gone to Wikimedia Commons at: `http://commons.wikimedia.org/wiki/Main_Page` and selected an image that requires I credit the photographer, which is what I will do.

Now that we have the audio file and the image ready, we will create our NanoGong activity. Go to the **Activities** drop-down and create a new **NanoGong**. On the NanoGong **Edit** page, we will give it the name 'Talking about Things'. In the description we will include the audio file and the image just like we did in the chapter on the Quiz module.

For fun, let's say we also want the NanoGong to be a shade of blue. We will choose a color that we like using the Hexadecimal system. We will use #2E9AFE, which is a light blue color.

We will leave the **Maximum number of recordings** set to **0**. We will set the **Maximum length of the recording** to **240 seconds** (four minutes), which should be much more than needed. We will also set the **Maximum score** to **10** points. We will score the sentences in one of three ways. We will give full credit, two points, for a complete and correct sentence. We'll give half credit, or one point, to a sentence with a couple of small mistakes, and an overall good effort. We will give no credit to sentences with multiple errors.

We will leave the **Common module settings** as they are. Once we are finished, we will click on **Save**. We will see the MP3 player, the image, and a list of students enrolled in the course. Since none of them have made an attempt at the NanoGong yet, there is not much to see.

Now, we will log into one of the student accounts I created and see what it looks like from the perspective of one of our students. You will want to use the **Switch role to** option to achieve this result. Here is what they will see when they open the activity. For spacing purposes, I have placed the images side-by-side, however, on the page they would be seen with the audio and image at the top and the NanoGong recorder at the bottom.

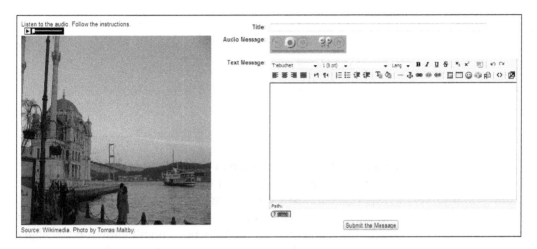

As you can see, our students will see the MP3 player and the image. They will listen to the audio and then they will create their own message responding to our instructions.

They will create a title for their post, then click on the red circle button and record their message. Once they have finished their recording, they click on the square **Stop** button. They can then listen to their recording by clicking on the **Play** button. If they are unhappy, they can repeat the process, which will overwrite the old version. When they are happy with the recording, they can then enter some text in the rich text editor if they'd like. This may be useful for adding additional information related to the recording, like references, their thoughts about the assignment, and so on. Once they finish recording their messages, they click on the **Submit the Message** button. Once the recording is submitted, the student is taken to the front of the NanoGong activity where they can see their work and have the option to make another recording if they'd like.

Now that there is a recording added to the NanoGong, go to the course page and click on the assignment titled **Talking about Things**. Here you can see which students have submitted work, listen to their recordings, and read their comments, if any. This is shown in the next screenshot:

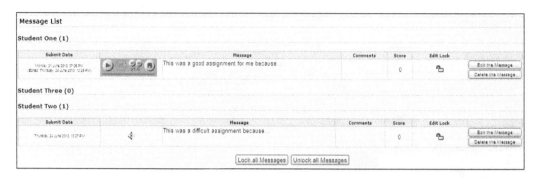

As seen in the previous screenshot, we have a list of the students enrolled in the course on the left, with the time they recorded their message, and a time of student editing, if any. Next to this you will see a speaker, looking something like you see next to **Student Two Submit Date**. Clicking on the speaker will load the NanoGong player, as done for **Student One**. Clicking on the **Play** button will allow you to hear the student's recording. You are also able to speed up or slow down the player by using the left and right arrows to the right-hand side of the **Stop** button. This can be useful to listen for specific sounds, for transcription or for several other reasons. Next to the recording, you see the **Message** column, where you or your students can leave text-based messages. Next to this is the **Comment** column, where comments you may have can be entered. Next we have the **Score** column, and here is where you are able to see the score the student received for their work. The **Edit Lock** column shows you whether or not editing is available in the NanoGong. This can be useful for many reasons, especially if you are testing and don't want any changes made after the initial recording by the student. To lock the messages, click on the **Lock all Messages** button at the bottom of the page. To enable editing, click on the **Unlock all Messages** button. The final column has two buttons. The top button allows you to edit the message and enter your own comment for the students. The bottom button will allow you to completely delete the recording from the activity.

When you click on the **Edit** button, you will be taken to a page similar to what the students see, where you will be able to enter your own recording by recording over the student's recording, enter a message to the student, enter the score, and make your own comments on the student's performance. This is shown in the next screenshot:

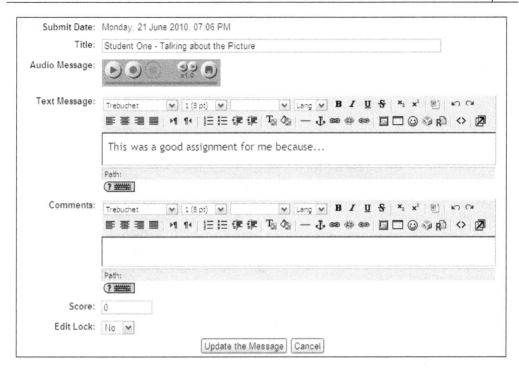

One concern when using this for testing is that you will be recording over the student's original comments. To alleviate this concern, you can click on the **Save** icon on the right-hand side of the recorder, the button that looks like a floppy disk, and keep the files for later reference.

When you have made your recordings, comments, and given your score, click on the **Update the Message** button and the information entered will be saved and available for student review.

> **Playback Speed**
> Students are able to adjust the playback speed of the recordings by pressing the left and right arrows located next to the Save icon. This can help if the listening speed it too fast or too slow for them. Very useful in language classes.

Possible NanoGong ideas

In addition to specific oral tests, NanoGong can play a role in speaking practice by creating an ongoing dialog with your students. Setting a NanoGong to unlimited attempts will allow you and your student to communicate throughout the term in this way.

Another activity you can set up, while not exactly testing is a student-to-student talk, where two students are paired up and discuss an issue or topic using NanoGong. As the instructor, you can listen in and assess their grasp of the subject matter and level of interaction. If you are a language teacher, you can use it to check listening comprehension, speaking skills, and pronunciation.

Voiceboard

Voiceboard is a new module for Moodle that is still in its beta stages, but offers some excellent options for testing speaking as well as offering self, peer, and teacher evaluations. The setup for this activity is very basic and is very similar to the NanoGong activity we just looked at. The difference between Voiceboard and NanoGong is that the Voiceboard activity offers the ability to record multiple audio files and track the comments. The recordings will all be kept in order, under the student's name, so it allows the instructor and student to easily follow a series of speaking assignments. You can see all the posts in context and are able to go back and review previous interactions and keep track of when items were posted. Here is the setup page, which as you can see is very simple in its design as shown in the next screenshot:

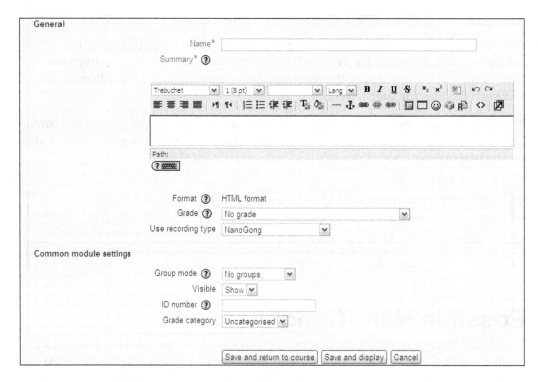

General settings

Now we will take a look at the **General** settings for the Voiceboard module.

Name

Enter the title of the Voiceboard activity here. This is what will be seen on the course page and how the students will identify it.

Summary

Here, you can describe the type of discussion that is going to take place, give directions, grading explanations, and so on.

Format

This is the default format for your text entry, and something we have looked at before. You shouldn't need to do anything here.

Grade

This drop-down offers two grading schemes. The first is the typical 1 to 100, where you will assign a numerical score based on a set of criteria and how well the students completed the assignment based on the criteria given.

The second method offered is called **Scale: Separate and connected ways of knowing**. This grading pattern is based on the idea that there is a separate and a connected system of knowledge. There are three possible 'marks' that can be given if this grading scale is selected: Mostly Separate Knowing, Mostly Connected Knowing, and Separate and Connected. These ideas require some reading up on if you are to make use of them. One place you can get a short overview of the topic is at http://docs.moodle.org/en/Separate_and_Connected_ways_of_knowing. These 'marks' are not added to the Gradebook and have no bearing on the students' grade. The value in using these scores is to help the students see how they use their knowledge and how it affects their interactions and communication skills.

Use recording type

This setting will allow you to change the type of recorder you are using. It will use NanoGong and Flash, although you need to configure a Flash recorder.

Common module settings

These settings have all been looked at earlier and function in the same way as in the prior activities.

We are going to be carrying on a discussion with our students in Turkish. We will cover a variety of topics based on what they have studied in class. Once we have the **Name**, **Summary**, **Grade**, and have selected our player (in our case we will be using NanoGong) we click on the **Save and display** button. The screenshot is as follows:

As you can see, since no one has made any recordings, there is nothing here yet. What we do see is the way the recordings will be organized and a tab for us and the students to make recordings.

We will now go to the **Record audio** tab at the top of the page to record the first message in the Voiceboard. A screenshot of the **Record audio** page follows:

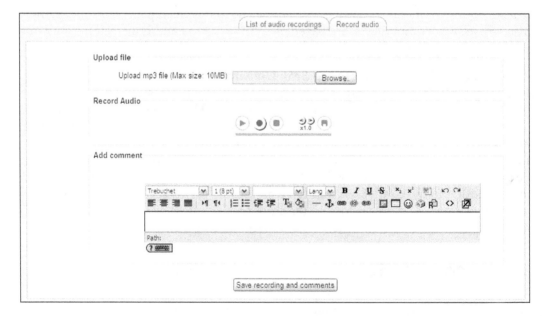

Upload file

As you can see, we have the option to **Upload file**. This can be useful if we already have an audio file with the instructions or whatever other audio we want, for example, if we wanted to use a file that we have previously recorded on Audacity and exported as an MP3. If we have this file ready, we simply click on the **Browse** button and locate the file on our computer.

Record audio

Here you see a NanoGong player. We can record just as before, by clicking on the **Record** button.

Add comment

You can make a comment regarding the recording here. This comment will be displayed in the **Comment** column on the **List of audio recordings** page.

We will not upload a file, but we will make our own recording using the NanoGong player. Again, every new recording will overwrite the previous one, and recordings can be reviewed by using the **Play** button. Once we have finished and are satisfied with the recording, we will add a comment then click on the **Save recording and comments** button. When you click on this button, you will get a small message on the top right of your screen telling you that the recording was saved and will be moved to the **List of audio recordings** page.

Once we are on the **List of audio recordings** page, we will see our new entry. This is shown in the next screenshot:

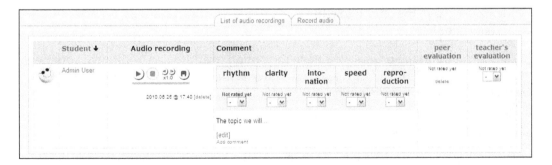

Now that we have some information in the columns, we can talk about them in more detail.

Student

This column, and the column to the left-hand side of it, show the student's name and a profile picture, if there is one.

Audio recording

This column holds the NanoGong player. Clicking on the **Play** button will allow you to listen to the recording.

Under the player, the date and time of recording are noted. There is also a **Delete** button. Clicking on it will allow you to delete the audio file. This could become necessary at some point, for example, if a student were to use profanity or something else offensive, but for the most part, you won't want to delete these files.

Comment

This is the where we can grade and comment on the student's work. As you can see, there are several categories available for assessing the student's performance. These categories are: **Rhythm**, **Clarity**, **Intonation**, **Speed**, and **Reproduction**. Each of the categories has an associated drop-down menu with numbers ranging from one to five, one being the lowest score possible and five being the highest.

These categories are used for self-evaluation and can be very helpful for teachers. Students who self-assess correctly are often hard on themselves and the scores they give themselves can offer you an insight as to where they feel they are lacking in skill. This can help you focus on helping them feel more confident in those areas or offering additional instruction or practice in the target sub-skill.

Students also have the option to edit their comments or even add an additional comment.

As an instructor in the course, you have the option of adding an additional comment as well. This comment will be displayed underneath the student comment and will be set off by a black border, so the student will be able to spot it immediately.

Peer evaluation

A student's work is also available for peer review. Another student in the course is able to listen to the recording and offer their own evaluation of the student's work. This can be a useful tool both for students and instructors.

Depending on the number of students making peer evaluations, this number will adjust. The first evaluation will always be a whole number because the drop-down menu where you select the score only shows these options. However, when a second student adds their score, the numbers will be added to the first score and averaged. The students will not see any individual scores, only the total. They will also not be able to see who evaluated them, which increases the chances of honest reporting.

As an instructor, you also have the option of removing obviously malicious or seriously flawed evaluations.

Teacher evaluation

Here is where your grade for the student's performance will be displayed.

If you feel afterwards that the evaluation you gave was incorrect, simply click on the **Edit** link and you will be able to change the score.

A completed assessment with comments and recordings is shown in the next screenshot:

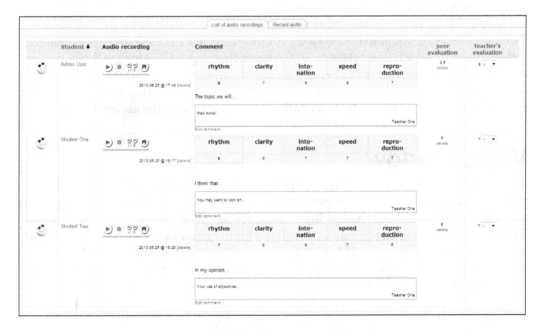

As seen in the previous screenshot, three people took part in the activity. They recorded audio, completed self-evaluations and commented on their performance. Each participant received peer and teacher evaluations as well as teacher comments.

This has the potential to be a very useful addition to your Moodle site, especially if you are interested in self and peer evaluations of student speaking skills. In addition, by keeping these items available for students over the course of a term or year, the students will be able to see progress in terms of their speaking abilities.

Notes on Voiceboard

This is still in beta, so there are a few issues that still need to be worked out. The first one is that the categories for evaluations are set. You can't make any changes to the category names. To get around this, in your **Summary**, you could tell students that the grade for the **Intonation** category will be used for X. This is something that has been noted by the developer and something they are considering changing. However, the intended use of this module is not the way I have presented it here. It was intended for language students to practice their speaking using pre-scripted material.

The second issue is the way the **Grading** drop-down functions. In most drop-down menus, you have the option of making adjustments to your grade if you decide later that you evaluated the item incorrectly. This is very important because there are times when this happens. However, in the Voiceboard, the choices once made are locked. There is a way around this, but it requires a couple more steps than is really necessary. If you make a mistake, you need to click on the **Edit** link under self-evaluation, which will take you to the recording page. Clicking on **Save recording and comments** will keep the recording and comments as they are, but will bring you back to the **List of audio recordings** page. The other option available is logging out and back in, which will allow you to revaluate the assignment.

Voiceshadow

This activity is similar to Voiceboard and is also just getting ready for release. It allows for self, peer, and teacher evaluations and can be a useful way to test speaking skills. It is envisioned as a shadowing activity for language learners. Shadowing is a technique used by language instructors that tries to get students to listen and repeat what they hear. A student will listen to an audio file or watch a video file and repeat what he/she hears, as soon as he/she hears it. If you are interested in learning more about this technique, a website describing this idea in more detail is `http://www.foreignlanguageexpertise.com/foreign_language_study.html#svd`. However, this module offers more possibilities than shadowing. We will look at how to use it for shadowing first, then at some testing possibilities. The setup page is shown in the next screenshot:

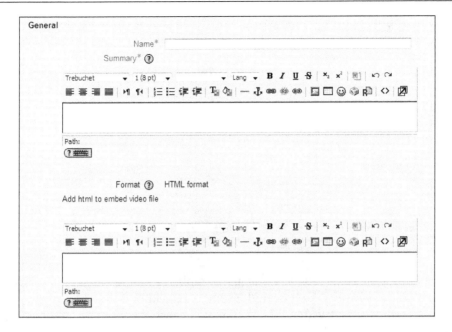

General

This section contains the basic information shown to students as well as a place to embed video for shadowing.

Name

Enter the name you want to use for the activity here. This will be what the students see on the course page.

Summary

The students will see this at the top of the page when they open the activity. Enter information about the activity and instructions for the activity here.

Add html to embed video file

If you want to embed a video to this activity, you have two options. The first is to enter some HTML code into the editor. To do this, you will need to use the `<embed/>` tag. This, while it isn't too difficult and you can find a variety of websites and online guides to walk you through the process, is not the easiest or best way.

The second option, and by far the easiest way to do this, is to locate the video you want on YouTube or some similar site. These sites will have a button or some other function that will allow you to embed the video. YouTube requires that you copy and paste a long piece of code into your site. In Voiceshadow, you will need to copy the HTML code from the YouTube embed code and paste it into the **Add HTML to Embed Video File**. I have found a video about Shadowing and now I want to embed it. Here is what the embed code will look like when copied and pasted from YouTube:

```
<object width="480" height="385"><param name="movie"
value="http://www.youtube.com/v/130bOvRpt24&hl=en_US&fs=1&"></
param><param name="allowFullScreen" value="true"></param><param
name="allowscriptaccess" value="always"></param><embed src="http://
www.youtube.com/v/130bOvRpt24&hl=en_US&fs=1&" type="application/x-
shockwave-flash" allowscriptaccess="always" allowfullscreen="true"
width="480" height="385"></embed></object>
```

It is a pretty long piece of code to write just to embed a single video clip, which is why it is easier to simply take it from the source instead of doing it yourself. Adding this HTML to the **Embed Video File** textbox will cause the video to be seen under the **Summary** you entered.

You can also do this if you have your own video that you want to use. By far the easiest way to do this is to upload it to a site like YouTube. Once it is uploaded, you will be able to get the embed code from them without having to type it out yourself. If you don't know how to upload a video to a site like this, check out this link from YouTube at `http://help.youtube.com/support/youtube/bin/topic.py?hl=en&topic=16560` explaining all kinds of things from how to upload a video to advanced features like tag formats.

Once you have the video file you want added, you can move on to the **Common module settings** to make any changes you want there or you can simply click on the **Save and display** button to see what you have.

If you don't want to use a video for this activity, move down the page to the next section called **Record audio** as shown in the next screenshot.

Record audio

This section allows us to create simple audio files for shadowing, allows us to change the type of recorder we are using, and is where we set our grades.

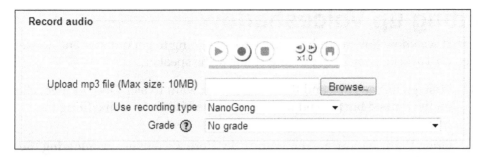

Player

As you can see, if we have installed NanoGong, there is a player embedded for use in this section. You are able to record audio for shadowing using this player. Whenever you record here it will be heard by students when they click on **Play**.

Upload mp3 file

This will allow you to upload an audio file you have previously recorded or any other MP3 file you would like to use for the activity. Click on the **Browse** button and follow the process we have gone through in the previous activities to upload audio files.

Use recording type

Here, like in Voiceboard, you can choose to use either NanoGong or another installed player. We will be using NanoGong again.

Grade

Again, this is the same as Voiceboard. It offers **No grade**, scores of 1 to 100 and the separate and connected ways of learning assessment.

Common module settings

Again, these settings are the same as we have looked at in the previous modules.

Setting up Voiceshadow

Now that we know how to embed video, we are going to get our students to watch a video on Turkish from YouTube and shadow the speaker.

1. First, go to YouTube and find a video you want to use. Once located, click on the **Embed** button and it will reveal the HTML for embedding the selected video.

2. Open Voiceshadow and enter the title. Here we will use **Shadowing the months in turkish**.

3. In the **Summary**, we will enter the assignment instructions and how it will be graded.

4. In the **Add HTML to Embed Video File**, we will include the HTML we got from the YouTube **Embed** button.

5. In the **Record audio section**, we will do nothing except assign a grade for the activity. We will use 5.

6. Leave all the **Common module settings** as they are.

7. When finished, click on the **Save and display** button.

We will be brought to a page that mirrors the Voiceboard's **List of audio recordings** page. At this point, there will be nothing here, because nothing has been added yet. From here, we will click on the **Record audio** tab and we will see the embedded video and all of our options. This is shown in the next screenshot:

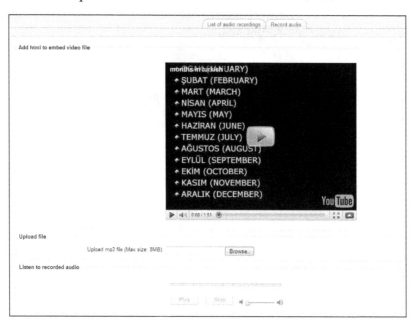

As you can see, the very top of the page shows the embedded video. Under this we see a place to upload files. This **Upload file** feature is useful if students have recorded audio on a different system or external recording device and want to use it. This could be the case if there are insufficient/non-functioning headsets but there are some handheld MP3 recorders available. While this feature may not be used extensively, it is a useful addition to the module.

Following the **Upload file** section we see the **Listen to recorded audio section**. If you have decided to use audio files instead of video files, the students will click on the **Play** button here to listen to the audio file uploaded. Under this button is the audio recorder as shown in the next screenshot:

The **Record audio** is where the students will shadow the embedded video or audio file. They will watch or listen to the file and press record to shadow the speech.

The final section to the **Record audio** tab is the **Add comment** section, where students are able to make comments on their performance, feelings, or anything else regarding the assignment.

Once the student has recorded his/her voice and added any comments he/she has, he/she will click on the **Save recording and comments** button to be taken back to the **List of audio recordings** page, which again is set up just like the Voiceboard, offering the same columns, options, as well as self, peer, and teacher evaluations.

The Voiceshadow and Voiceboard are two new modules that will help with testing and assessing speaking using Moodle. Voiceshadow has applications other than shadowing. For example, you could have students view a video clip and comment on it. You could upload a news file and have students listen and summarize the story, or have students listen to a piece of music and describe how they felt while listening. There are many applications for this module outside of shadowing, and if the developers offer a method to alter the names and number of assessment items, it will be even better.

Speaking tests in Forums

Another way to use NanoGong is in Forums. Using Forums can be a useful way to track conversations, practice pronunciation, or have a Q&A session with your students, and this can function much like an audio log. This type of speaking test or activity can be done as a class, in groups, or individually.

In addition, using the Forum's **Grade** settings, you can give grades and those scores will be included in the Gradebook. The Forum's **Grade** section is shown in the next screenshot:

- **Aggregate type** is as we have seen before, the options being: No ratings, Average of Ratings, Count of Ratings, Maximum of Ratings, Minimum of Ratings, and Sum of Ratings.

- The **Grade** scale can be set as we have seen in the Voiceboard and Voiceshadow, the options being: Separate and Connected Ways of Knowing, No Grade, or on a scale from 1 to 100.

- If **Restrict ratings to post with dates in this range** is selected, it will ensure the students complete the assignment within the time period provided, and if they don't, they will be penalized.

Once we have decided that we want to create a speaking test or activity in a Forum, the first thing we will need to do after initially installing NanoGong is to set up the Filters and HTML area. Setting up the HTML area will allow NanoGong recordings to happen directly in the forums. The process for doing this is fairly simple; all you need to do is extract the appropriate files to the appropriate places. The instructions for doing this are located at http://gong.ust.hk/nanogong/moodle_inst.html.

Once you have it installed, and this is something the site administrator will need to do, you will see a new icon button added to the HTML bar in your Forum. This is shown in the next screenshot:

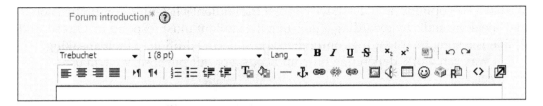

As you can see here, there is now an **Insert/Modify Sound** icon located between the **Insert image** and **Insert table** icons. Clicking on this icon will open a pop-up window containing a NanoGong player. You will be able to record directly into this and it will be added to the Forum. Let's walk through setting one up. Here is what the pop-up window looks like:

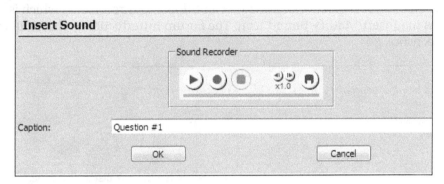

As seen from the previous screenshot, this simple pop-up gives you access to the recorder and allows you to enter a **Caption**. I have entered **Question #1** for ours. Note that the sound file is automatically saved after recording. The **Save** button is only used if you want to export the file.

Setting up an Audio Forum

I am going to assume everyone is, at this point, comfortable setting up Forums, but if you aren't please check out this link: `http://docs.moodle.org/en/mod/forum/index`. We are going to call ours 'Turkish Q&A Test #1'. We want this to be individual student tests, so we will set our Forum up as Each Person Posts One Discussion. In our Audio Forum Introduction, we will explain the test directions and guidelines.

For the grading, we will set it to an **Average of Ratings** and the **Grade** will be out of a possible 20 points.

We have two options now. First, we can test the student's listening comprehension and speaking skills by recording a question the student must respond to. Our second option is testing their reading comprehension skills in addition to their speaking. Either way can work, depending on your needs. For our purpose, we will use the former.

Now, we will record our initial question and wait for the students to respond. Our initial question will be something simple, and from there we will move on to more complex or advanced grammar and vocabulary. We will give our question the caption Question #1.

When we have recorded our question and are happy with it, we will click on the **Save and display** button. When we do this, we will see our new Forum displayed, showing any text or image we've added, in addition to our recording, which is shown as the **Insert/Modify Sound** Icon. The Forum Introduction is shown in the next screenshot:

Once the speaker icon is clicked on, the player will load and the students will be able to listen to the recording you've made. Once they listen, they will need to click on the **Add a new discussion topic** button to make their response. They will follow the same pattern, clicking on the **Insert/Modify Sounds** button, recording their response, and posting it.

Once the student posts their response, you can go to their post and listen to what they said. Once you have listened, you can rate the student's performance and make another post yourself. An example of a forum with the instructor interacting with multiple students is shown in the next screenshot:

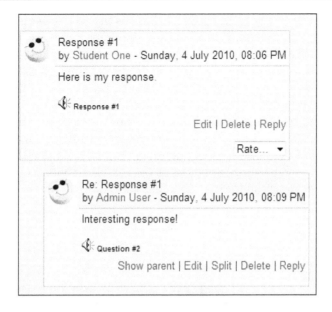

This is a good way to keep track of performance and language development, especially if done over an entire course or term.

Real-time conversations

Of course, testing speaking skills is best done when actually interacting with your subject in real time. Using computers takes away the physical face-to-face component of this interaction, but we can still have synchronous conversations, like on the phone, and we can still see our conversation partners if we have the correct setup. One of the modules that allows this is the Skype module.

Skype module

Skype allows real-time conversations to take place over the Internet for free with other users of Skype or for low rates to non-users. The Skype module for Moodle allows you to set up video conferences with your students or have them video conference with each other. They can also chat and send files. The Skype module offers teachers the ability to engage their students in real conversations from anywhere. In a lab setting, this allows the teacher to interact with specific students and assess their skills while the rest of the class is working on some other assignment. This is one of the best methods available for real-time, synchronous assessment of speaking.

One thing to be aware of before using this module is that all students and teachers who want to take part in the module are required to have Skype installed on their computers and create a Skype account. It is easy and free and takes about five minutes or less. To download Skype and to create your Skype account, go to Skype.com. Once you have an account, you need to go to your Moodle profile and in the **Optional** section towards the bottom, click on the **Advanced** button, which will show a list of additional, personal, and contact information. One of the options is **Skype ID**. In the **Skype ID** textbox, enter your Skype ID. If you do not do this, you will not be able to access the Skype module. Make sure all the students that you want to take part in the activity have also done this. Once everyone is part of the activity, you can go forward and create it. The setup screen for the module is shown in the next screenshot:

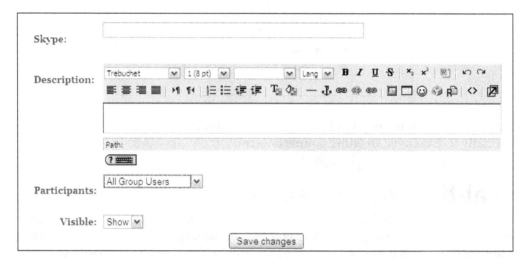

As shown previously, it is very simple to set up.

1. In the **Skype** textbox, add the name you want the students to see.

2. In the **Description**, give instructions for how the activity will run and any other pertinent information the students will need to know.

3. In the **Participants** section you have the option to leave this at its default setting, **All Group Users**, which will allow everyone in the course access to the Skype activity, or you can change this setting to **All Course Teachers**, which will only allow the teachers to access the activity.

4. The **Visible** option, as before, simply shows the activity or hides it from students.

5. Once you click on the **Save changes** button, you will be directed to a page where you can initiate the activity.

What you will see is shown in the next screenshot:

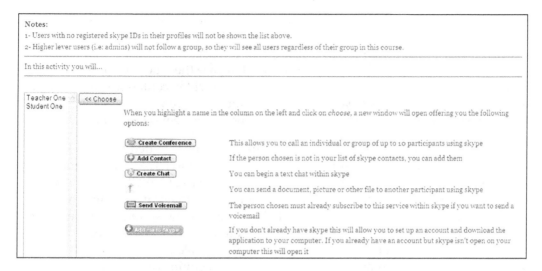

There are a lot of options and information on this page, but the one we are going to look at is the **Create Conference** button.

To begin your speaking test with your student, you will click on the student's name, in our case, **Student One**, and click on the **Choose** button. This will open a small window with each of the module options available. In this window, you will click on the **Create Conference** button. A second window will open, this one asking which application to launch. Skype should already be selected, so you should simply have to click on **OK**. If for some reason Skype is not shown, click on the **Choose** button and locate and select **Skype**, then click on **OK**. Once you do this, Skype will open and the conversation can begin.

In addition to teacher to student or student to student conversations, you can create groups of up to ten users who can all be active participants by using the **Create Conference** call feature. This can be very useful in assessing dynamic speaking skills such as speaking strategies or group fluency and interactions.

If you want to grade this student, you will need to create an offline assignment to grade it. You may also want to record the conversation to review later. There are many ways to record conversations on Skype. CallBurner, which can be found at `http://www.callburner.com/`, and HotRecorder, found at `http://www.hotrecorder.com/`, are two programs that allow you to do this. Both of these are easy to use and free and can be set up in minutes.

Skype is an easy way to do real-time conversational or speaking assessment in Moodle. If you are looking to test your students' speaking ability, this module is highly recommended.

COVCELL

COVCELL means Cohort-Oriented Virtual Campus for Effective Language Learning and its development was funded by the European Commission. It is a collection of activities, with applications such as Audio Recording, Whiteboard, Chat, and a few others. The important ones for testing speaking are the Audio recorder and the Audio-Video Conference. This is similar to the Skype video conference, in that you are able to invite members of your course to a video conference. This is a very useful tool for testing speaking skills such as conversational strategies or fluency.

The big drawback to the COVCELL is that it has not been updated for a while and it is fussy about system requirements. You will need to have your system administrator install a specific server, Red5, in order to use COVCELL. If you are on a hosted server, chances are that you will not be able to use it, and since many people are using hosted servers or are not able to change the system they are using, this isn't practical for many users. However, if you have your own server, you can install the appropriate software and then you will able to use it. To find the system requirements and an overview of COVCELL activities and features, go to `http://covcell.org/images/documents/srs2-final.pdf`. You might also look on the Moodle.org pages related to language teaching, which go into discussion about the module located at `http://moodle.org/mod/forum/view.php?id=5368`.

If you are able to install COVCELL Audio-Video Conferencing, you will be able to choose members of your course and speak with them individually or in groups, as you can in the Skype module, although the COVCELL does offer the benefit of not requiring students to register for an outside application.

Summary

As you can see, there are a lot of activities and modules that can be adapted to test and assess your students' speaking abilities. We have looked at a few modules here that I feel are useful for testing students' speaking skills and also offer varied approaches to interacting with the students via Moodle. However, we have only looked at a few modules here. There are many more options you could use, some inside of Moodle and some external. Now that you have a basic grasp of several methods to test speaking with, you will be able to begin to use Moodle for speaking tests and from there, you will begin to experiment with alternative methods and new modules. There are always modules being developed, and some will work better for you and for your situations than others will. Once you are comfortable using Moodle to test your students speaking ability, I highly recommend looking for alternative methods. If you find that nothing meets your needs, start a discussion about it; maybe you or someone else will develop what you envision. Finally, if you want to interact with some people regarding speaking activities and methods, get on Moodle's site and start searching for what you want to know; chances are someone else will have already asked and answered it. Now, we will move on and take a look at ways we can use Moodle to test writing.

10
Testing Writing

Testing writing is a tough task, whether on paper or on computer, but can be one of the most fulfilling for students and can really show you the range of language skills and knowledge the student has regarding the target language or topic. Assessing a student's writing skills requires the instructor to first instruct a student in the type of writing they will be assessed on, create and explain the parameters of the assignment and how the grading will be done. Then, you need to give the students time to write, edit, and rewrite, then submit their work. The components that will be assessed in a writing assignment can be varied, but may include: clarity of thought, content, grammar, paragraph or essay organization, and vocabulary. Once this has been decided on, it is your job to carefully read through each piece of writing, evaluate it, and give effective and useful feedback. Moodle can help this process but, unfortunately, you still need to do most of this manually. We will look at testing writing in stages. In this chapter, we will learn about:

- Setting up a Forum as a writing portfolio
- Pre-writing assignments
- Writing assignments
- Finding plagiarism

Choosing a portfolio

There are many ways in which writing can be assessed. I prefer to teach writing using a process strategy, and I feel that this is also a good way to assess students' writing skills. One of the ways I do this is by creating a writing portfolio. Writing portfolios are collections of a student's work, which showcase their writing, and while a portfolio can contain all of their writing samples, it usually contains only select pieces. The pieces included usually show writing assignments from the beginning of the course until the end, which shows their growth as a writer.

Using Moodle, there are many ways to do this. You have the option to use external portfolio software like Elgg or Mahara. Elgg is an open source social network package that allows you to create local or school-wide social networks. This can be used in different ways and could be set up to act as a portfolio. For more information about Elgg, check the following site: `http://elgg.org/`. Mahara, however, was created to be a free and open source e-portfolio package that offers a lot of options for personalization and acts as a social networking system, and most importantly, it integrates very well with Moodle.

So, what can Mahara do? Well, like Moodle, it allows users to set up personalized profiles including usernames, contact information, messaging options, and so on. It also allows users to make decisions on who can access their work and network and allows for easy teacher-student and student-student communication.

In the portfolio section, Mahara has developed an easy and intuitive way to lay out the pages. Students can choose which blocks they want to display by simply clicking and dragging the blocks into their display layout. Students have the option to include: files, folders, images, RSS feeds, blogs, and so on.

The drawback with Mahara is that it requires a server to run it and if you are using a hosted site, this could prove problematic for you. We did not go into too much detail about Mahara here other than a brief overview, but I recommend going to its site at `http://mahara.org` to look at the demo, sign up for a free portfolio, and see if it is something you would like to use in your class or school. If it is, the installation process is well-documented and fairly easy to follow. You can find more information about the installation process at: `http://wiki.mahara.org/ System_Administrator%27s_Guide/Installing_Mahara`.

Another option for creating writing portfolios is using a blogging site. Blogging sites like `Blogger.com` or `Wordpress.com` offer free blog hosting and using these services, you can upload your work, comments, images, as well as allow others to read and comment on your posts.

Moodle also offers contributed portfolio modules. One of the more useful options available is the Exabis e-portfolio block. It can be used for nearly everything you could want in a portfolio, from note-taking and uploading files to a place to store all your favorite links. It is well-documented and we will not go into how to set it up since all the information related to it is available in detail on the `Moodle.org` site by going to this link: `http://docs.moodle.org/en/Exabis_e-portfolio_block`.

Another option, and the one we will look at, is using Forum to create portfolio-type activities. We can use Forums to create places where students can show their work as well as give and get feedback. Personally, I find Forums to be some of the most useful places to write and assess writing, since the entire interaction and all the drafts are included in the thread, which can be browsed anytime, allowing feedback to be reviewed and acted on, as well as allowing the instructor to rate each thread in a variety of ways. We will go through how to set up a very basic way of creating a portfolio for your students using Forums.

Forum-based writing portfolios

Using Moodle's Forum is one way to create simple portfolios of your students' writing, and it is an easy way to integrate portfolio-type work into your course. Students will be able to upload images, audio, video, and files, and classmates and teachers will be able to comment.

Step 1

First, you will need to set up the Forum for the portfolios. Open your course and create a new Forum with an appropriate title; here we will use 'Writing Portfolio'. In the Forum Introduction, we will write an explanation of the purpose and use of the Writing Portfolio Forum.

When you are setting this up, make sure to change **Forum Type** to **Each person posts one discussion**. This will allow each student to set up their own thread to work with. This thread can continue throughout the course, used for a series of assignments, or it can be used for a single assignment.

For grading, and this will depend on your needs for your class, but for now, we will use the **Count of ratings**, which is important here because we want to make sure the students submit each of the stages of writing we will be going through. For grades, we will select an appropriate score from the **Grade** drop-down menu. For our example we will use 5, which will include a pre-writing stage (1), the initial draft (1), peer editing (1), a second draft, which will include teacher comments (1), and a final draft (1).

We will leave all the other settings as they are for now, then click on **Save and display**.

Step 2

Once students enter the newly created portfolio they will see a button titled **Add a new discussion topic**. Clicking on this button will bring them to where they need to be to create their first entry in the portfolio.

In the subject line, I find it best to have students enter their name and the title of their writing since this makes it easy to quickly identify whose work you are looking at and what you're reading about.

In the message section, students will enter the text of the first draft of their writing assignment. This can be done in several ways. The simplest way is to type directly into the Message area in the forum. Some people are more comfortable typing in word processors. Typing in a word processor and then copying and pasting it is another option; however, this often includes formatting information that is invisible in the word processor itself. Occasionally, when copied and pasted in the forum, it can leave sections of junk characters at the top or bottom of the post. To get around this, you may open a simple text editor and copy and paste the writing from the word processor into the text editor, which can then be copied and pasted directly into the Message area. This will eliminate any of the formatting junk at the top or bottom of the post.

If you want to keep the students' documents in their word-processed form, you can have your students simply upload their files using the **Attachment** option under the Message textbox.

Once the writing has been successfully added to the Message area, students will click on the **Post to forum** button.

Once students post the entry, they have up to 30 minutes to edit. Once this time has elapsed, students will no longer be able to make any changes to the original posts.

Here is an example of an initial posting in the Forum from the instructors view. By adding the student name, here seen as **Student One**, and the title of the work to the subject line, you have immediate access to who and what you are working with. I know this may seem redundant since the profile name is located directly below, but some students may go by nicknames or change their profile names, which can occasionally cause confusion.

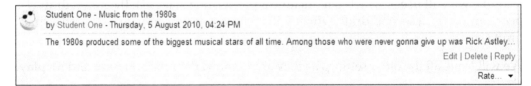

Student One - Music from the 1980s
by Student One - Thursday, 5 August 2010, 04:24 PM

The 1980s produced some of the biggest musical stars of all time. Among those who were never gonna give up was Rick Astley...

Edit | Delete | Reply

Rate... ▾

Step 3

Once the 30 minutes for editing has elapsed, you can go into the post and begin to assess the student's work. For our assignment here, you, as the teacher, will not be making any comments yet. We will do a little peer editing. You should decide on partners for the students and have them enter their partner's post, read the post, and comment on it. Once the reply to the original post has been made, there will be a 1 shown in the **Replies** column, notifying the student that their work has been reviewed.

The student should then look at the new comments from their partner and make any necessary changes or respond with comments or questions of their own.

Here is an example of how this would look to a student looking at their first feedback.

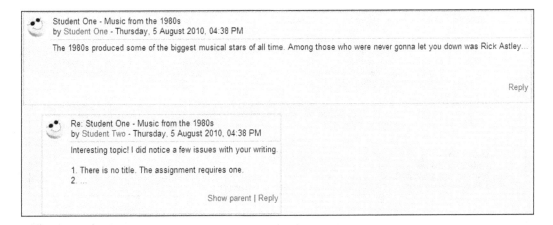

Step 4

Student One will then go back and make the necessary changes and repost. This could happen multiple times depending on the time available and the type of assignment the class is working on. When all peer editing is completed, the instructor would then go in and make some additional comments and assess the work.

This stage is one of the reasons why Forums are so good for writing assessment. As an instructor, you have the option to edit the content of the student's work. You can take a student's work and copy and paste it over to a new post in which you will be able to highlight sections you want to point out, change font colors or font type, underline text, and boldface certain points or for emphasis. You are also able to go in and make comments in the text itself. This is an important part of giving feedback and can be valuable to the writer.

An example of how an instructor has marked up a piece of work is shown in the next screenshot:

Re: Student One - Music from the 1980s
by Admin User - Thursday, 5 August 2010, 05:18 PM

Music from the 1980's *(Delete apostrophe; Center title)*

The 1980s produced some of the biggest musical stars of all time, some of which we are never gonna *(going to - do not use gonna, wanna, or the like in writing)* give up. Among those who were never gonna *(same as above)* let you down with a performance was Rick Astley. He was a solid musician and had the voice to prove it. *(How do we know he was a 'solid musician'?)* He was seen as a performer who was never gonna *(same as above)* run around or desert you or any of his other fans. In fact, he promised to never make anyone cry or say goodbye to performing. He didn't tell a lie there. *(This seems strange. What exactly do you mean here? Please rewrite this part.)* He kept his promise and kept from hurting the fans by continuing to play shows around the world.

Unfortunately today, there are those who make fun of him, his hair, and his lyrics. This was termed 'Rickrolling' and it is not funny. Rick Astley was one of the great musical talents of the 1980s, and while we may have different musical tastes today, we should not disparage him for doing what the people and time wanted. He knew the game and he played it - and won! *(I like this ending!)*

Student One:
1. Make the changes I suggest.
2. Some parts of this don't seem to make sense. Please read through it and make sure this flows as it should.
3. If you are going to focus on Rick Astley, please add more facts about him, his life, etc.

As seen in the previous screenshot, the student will be able to quickly spot points of concern from the teacher and know exactly which aspects of his/her writing need to be reviewed.

This technique is not available only to instructors. Peer editors can do the exact same thing, and should be encouraged to use this format to help their classmates in improving their writing.

Once the student has reviewed the comments and adjusted his/her work, he/she will be able to reply to the post and add his/her final draft to the same thread.

By using the Moodle Forums to create a series of steps in the writing process, you and your students will be able to review all the steps taken to get to the final draft. This, in and of itself, is a valuable tool for learning how to write and practicing the writing process.

If you decide to have students add files as attachments instead of adding the text to the Forum Message textbox, students should be able to use the track changes function in their word processor to do the same thing as we have just seen. It will simply mean that they will have to go through extra steps and the writing will not be immediately visible in the Forum thread.

You have four options on how to view the threads. You can display them flat, with either oldest and newest posts being first. You can also view them in threaded form, showing only the post you are currently reading with the others shown as links. The final option is to view them nested, which will show you all the posts nested in a chronological order.

Now we have only looked at one way to create a single thread in Forum, which can be used to hold all stages of a student's writing. There are, of course, other ways to set up portfolios. You could use the database module to file work away, you could use one of the contributed portfolio modules, or you might devise a way I haven't even considered. However, using Forums, especially if you have used them in your courses already, is a simple and easy way to set up collections of student work. What we have seen here is only an example, and there are other ways to set it up. Allowing multiple threads to be posted by each student is one option. What really matters is that you choose a way that will work for you and your context, as well as something that makes it easy for you to review and assess.

Pre-Writing

When you begin writing, it is important to prepare to write. To do this, many students are taught mind mapping or brainstorming activities, which help focus thought and bring out what you know about a topic or subject.

What is a mind map? A mind map is a visual way of organizing thoughts and ideas, which help students develop ideas for writing; all of the ideas developed are extended from a core idea or theme. This is usually done with paper and pen; however, there is a third-party module available in Moodle that will allow your students to create theirs in the course and allow it to be visible to other course members.

Another technique used is brainstorming. This is usually done in groups with the object of helping develop ideas for some type of project or assignment. Since we will be looking at collaboration between two or more students, in Moodle, one way to ease this process along is using the Wiki module, which allows multiple users to edit a document.

We will first take a look at mind mapping, then look at brainstorming.

Mindmap module

The Mindmap module was developed by Ekpenso.com. It allows you to create mind maps as well as export the maps in several different formats. This module is not part of the core Moodle package so you'll need to download it and add it to your site. To download the Mindmap module go to http://en.ekpenso.com/downloads and follow the installation instructions.

Once the Mindmap module is installed, enter your course and turn editing on. Go to **Add an activity**, and click on the drop-down menu and the **Mindmap** module is available for use.

Select the **Mindmap** and you will be brought to the Mindmap creation page, which is shown in the next screenshot:

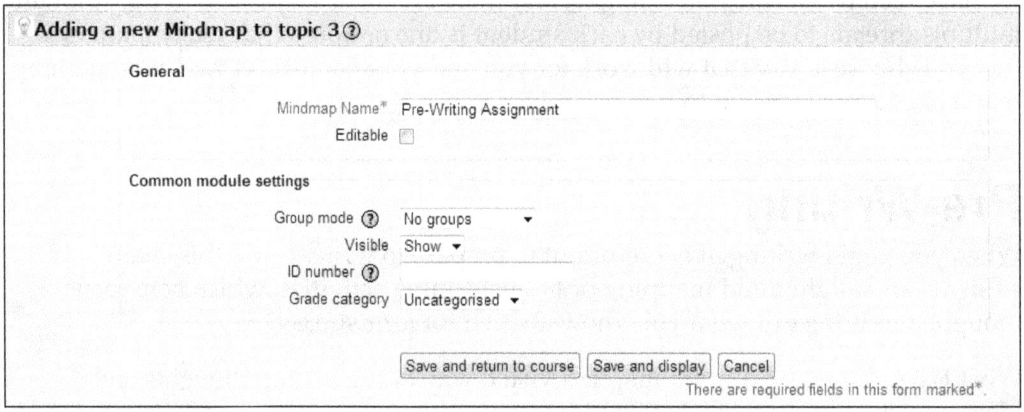

As you can see, this is a very simple setup page. All that really needs to be done is to give the Mindmap a name and determine if it is editable or not. If you leave the **Editable** setting unchecked, students will only be able to view the Mindmap. Leaving it unchecked is useful if you're planning on giving them examples of how a Mindmap should look. However, if you want them to create their own Mindmaps you must check the **Editable** box.

However, if you do nothing to the **Common module settings**, there will only be one Mindmap available for all users. You may set up groupings or create multiple mind maps available to individual students. For information on groupings and setting them up, visit: http://docs.moodle.org/en/index.php?title=Groupings&old id=75013.

Once you have decided on how you want to set up the Mindmap, click on the **Save and return to course** button.

When you get to your course page, you will see the new mind mapping exercise available. Once you click on the Mindmap link, you will see the following screenshot:

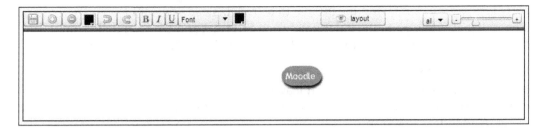

Before any changes are made, the word Moodle will always be shown as a red text bubble in the center of the mind map.

At the top of the box, you will see several commands available. Looking from left-hand side to right-hand side, you can see:

- **Save**: Clicking on this will save the mind map.
- **Add**: Clicking on this will add an additional text bubble.
- **Subtract**: Clicking on this will delete the last text bubble created.
- **Palette**: Clicking on this will open up the color options for the text bubbles. This uses the hexadecimal format so if the color you want is not visible simply enter the code.
- **Undo**: Click on this to undo the last action done.
- **Redo**: Click on this to redo the last step undone.
- **Bold, Italics, Underline, Font**: These are the formatting options available for text and the mind map.
- **Palette**: This is the text palette. It functions same way as the one for the bubbles.
- **Layout**: This button will organize the mind map to make it look as balanced as possible.
- **All**: This drop-down menu will show the number of levels reaching out from the central point. The options are 1, 2, 3, 4, and All. Clicking on option 1 will only show the first level of ideas. Clicking on option 2 would show the first and second level of ideas, and so on.
- **Plus / Minus Slide**: This will make the mind map look either larger or smaller depending on which direction we slide the arrow.

We are going to change? Moodle? to? Testing Writing?. To do this we need to click on the red bubble with the word Moodle. This will highlight the text. All we need to do is type? Testing Writing? and the text will be changed.

Now let's say we don't want the bubble to be red, instead we want to change it to something else. We go to the **Palette** between **Subtract** and **Undo** and click on it. We choose the color we want, in this case I have selected **#0066ff**, a shade of blue.

We do the same thing if we want to change the font or the font color. We are going to change our font to one we like, but leave the font color as it is. Now that we have changed our central theme, the color, and font to what we want it to look like, we can begin to add ideas to our mind map.

Changing colors and fonts

Having each member working on the Mindmap choose a different color or font to post in is a good way for groups to work together. Requiring each group member to choose a specific color or font, can help to determine who put ideas where. If you're assessing the mind map, it also allows you to see how much effort was put into it by each member of the group.

There are two ways to add ideas to the mind map. The first way is to click on the **Add** button located between **Save** and **Subtract**. Clicking on the **Add** button will cause a new bubble to appear. A second and faster way to create more text bubbles is to simply click on any white space inside the mind map. This will create a new text bubble exactly where you click on your mouse.

Each new text bubble will appear with an ellipsis (**...**) already entered. Clicking on the bubble will highlight the **...** enabling you to enter text. Once you finish entering your text, you may want to move the bubble somewhere else. Using your mouse you'll be able to drag this new bubble anywhere you'd like on the screen. You will also see a gray line leading from the central idea to each of the sub-ideas included.

For our mind map, we will use Testing as the central idea. From our central idea, we will create four text bubbles, each containing a separate testing area: **Testing Writing**, **Testing reading**, **Testing Listening**, and **Testing Speaking**. Now, we have four topics in our first level of the mind map. Since we are looking at testing writing, we will add more levels to this subtopic.

To add ideas to the second level we follow the same process, that is, adding the text bubble and entering text into it. Once we've entered the text, we drag the text bubble on top of the topic we want it to be grouped with. For example, we want to include **Pre-Writing Activities** as a subtopic of **Testing Writing**. We create a new text bubble, insert **Pre-Writing Activities** in the text bubble, then drag the bubble on top of **Testing Writing**. By doing this, we will change the connection origin from the central idea or theme to the topic that it has been dragged over. So now our **Pre-Writing Activities** text bubble is no longer directly connected to the central idea, Testing, but is now connected to **Testing Writing**. We will follow this up by including two topics as subcategories of **Pre-Writing Activities**: **Mind Mapping** and **Brainstorming**.

This process can continue as deeply as needed. However, occasionally the ideas added to the mind map will be extensive and you may want to focus on a specific aspect. The Mindmap module allows you to do this by including a plus/minus sign (+/-) next to each topic that has ideas extending from it. By clicking on the minus sign, all the ideas associated with the subtopic will be hidden from view. Clicking on the plus sign will return those ideas to view.

A completed mind map is shown in the next screenshot:

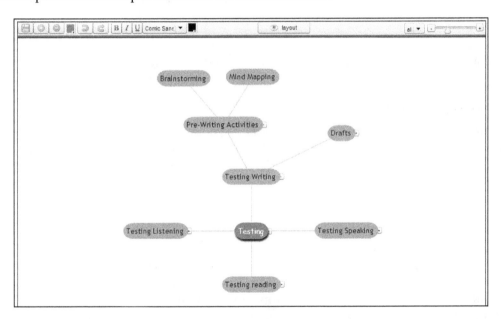

Here, you can see that there are subtopics related to **Testing Listening**, **Testing Speaking**, and **Testing reading**; however, they have been hidden so we are able to better focus on the writing topic.

The Mindmap module is a valuable tool for students in the pre-writing phase. It visually represents ideas and allows sharing between classmates, groups, and the instructor. As an instructor, you will be able to easily see how your students are approaching the topic and what they're likely to include in their writing. Being able to quickly view students' thought patterns may help you to guide them to areas they hadn't previously considered and help them become better writers.

More writing tasks

There are other places where we can test our students' writing skills. The following activities are particularly useful in one-time assignments, such as essays.

Quiz module

Remember the Quiz module Essay item type? In Quiz, this is the easiest way to create writing prompts and give students writing tasks.

This item type is particularly useful for writing-prompt type questions, for example, something like 'Explain how solar panels work.' or 'Why is the sky blue?' The student reads the question or prompt and then sets to work on composing his/her response.

Once the students have submitted their work, you will need to enter the quiz, read and assess their work manually, using the **Manual Grading** tab, then enter a grade.

Assignment

Assignments are an integral part of Moodle and one we have not looked at yet. There are four basic Assignment activities available: **Offline activity**, **Online text**, **Upload a single file**, and **Advanced uploading of files**, which is great for writing assignments with multiple drafts.

Offline activity

This type is used for activities that are not completed online. Typically, this is used for explaining assignment to students via Moodle as well as adding a grading place in the Gradebook, which we will look at in the next chapter. For testing writing, this could be used to provide an essay prompt, to explain the assignment parameters, and the like. So, students access the assignment in their Moodle course, then complete the assignment using their own resources. When the students complete their work, they will physically turn in their writing to the instructor. Once the instructor has completed the assessment of the writing, he/she can go in and add a score to the Gradebook, which the student will then be able to see.

Upload a single file

In this assignment type, students upload a single file to the course. Once a file is uploaded, instructors are able to access the file and assess it. Like the **Offline activity**, this will also include a grade slot in the Gradebook. The setup for this is very simple. The setup page is shown in the next screenshot:.

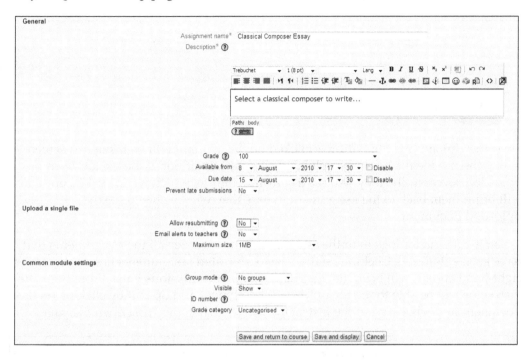

As you can see, in the general section we have the standard name, description, grade, dates, as well as the ability to prevent late submissions.

In the **Upload a single file** section, we have the ability to allow students to resubmit their work and e-mail teachers when the work has been submitted, as well as to limit the size of the files uploaded.

When the student accesses the page, he/she will see the description of the assignment at the very top. If you have enabled the date settings, directly under the assignment description, students will see the date the assignment is available from and when it is due.

Under this, they will see an **Upload a file** textbox, where they can manually enter the file location or browse to locate it. Once they have added it, click on the **Upload this file** button. This is shown in the next screenshot:

Once the **Upload this file** button is clicked on, the student will be taken to a screen telling them if the file has been uploaded successfully or not. If the file has been uploaded successfully, they will see a **continue** button, which when clicked on will bring them back to the assignment, where they will be able to see the uploaded document.

When the instructor logs in to the assignment, they will see all the assignments that have been submitted. Clicking on the **View submitted** assignments link in the upper right-hand corner, will bring the instructor to the **Submissions** page. From here, the instructor will be able to see the uploaded assignment and open it by clicking on the document link. This is what the instructor will see when they first open the page:

Once the teacher has read the assignment, they click on the **Grade** button in the status column. This will bring up the grade and feedback menu. At the top right-hand side of the screen, you will see a drop-down containing all the grade options available. Choose the grade desired from the drop-down menu. This will be displayed to the student in the Gradebook. There is also a large textbox for assignment feedback, which can be used to give comments and observations on the quality or any other aspect of the work. The menu is shown in the next screenshot:

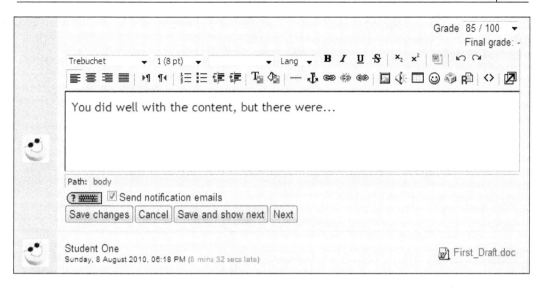

Clicking on the **Save changes** button will return you to the Submissions page. This will be updated with the grade, comments, the time the assignment was reviewed, and the option to update again. Note the **Send notification emails** checkbox under the rich text editor. Uncheck it if you are working on feedback and just want to save it without having an e-mail sent to the student. Here's what the Submissions page will look like after the assignment has been assessed:

Online text

The **Online text** assignment type is an option for creating journals that allow teacher-student communication as well as assignments that will have multiple rewrites before being assigned a final grade. It can also be used as a place for collaboration and reflection. There are many options available with this form of assignment, and ultimately how useful it is and how it is used will depend on your situation.

The setup for this assignment type is very similar to setting up the **Upload a single file** assignment type. The difference is that instead of an **Upload a single file** section we now have an **Online text** section. This is shown in the next screenshot:

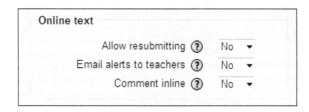

In this section, we see one new option, **Comment inline**. The e-mail alerts and resubmitting options are the same as shown previously.

Comment inline is a useful feature when grading or editing student work. The default setting for this is **No**, which will display the same grade and feedback menu as in the **Upload a single file** activity.

If this option is set to **Yes**, the student's work will show up in the feedback textbox as well as below it. This allows you to make comments directly in the text, while simultaneously keeping an unedited version visible below. You can choose to highlight text, strikethrough, delete, or any of the other options that you have while writing. This can prove a valuable tool for both the student and the teacher. The teacher can quickly highlight issues that each of his/her students have and help them focus on improving those areas. For the student, he/she can quickly and easily see where he/she has made mistakes in his/her writing, which allows him/her to focus on the changes needed.

Assuming that the **Allow resubmitting** option is selected, this can happen as many times as needed. Once the final version has been submitted, the final grade from the teacher will also be given. However, during the process of writing and rewriting, a grade can be given by selecting the score from the drop-down menu.

Advanced uploading of files

This assignment type is similar to the single file assignment type except that it allows students to upload one or more files. Using this assignment type will allow you to work with students going through first drafts, rewrites, and final drafts. There are three sections involved in creating this activity. The **General** and **Common module settings** are identical to those for the single file assignment. The difference between the two activity types is seen in the **Advanced uploading of files** section of the activity. This is shown in the next screenshot.

Advanced uploading of files

Maximum size	1MB ▼
Allow deleting ⑦	Yes ▼
Maximum number of uploaded files ⑦	3 ▼
Allow notes ⑦	No ▼
Hide description before available date ⑦	No ▼
Email alerts to teachers ⑦	No ▼
Enable Send for marking ⑦	Yes ▼

There are several new options here, so will go over each one individually.

Maximum size

This setting determines the largest file size the students will be able to upload. Keep it small if you want students to focus on content rather than formatting or images.

Allow deleting

This allows students to delete files that have been uploaded. The default setting is **Yes**, which will allow students to delete any files uploaded until the assignment deadline has passed or their work is submitted for a grade. If this is set to **No**, students will not be able to make any changes to the files that have been added.

To delete a file, students simply need to press on the **X** icon located to the right-hand side of the files that have been uploaded. Once they click on the icon, they will be prompted to confirm the deletion of the file. Clicking on **Yes** will delete the file from the course.

Maximum number of uploaded files

This determines the maximum number of files a student can upload. The number of files a student can upload ranges from 1 to 20. Also, students are not shown the maximum number of files they can include. You will need to indicate the number of files they will be able to upload somewhere in the assignment description.

Allow notes

The **Allow notes** setting determines whether or not students will be able to make notes in their textbox. You must inform the students about this, or they will not use it. The notes students are able to enter in the textbox function in the same way as in the **Online text** assignment. This can be useful for students so they can remember important points, things to come back to, or to communicate with their instructor.

Hide description before available date

This option allows you to hide the description of the assignment until the assignment is made available. The default here is **No**, which means students will be able to see the description of the assignment at any time. If there is a need to hide this description from students until the beginning of the assignment, change the setting to **Yes**.

Email alerts to teachers

This setting functions exactly as previously stated. By default it is set to **No** and this is where it is usually best to keep it. However, if you really want to receive e-mail announcements whenever students update or submit work, set it to **Yes**.

Enable Send for marking

This allows the student to tell their instructor that they have completed their work and it is ready to be graded, but you must first teach the student how to use it. To be able to **Send for marking**, students must first upload a minimum of one file. Once a file has been added to the course, at the bottom of the assignment page, they will see a new section entitled **Final submission for assignment marking**. Students click on this button to send their work for grading. After clicking on the button they will be brought to a confirmation page where they have the option to confirm or cancel their submission. Clicking on **Yes** will submit the assignment for grading and the students will no longer be able to do anything to the attached files.

There is also an option for you to change the assignment back to an unfinished assignment by clicking on the **Revert to draft** button on the feedback and grading page. An example of what the feedback and grading page looks like in the Advanced uploading of files assignment is shown in the next screenshot:

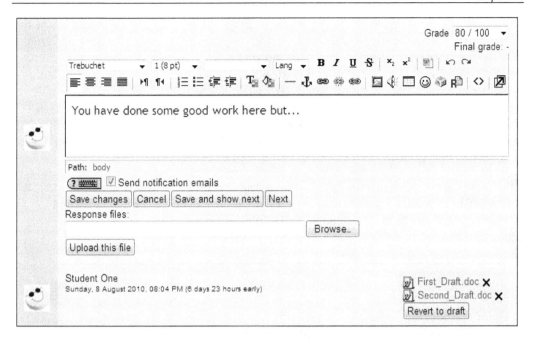

As you can see on the bottom right-hand side, you have the option to delete the drafts or to revert to a draft form. In addition, under the rich text editor you have the option to include additional files for review by the student.

Adding a grade and feedback and clicking on the **Save changes** button will bring you back to the Submissions page and a screen identical to the one seen in the **Upload a single file** assignment.

Using this assignment type for essay writing or extended writing projects is a very good way to assess students. It allows you to keep all files in a central location and review them at any time. It also allows you to follow the progress of the students from the beginning of the project until the end. Note that no peer review is possible unless you override the student permissions on the assignment.

Plagiarism

Plagiarism is a perennial problem for writing instructors. As an instructor you want to ensure that your students are not plagiarizing anyone's work. With the advent of the Internet, more and more material is available for students to access, and it is growing on a daily basis. If you find something that you may feel is not consistent with the student's normal production, you can search the Internet for it, and you may find the original source. However, this can prove to be a time-consuming task.

The most basic way to search for plagiarized material is to simply copy and paste the suspected sentence or paragraph into a search engine and see what comes up. This is often the only way for many of us to find plagiarized material. Sergey Butakov began development of a new block for Moodle called Crot. The block is intended as an anti-plagiarism measure and has two functions. The first function is that it will search local-level submissions to find possible matches. The second function uses the Internet to search for similar work online. In both of these modes, the results will be displayed next to the original submission allowing you to compare the suspected work with another source.

The Crot block is currently in development and it only works with the **Upload a single file** type assignments now, but it can be very useful for many teachers in many situations. You will need site administration privileges to install this block. The link to download the file is `http://moodle.org/mod/data/view. php?d=13&rid=2141filter=1`.

Once Crot is installed, go to **Site administration | Modules | Blocks | Manage blocks | Anti-Plagiarism**. In the settings column of the **Anti-Plagiarism** block click on the **Settings** link. Clicking on this link will take you to the settings for the **Anti-Plagiarism** block. You should see something that looks like this:

Anti-Plagiarism

Be careful modifying these settings - strange values could cause problems.

Settings	
Grammar size:	30
Window size:	60
Colours:	#FF0000,#0000FF, #A0A0(
Max Distance between hashes in the text cluster:	55
Minimum cluster size:	10
Defaul Threshold:	0
Global Search settings	
Global Search Threshold:	90
MS Application ID key:	CHANGE ME!
Global Search Query Size:	7
Percentage of search queries for Web search (1-100):	40
Number of web documents to be downloaded(1=<):	10
Culture info for global search:	en-us
Tools	
Clean tables (WARNING! It removes all Crot data except assignemnts set for check up! Recalculation of fingerprints may cause heavy load on the server)	☐
Check it to perform quick test of global search	☐

Save changes

Initially, you will want to leave the settings as they are. Once you become familiar with the block, then you may want to play with the window size, colors, and so on.

Under the global search settings you will notice an **MS Application ID Key** entry. In the textbox you can see the phrase **CHANGE ME!** entered. You will need to have an MS Application ID number to use this block. To create Microsoft Bing MS Application ID, you'll need to go to this link `http://www.bing.com/developers/appids.aspx` and follow the instructions on how to create an AppID. When you make an AppID, your new ID number will be immediately available. Once you have that number, copy and paste it into the **MS Application ID Key** textbox.

Once you have your ID Key entered go to the **Tools** section and find the option called **Check It to perform quick test of global search**, select the checkbox, and click on **Save changes**. If everything has been set up correctly and your Internet connection is functioning properly, you will see a series of test results from the search. You will see a message telling you the test is complete. When you click on **OK**, you will be brought back to the block management page.

Now go to the course in which you want to enable the new block. Once in the course, click on the **Turn editing on** button. Find the **Blocks** drop-down menu, click on it, and find the **Anti-Plagiarism** option. This will enable the block in the course. The screenshot of the block is as follows:

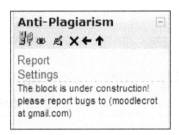

As you can see, there are two options here: **Report** and **Settings**.

First you will click on the **Settings** link. Once you click on this, you will be taken to the list of all the **Single file to upload** assignments. The next screenshot shows this:

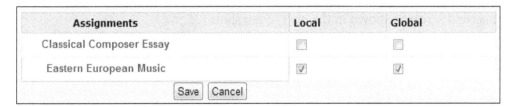

You can see that there are three columns. The first column lists the name of the **Assignments** available for checking. The second column, **Local**, allows you to search local files to see if there has been any plagiarism inside the course. The third column, **Global**, will perform the same action using an Internet search. The block will scan everything that has been checked. As you can see here, we have made our selections, and we will be checking our **Eastern European Music** assignment both locally and globally. Now all we need to do is click on the **Save** button.

Once we click on the **Save** button, we will receive a message telling us that the anti-plagiarism assignment has made the appropriate changes to the settings.

We will be brought back to the course front page. Now we need to click on the Report link in the **Anti-Plagiarism** block.

After clicking on the **Report** link you will be brought to the **Anti-Plagiarism – assignments** page. There'll be a drop-down menu titled **Select the Assignment** in the top center of the page. Pressing on the drop-down menu will list all the assignments that have been selected for scanning by the **Anti-Plagiarism** block. Choose the assignment you wish to scan. The scan will take place the next time the cron.php jobs runs. Once the Cron has run, you will see a report determining whether or not something has been plagiarized or has a high percentage of similar content.

You will see one of two screens. The first one you see is seen in the next screenshot:

Student name	Similar assignments
User Admin	no plagiarism have been detected OR check up was not performed yet
One Student	no plagiarism have been detected OR check up was not performed yet

There are two reasons you may see this screen. The first is that no plagiarism has been detected. The other possibility is that the cron.php may not have been run yet. If you have site administration privileges, run the cron.php and this should be updated. One thing that is important to note is that, depending on the number of assignments and size of the site, it may take a while to run the script. Be patient.

The second screen is shown in the next screenshot:

Student name	Similar assignments		
One Student	Name	Course	#
	WWW: http://www.experiencefestival.com/a	Web document	84 %
	WWW: http://www.evansvillefolkdancers.co	Web document	84 %
	WWW: http://www.evansvillefolkdancers.co	Web document	84 %
	WWW: http://www.wordiq.com/definition/Mu	Web document	80 %
	WWW: http://www.europopmusic.eu/Poland_p	Web document	76 %
	WWW: http://en.wikipedia.org/wiki/Music_	Web document	76 %
	Two Student	Testing Writing	44 %
	WWW: http://www.humanitiesweb.org/human	Web document	28 %

Here, you can see three columns. The first column shows the name of either the local source or the global source. Local sources list the profile name of the person who submitted it. Global sources are headed with **WWW:** and supply a link to the site. The second column shows the source of the document. This may be the course it came from or a document from the Web. As you can see here, seven documents are **Web document**, and one is a local document from the **Testing Writing** course. The final column shows the percentage of matched words in the documents. As we can see here, there are several sites that appear to have plagiarized large portions of an original document. We can also see that **Two Student** in the **Testing Writing** course has submitted a document with a **44%** match rate.

Clicking on the local search link that revealed a high match rate by **Two Student**, we will be shown both works side by side. The original post will be shown on the left-hand side and the comparison item selected will be shown on the right-hand side. After clicking on the link, we can see the following screen:

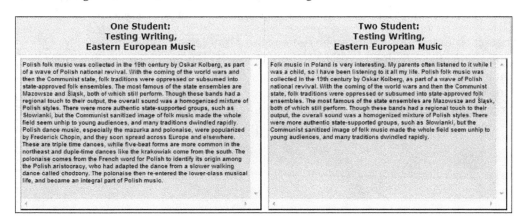

Source: Wikipedia. Retrieved on August 8, 2010 from: `http://en.wikipedia.org/wiki/Polish_folk_music#Traditional_music`

In an amazing coincidence, or a rather blatant plagiarizing attempt, **Two Student** has written an almost identical paper to **One Student**. From here, as an instructor you can make decisions as to how to best deal with the students depending on the class and the situation.

Clicking on any of the global links will create an identical screen to the local link, except that it will show text from the web document.

This new block, even though it's still in development, offers instructors an extremely useful tool in hunting down and stopping plagiarism in their courses. It is worth taking the time to install, set up, and use in your classes.

Summary

Teaching and testing writing is a time-consuming task; however, it can also be a very rewarding one. Watching students grow from using simplistic structures and basic patterns to more complex and daring creations is something that makes many writing instructors feel it was all worth it. Using Moodle can help make this task easier, by offering a variety of tools to use in your courses. From using basic Forums in setting up simplistic portfolios to testing using the Quiz module, Moodle offers students and teachers several effective techniques for writing instruction and assessment.

There is so much more that can be done using Moodle and other third-party applications that we don't even have time to touch on here. However, the more you use Moodle for your writing courses, the more tricks and ideas will come to you. You will discover through trial and error, or hopefully through trial and success, alternative methods for helping students succeed in writing and innovative methods for grading the work the students produce.

11
Using Gradebook

As an instructor or student, grading and grades are important. Grades are important for many reasons; educational and professional opportunities are two major uses for them. Grades can at best motivate us to work harder, at worst, make us give up. However, what is important to most students and instructors is the ability to see where they stand in relation to others in the class and where they stand in relation to the course standards.

We have been looking at testing, question creation, and setting up tests up to this point, but we have not really talked about how to grade in Moodle or how teachers and students can view their results. We have looked at how scores for Workshops, Lessons, and Quizzes are calculated and how to enter them, but we have not looked at the output and how the results are shown. In this chapter, we will look at Moodle's answer to the old, hard-covered, neatly lined and divided teacher's Gradebook. In this chapter, we will:

- Learn about Gradebook
- Create grade categories
- Create grade items
- Set up a complete Gradebook

What is Gradebook?

In short, Gradebook allows teachers and students to view grades on all assignments submitted and graded. For many types of quizzes and tests, this is automatic and grades are usually available for viewing immediately.

Workshop is one example of where this is typically not true. Gradebook can be of great use to instructors and students, but it will not do everything for you; it will not automatically grade everything, stop mistakes from happening, make students use it, or replace hardcopies of work. What it can do is help you with your grading and grade organization, allow you and your students quick and detailed access to grades, allow you to give feedback to students based on their scores, allow a quick review of students' or an entire class's grades to spot problems, and generally make grading a bit easier.

Gradebook can be used in several ways, but to get the most use out of it, we need to understand the basic options available and how they work.

Gradebook options

Setting up a Gradebook takes time and patience. There are many issues involved and many things to consider before finalizing a student's grade. Let's begin by looking at the two broad Gradebook options: Grade Items and Grade Categories.

Grade Items

Grade Items are the work items submitted by the students that are scored and when combined make up the student's final grade in the course. Some of the Grade Items are Assignments, Quizzes, and Lessons. Grade Items can be either automatically graded or manually graded. The grades submitted can be changed at a later date should that become necessary.

Grade Items are listed in columns, and we will see later how the Grade Items are displayed in the Gradebook.

Grade Categories

Grade Categories are a number of Grade Items, which are combined into a single category to make up a percentage of the student's total grade. For example, using a Grade Category would allow you to take several tests and combine them into a Test Category, which was worth a set percentage of the student's grade. It is important to note that each Grade Item can only added to a single Grade Category. So, you can't have your Algebra of Vectors test as part of your Participation category and your Test category.

There is no limit to the number of categories you can have in your course and there is also no limit to the number of nested categories that can be used. For example, if you are planning on giving several quizzes and you want them to be worth a percentage of the Testing Category, you can put them into a Quiz Category, give the category the value you want, and nest it inside of the Testing Category.

The top category in each course is called the Course Category, and all other categories are necessarily nested inside of it.

Accessing Gradebook

To access Gradebook, you need to go to the **Administration** section and click on the **Grades** link. It is located on the left side of the screen and looks like this:

As you can see, **Grades** is the fourth option from the top, between **Assign roles** and **Groups**.

Once you have clicked on this link, you will be taken to the Gradebook and what is known as the **Grader report**. Note that this is the Teacher View.

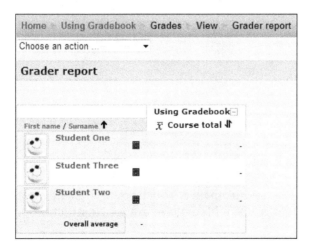

As you can see, we have enrolled our three imaginary students. We can also see that there is no grade for any of them yet, since we have not created any Grade Items. We will do this shortly. First, I'd like you to look at the **Choose an action** drop-down menu located directly under the **Home | Using Gradebook** breadcrumbs. This drop-down menu has all the possible actions we can take in the Gradebook, and I'd like to take a few pages to discuss all the options available here.

View

View is the first section visible in the drop-down menu. As you can see here, there are three options available, **Grader report**, **Overview report**, and **User report**.

Grader report

The **Grader report** is what we were just looking at. It contains the list of students in the leftmost column and a row of assignments listed just above the names. This will display all the student scores, for all assignments, in all categories. We will see a full example of this later, once we have added some assignments and categories.

This is a very useful view for teachers because it allows you to look at trends in the grades across assignments and classes. The only drawback to this view is that it can get long and you can lose sight of which student's grades you are reviewing. There is an **Expand/Collapse** function available next to the course name just above the assignments. When the grades are in the expanded view, there will be a **+** visible. Clicking on this sign again will change the view to the collapsed view and leave a minus sign **-** visible, which when clicked will revert the page to the expanded view. The expanded view is shown in the next screenshot:

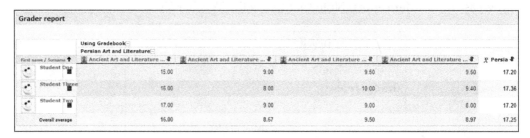

Another useful feature of this page is the averaging feature. Each Assignment column will be totaled and averaged at the bottom. For instructors this can be a very valuable tool because, not only is the calculation done for you, but it enables you to see any major changes in performance, which could indicate a particularly easy or difficult assignment, or issues with the preparation, instructions, or grading.

The last column is titled **Course total**. This column totals all the student assignment grades and gives the student's current score in the course. At the bottom of this column, you can see the course average grade. This can be extremely useful to determine where students fall in the course and can help you quickly determine which students may need additional assistance or student-teacher conferences.

Missing Grades

There are several reasons why you might not see a student's grade. They might not have completed the assignment, it may not have been graded yet, or it could be something else. If you see missing grades in the Gradebook, the first thing you want to do is look at the assignment that has no grade to find out where the problem lies. If the assignment isn't there, then talk to the student about it.

Overview report

The **Overview report** allows you to look at all the courses the student is enrolled in and see his/her grades in each. It also allows the student to see his/her grades in all the courses. You, and the students, are able to access the **Overview report** from any course enrolled in. The report itself creates a list. This is shown in the next screenshot:

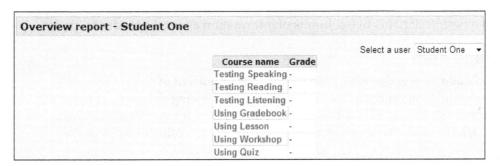

As you can see here, our student, **Student One**, is enrolled in seven courses. The student has received no grades in any course as of yet.

Also, on the far right, you can see a drop-down called **Select a user**. This drop-down lists all the students, and you select which student you want to view here. We will see another example of this later, once we have given the grades.

User report

The **User report** view provides much more detailed information about assignment grades than the Grader report. It also breaks down the view to a single individual. Selecting this view will bring you to a new page with a list of course assignments, quizzes, and so on, listed in their categories. The categories are nested in color, making it easy to see how the grades are organized and how the final calculation is broken down. The report is a very useful way to look at student grade information. An example is shown in the next screenshot:

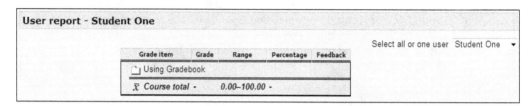

In the upper left-hand side, we can see the name of the user we are working with. On the right-hand side of the screen, we can see a drop-down with the title **Select all or one user**. Clicking on the drop-down will enable the instructor to select the student's grades he/she wants to look over. The instructor also has the option to select all users, which will show the user reports of all the members in the course listed in an alphabetical order.

The report itself holds five columns of information about the student's grades.

Grade item

The **Grade item** is the assignment name. It is important to create clear and meaningful assignment names because when reviewing the user or grader reports, assignments named 'H1', '12', and so on, don't allow for quick recall or recognition of the task the students were assigned. This reduces the value of the reports.

Grade

Grade is, obviously, the grade the student has been given for the assignment. It is shown as a total number of points received from the assignment. This number is calculated out to two decimal places.

At the very bottom of this column, we see a point-based grade based on the total number of assignments, the assignment's weight, and the assignment's point value. If you have not used categories, and all assignments are worth equal weight, this number will be the same as the percentage score.

Range

The **Range** column shows the possible range of scores available for the given assignment. For example, a test with a maximum possible value of 20 would show '0.00 – 20.00' in the **Range** column.

At the bottom of the **Range** column, you will see a range. The numbers in the range will be based on the lowest and highest numbers available in grading. For example, if we had ranges of '0.00 – 5.00', '0.00 – 20.00', and '0.00 – 100.00' the range displayed at the bottom would be '0.00 – 100.0'.

Percentage

The **Percentage** column shows the percent score the student received for the assignment. For example, if an assignment was worth a maximum of four possible points and the student got three points, this column would show 75.00 percent.

Feedback

In Gradebook, you are able to make comments on student grades. If you have decided to comment, whatever comments you added will be seen in this column.

Outcomes report

You might remember that I mentioned only three reports earlier. There are, in fact, four reports; however, the Outcomes report is not initially visible in the drop-down menu. The Outcomes report is used to track student achievement and to see if they have reached certain course goals or standards. These can be very useful in courses if you need to determine whether or not a student has reached the minimum acceptable level of competence in the course.

First enable the Outcomes feature. You must have administrative access to do this, so if you don't, ask your site administrator to do it. To enable the Outcomes you need to go to **Site Administration | Grades | General settings**.

Go to **General settings**:

1. Click on the **Enable outcomes** feature, located one down from the top of the list.

2. Once you have enabled this, save the changes and return to your course.

3. Once you are back in your course, you will notice a change has been made in the **Administration** block.

Between the **Grades** and **Groups**, you will see a new link called **Outcomes**. The updated block is shown in the next screenshot:

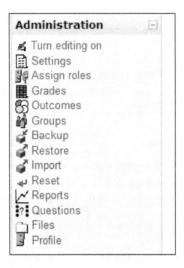

Once you have done this, to get to the Outcomes report, you just go back to the drop-down menu and the Outcomes report will be there. The Outcomes report is shown in the next screenshot:

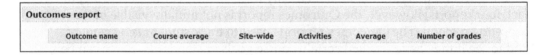

Outcome name

This is the short name of the outcome being used.

Course average

The column displays student averages for each of the outcomes in the course.

Site-wide

This column shows whether or not an outcome is used only in the course or if it is a **Site-wide** outcome.

Activities

The column here displays all the activities associated with the particular outcome being viewed.

Average

The **Average** column lists the average score for all the activities that use the outcome being viewed. This average is only related to activities in the course.

Number of grades

This column displays the number of grades given to the participants in each activity that makes use of the outcome being viewed.

Creating Outcomes

Now that we understand how outcomes will be displayed, we will look at how to create them. When we create Outcomes, we can make either course-based or site-wide ones. We will look at creating course-based Outcomes first, then we will look at site-wide Outcomes.

Course Outcomes

To create course-based outcomes, we need to click on the **Outcomes** link in the course administration block. This will open a page displaying two columns. On the left-hand side are the Outcomes already associated with the course. On the right-hand side are any outcomes you are able to add. Since we have not created any outcomes in our course yet, we will not see anything here right now. This is shown in the next screenshot:

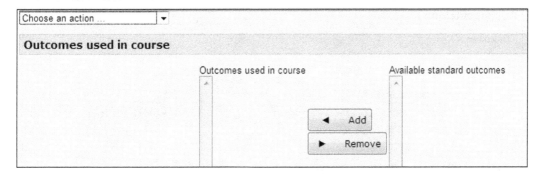

Since we have nothing here, we need to go to the **Choose an action** drop-down and scroll down to the **new Outcomes** section. You will see two options, **Outcomes used in This course** and **Available standard outcomes**. If we click on **Edit Outcomes**, we will be taken to the Outcomes page, as shown in the next screenshot.

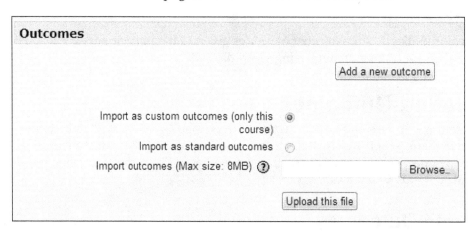

Here we have two options, we can either import Outcomes from other courses as .csv files or we can create a new one. Since we have no Outcomes to import, we will create a new one. To do this we will click on the **Add a new outcome** button. Once we click on the button, we come to the **Add an outcome** page, as shown in the next screenshot:

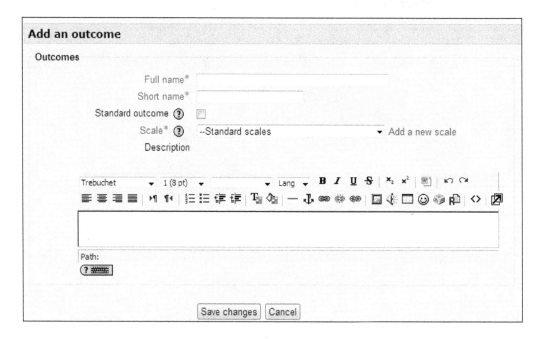

Full name

This is the complete title of the Outcome.

Short name

This is the name that will be displayed in the Outcomes report

Standard outcome

If you click on the box here, the Outcome will be made available to all courses on the site.

Scale

This is where you can select the type of grading scale to use with the Outcome. Until you add scales, the only visible option will be **Separate and connected ways of knowing**, which we have looked at before. If you want to create a new scale to be used for the outcome, click on the **Add a new scale** link, which will open a new window where you can create your own scale. Clicking on the button will bring you to the **Add a new scale** page, which we will look at in a moment.

Description

Here, you will enter a clear description of the Outcome. You need to make sure it is clear and will be useful for anyone who is using it.

Add a new scale

By clicking on the **Add a new scale** link, you will be taken to a new page where you can create a new grading scale. This is shown in the next screenshot:

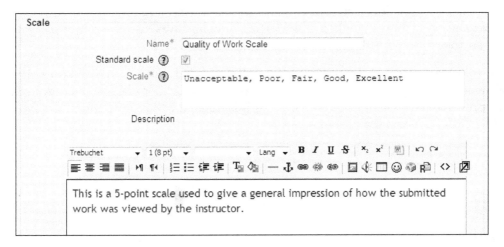

Name

This is the name of the scale and it will be listed in the **Scale** drop-down menu. You should make it something from which you, and anyone else on the site, will be able to quickly and easily identify how it will be used.

Standard scale

This will, like in the **Add an outcome** page, allow the scale to be used site-wide.

Scale

This is where you enter the scale you want to use. Each option you include should be separated with a comma from the following one. In addition, your scale should start from the lowest possible option and move to the highest possible one. For example, if want to create a list of five words describing your evaluation of the student's work, it might look like this: **Unacceptable, Poor, Fair, Good, Excellent**.

Description

Here, you will need to give a clear explanation of how the scale is intended to be used and the rationale behind the scale, if needed. The information here will be listed on the **Help** pages for the students, and other teachers, to use if needed.

Standard Outcomes

Standard Outcomes are used to enable site-wide outcome scales; however, only administrators can do this. If you have administrative access, you can go to the **Site Administration** block and click on **Grades**. Once in **Grades**, click on **Outcomes**.

On this page you will be able to do two things. The first option is to **Add a new Outcome**, which works just as mentioned earlier. The second option is to **Import Outcomes**. We have not looked at importing or exporting Outcomes, but this can be done.

We will add a new scale here, giving it a **Full name** and **Short name**, and for scale, we will use the **Quality of Work Scale** we used earlier. After we give it a description, we press the **Save changes** button. Once this is done, the **Standard Outcomes** page is shown as in the next screenshot:

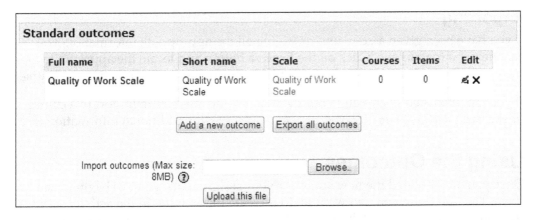

As shown in the previous screenshot, we can see the **Full name** and **Short name** given, the type of scale being used, and how many courses and items are using the new scale. In the **Edit** column, we have the option to either edit the Outcome or completely delete it.

Right now our **Courses** and **Items** columns are empty because we have not added this to any yet. If we go to a course we are teaching in, and click on the **Outcomes** link now, we will see the **Quality of Work Scale** is visible on the **Outcomes used in course** page in the available **Standard outcomes**. If we highlight the new scale and click on the **Add a new outcome** button, it will be moved to the **Outcomes used in this course** column, which will make it available for use in nearly all activities.

Exporting and importing Outcomes

You are able to import and export Outcomes for use in other courses, sites, or to make them available to others.

Exporting

Exporting the information is simple. As you can see from the previous image, there is an **Export all outcomes** button. Clicking on this button will allow you to save the file as a .csv file, which can be opened with a spreadsheet program like Excel or a text editor. The default naming for this is outcomes.csv.

Once it is exported, you will be able to open and view the file, make changes if you want, or give the file to other teachers who may want to review the scale, or upload it to their own sites.

Importing

If you have been given a `.csv` file containing all the appropriate information, you can import it to your site. Click on the **Browse** button and locate the appropriate file, then press the **Upload this file** button and the Outcomes will be added to the course.

If you are interested in creating your own `.csv` Outcome files to import to a course or site, see `http://docs.moodle.org/en/outcomes` for additional information.

Using the Outcomes

Once you have created the new scales for your assignments, you can begin to use them. The first thing you will want to do is create the activity. In the activity settings, the newly created scale will be available for use. We will use an Offline activity to show how this is done.

First, we go through and add all the information necessary for the activity. In the **Grade** drop-down, we will see the new scale we created earlier. Simply select that option and the new scale will be how we assess the assignment.

Once we have received the student's work, we review it and in the assignment's **Grade** drop-down, we will see our Outcome choices available for use.

The number of items added to the scale will determine the score the students receive. For example, in our created scale, an **Excellent** would be worth 100 percent, or five points since we entered five items, and an **Unacceptable** would be worth 0 percent, or zero points.

Outcomes can be a very useful tool for assessing your students and can help make them aware of their performance in the course and in specific assignments.

Categories and Items

The next area we will look at is the **Categories and Items** section of the Gradebook. Under this heading, there are two options, **Simple View** and **Full View**. This is where we are able to create categories and add individual items for assessment. The Simple View is shown in the next screenshot:

Name	Aggregation (?)	Extra Credit (?)	Max grade	Actions	Select
☐ **Using Gradebook**	Simple weighted mean of grades ▾	-	-	✎ ✖ ⌷	All None
☑ Ancient Art and Literature - The Greeks	-	☐	10.00	✎ ⬍ ✖ ⌷	☐
◈ Ancient Art and Literature - The Romans	-	☐	Excellent (5)	✎ ⬍ ✖ ⌷	☐
⚒ Ancient Art and Literature - The Persians	-	☐	20.00	✎ ⬍ ✖ ⌷	☐
☑ Ancient Art and Literature - The Egyptians	-	☐	10.00	✎ ⬍ ✖ ⌷	☐
⚒ Ancient Art and Literature - The Sumerians	-	☐	15.00	✎ ⬍ ✖ ⌷	☐
☑ Ancient Art and Literature - The Phonecians	-	☐	10.00	✎ ⬍ ✖ ⌷	☐
$\bar{x}$ Course total	-		100.00	▦ ✖ ⌷	

Name

This is the name of the course, category, or item that is part of the student's grade in the course.

Aggregation

This is where you decide how the grade calculations will be done. By choosing different **Aggregation** strategies, you are able to determine how each item and category will be calculated to arrive at the students' final score. There are nine choices available in the **Aggregation** drop-down, so there are many options in how you can calculate the student's score. The options available are: **Mean of grades**, **Weighted mean**, **Simple weighted mean**, **Mean of grades (with Extra credits)**, **Median of grades**, **Smallest grade**, **Highest grade**, **Mode of grades**, and **Sum of grades**.

We have looked at the **Aggregation** methods before, so please refer back to the explanation if you need to refresh your memory.

Extra Credit

This column is used if any of the assignments has been given an extra credit value. If it is to be used as extra credit, check the box in the column to signify this.

Several detailed examples of how extra credit is calculated into the overall score are given on the Moodle.org site.

Max grade

The **Max grade** setting shows what the maximum score possible for the assignment is.

> **Grades over 100 percent**
>
> If you want to give a grade over 100 percent, you can. You need to get whoever your administrator is to go to the **Administration | Grades | General settings** area of the site. At the very bottom of the page, there is a setting called **Unlimited Grades**. By default it is set to **No**, but by turning this on, you will be able to enter in any score you would like, 105 percent, 121 percent, and so on.

Actions

Here are your administrative possibilities. You have the option to **Edit**, **Hide**, **Move**, or **Lock** the item.

Select

This column allows you to select multiple items to work with.

Course total

Underneath the items being assessed, we can see the **Course total**. The number in the box represents the total number of points the student can get from the course.

Note that this number will not always equal the total for the **Max grade** column.

Full view

The full view offers a far more detailed view of how the grades will be calculated. Here is our previous example put into the **Full view** mode.

Name	Aggregation ⑦	Extra Credit ⑦	Max grade	Aggregate only non-empty grades ⑦	Aggregate including subcategories ⑦	Include outcomes in aggregation ⑦	Drop the lowest ⑦	Multiplicator ⑦	Offset ⑦	Actions	Select
Edit categories and items: Full view											
☐ Using Gradebook	Simple weighted mean of grades ▾	·	·	☑	☐	☐	0	·	·	🖉 ☁ 🔒	All None
☐ Ancient Art and Literature - The Greeks	·	☐	10.00	·	·	·	·	1.0000	0.0000	🖉 ↕ ☁ 🔒 ☐
☐ Ancient Art and Literature - The Romans	·	☐	Excellent (5)	·	·	·	·	1.0000	0.0000	🖉 ↕ ☁ 🔒 ☐
☐ Ancient Art and Literature - The Persians	·	☐	20.00	·	·	·	·	1.0000	0.0000	🖉 ↕ ☁ 🔒 ☑
☐ Ancient Art and Literature - The Egyptians	·	☐	10.00	·	·	·	·	1.0000	0.0000	🖉 ↕ ☁ 🔒 ☐
☐ Ancient Art and Literature - The Sumerians	·	☐	15.00	·	·	·	·	1.0000	0.0000	🖉 ↕ ☁ 🔒 ☐
☐ Ancient Art and Literature - The Phoenicians	·	☐	10.00	·	·	·	·	1.0000	0.0000	🖉 ↕ ☁ 🔒 ☐
✗ Course total	·		100.00	·	·	·	·			☑ ☁ 🔒

The **Name**, **Aggregations**, **Extra Credit**, **Max grade**, **Actions**, and **Select** columns are identical to the Simple view. Here, we will look at the six new features visible.

Aggregate of non-empty grades

This setting is used to determine whether or not assignments without grades are included in the overall course grade. By default, this is turned on and any assignments without a grade are not included in the **Course total**. If the setting is turned off, ungraded work will be included in the final grade.

Aggregate including subcategories

This option is mainly used to include the subcategories in the category you are working with. However, you do have the option to include every subcategory while excluding any aggregated grades.

Include outcomes in aggregation

If you include all Outcomes in your grading, your grade results might be different than you want. For example, the score associated with an Outcome could be very different than scores for other assignments. Using this setting, you have the option to exclude Outcomes from the aggregation.

Drop the lowest

If this setting is used, the lowest grade or grades will be dropped from the overall calculations. The number of lowest grades dropped is determined by the number you enter into the textbox.

Multiplicator

Using this setting allows you to multiply the assignment's value by whatever value is placed in the textbox.

Offset

This setting allows you to enter a number into the textbox, which will be added to the grade after the **Multiplicator** is calculated. This can be useful if you need to make a change to all grades for a particular assignment.

Setting up categories

Now that we have seen the Simple and Full views in the Categories and Items, let's make some categories. We will be using the Simple view to do this, although you are able to do it in the Full view as well.

The first thing we want to do is determine which categories to make. I have gone ahead and added a few new assignments to our course, which we will add to a category.

At the bottom of the page, click on the **Add category** button. Once this is done, we will be brought to a new page called **New category**. It is divided into two sections, **Grade category** and **Grade item**.

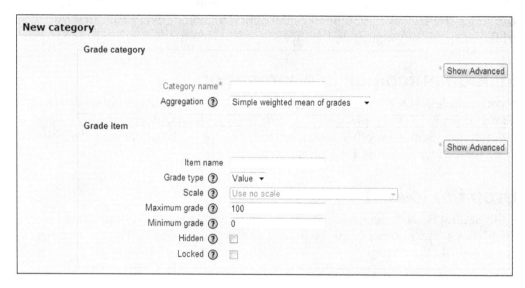

Note that we are looking at the basic view. Clicking on the **Show Advanced** buttons will add many new options. Feel free to experiment with these advanced options when you are comfortable with the basic settings.

Grade category

In this section, we have two items to work with: **Category name** and **Aggregation**.

Category name

This will be the title of the new category we are making. Something clearly defining the parameters of the category is a good idea. For example, since we are going to be working with Ancient Persian Art and Literature, something along those lines would be useful. Alternatively, a general category containing different activity types could be used, for example, a category with only tests or one with only forums. However you decide to break down the activities in your course, a name that clearly defines the category is useful.

Aggregation

This feature allows you to choose how the grades will be calculated for the category. The options available here are all aggregation methods we have gone over already.

Grade item

Here is where the information about the **Grade items** is entered.

Item name

Enter the name of the item here. Again, it is important to be clear about the item so there is no confusion about the assignment.

Grade type

This menu offers four options for the type of grading that will be used:

None

This setting does not allow the item to be graded.

Value

Selecting this setting will use the **Maximum grade** and **Minimum grade** settings to determine the student's grade on the activity.

Scale

If this option is selected, the **Scale** drop-down menu will be enabled and will determine how assignments are assessed.

Text

This option disables grading and only allows for feedback to be given to the participant.

Scale

This drop-down menu holds a list of scales for use with the assignment. Any scale previously created in the course, either **Custom** or **Standard**, will be available for use in the menu.

Maximum and Minimum grade

These two settings determine the highest and lowest grade available. The minimum is typically set to zero, with the maximum changing depending on the course and your needs.

Hidden

This will allow you to hide grades from the students enrolled in the course. If you decide to use this, click on the **Advanced** button. There you will see a **Hidden until** feature, which will automate the process of showing the activity results to the students when you are ready.

Locked

This setting is used to lock assignments, meaning that students will no longer be able to make changes after a certain point. This setting is usually used after a deadline is set. If you decide to lock the assignment, again, click on the **Advanced** button. This will show a deadline setting, which will automatically lock the assignment at the time of your choosing.

We are looking at Ancient Art and Literature in this course. We have several assignments on Ancient Persia that we want to be grouped together into a category. For our Category name, we will enter "Persian Art and Literature".

For our **Aggregation**, we will use the default, **Simple weighted mean of grades**.

For **Item name**, we will enter "Persia".

For **Grade type**, we will use **Value**. In our **Maximum** and **Minimum** grade settings, we will set the maximum to 20 and leave the minimum at zero.

We will leave **Hidden** and **Locked** disabled.

Once we have done all this, we will click on **Save changes**. Here is what our Simple view looks like after we have added our new category:

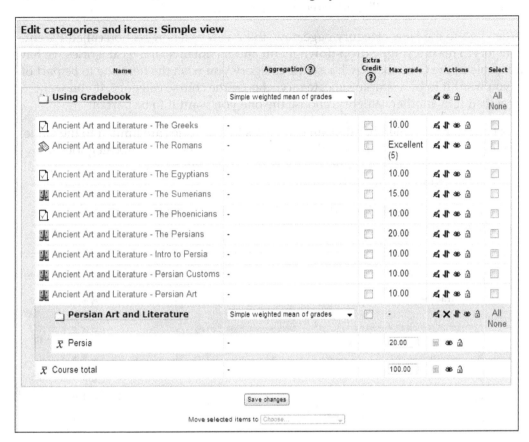

You can see that our new subcategory has been added and is clearly a subcategory in the larger **Using Gradebook** category.

Now, you can see that there are several Ancient Art and Literature activities related to Persia. We want to move those files from where they are now into the new category. We have two options here. The first is that we can click on the up or down arrows to move individual files to where we want them. This works, but it can be time consuming. Do you see the **Move selected items to** drop-down menu? Now that we have a second category, we can select multiple items and move them to where we want them. We will click on all the Forums related to Persia and, using the drop-down, place them all in the new subcategory at one time.

I am also going to make a few small changes. I'm going to change the scale grades we were using on the Romans to a 20-point values scale, I'm going to add a few more Forums, and then I'll add three more categories.

When I go to the **New category** page now, there will be a new section called **Parent category**. This is a simple drop-down menu and it contains all the categories we have available in the Gradebook. Choose the category you wish the new one to be part of. If you want it to be a simple subcategory, choose the course category. If you want to embed it in another category, choose the one you want it to be part of.

It is important to remember that subcategories in categories are limited to the value of the parent category. For example, if we were to place several subcategories into our Persia subcategory, the subcategory itself would still only be worth the original points assigned to it, that is, 20 points.

When we have finished, the part of our Gradebook appears as shown in the next screenshot:

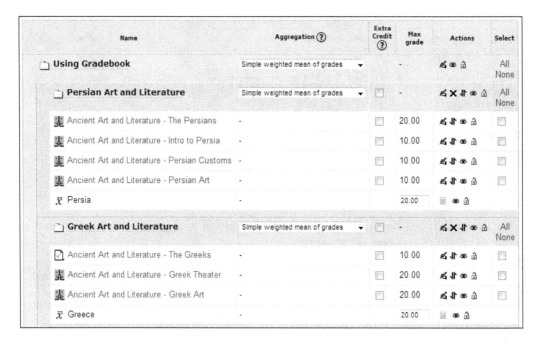

As seen from the previous screenshot, both sections are worth a total of 20 points. I have made four sections, each worth 20 points giving us a total of 80 points. However, the course itself is worth 100 points. We have two options here. The first is the easiest, leave everything as it is. If it is left as it is, Moodle will calculate everything and make each section worth the correct portion of the total. Our other option is to make the totals add up. We can go in and change each section to reflect the percent weight we want it to have. In our case, with four sections, we would simply need to add 5 points to each section bringing the total to 100 points. However, we will choose the simple route and leave it as it is.

Now, we need to go in and give our students grades for all their hard work. I am going to go into the **Grader report** and turn editing on. I will manually enter grades for all three of the students enrolled in the course. I am not going to enter feedback, just the scores. This is shown in the next screenshot:

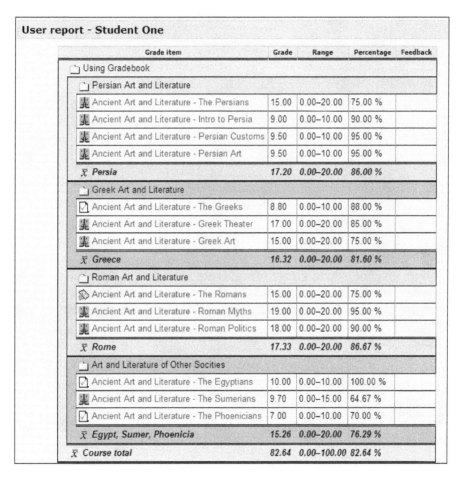

As you can see here in the **User report - Student One**, each section has been broken down into a percentage, then that percentage is calculated into a total number of points. This is then calculated into a percentage score.

Going back to the Grader report, we can now see all the participants in the course and all the grades they have received for each of the assignments, but this view is not as useful as the User report because it only gives raw scores. However, if the course category +/- icon is clicked, you will see only the course grade. This is a very useful feature and will allow you to quickly see which students are excelling and which you may need to meet with. It also shows the course average. The collapsed view of the **Grader report** is shown in the next screenshot:

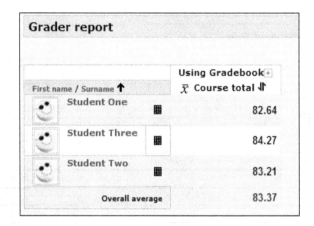

Scales

In this option, you are able to view the scales associated with the course. There are two types of scales: **Custom** and **Standard**. We have looked at how to set up scales in the Outcomes section. The scales page is shown in the next screenshot:

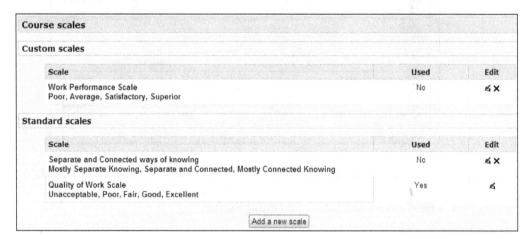

Custom scales

These are scales that are custom-made for the course. They are not used site-wide. In the previous example, you can see that I have added a custom scale titled **Work Performance Scale**. This was done by not selecting the **Standard scale** checkbox. You can see the title of the scale in the cell directly under the **Scale** header and the rankings/results under the scale's title.

In addition, you are shown whether or not it is used under the **Used** header. You also have the option to edit or delete the scale from here.

Standard scales

These scales are set up just like the **Custom scales** except that the **Standard scale** option is selected.

The **separate and connected ways of knowing scale** will always be an associated **Standard** scale unless you delete it or edit it.

Letters

This section displays the percentage score assigned to letter grades and how they are assigned in Moodle. This section has two options: **View** and **Edit**. Note that **Grade letters** are set at the site level, but can be overridden at the course level as we will see next.

To enable letter grades in your course, log in and on the front page **Administration** block, go to **Grades | Grade item settings**. Once you are there, you will see an option called **Grade display type**. Change the display type to **Letter** and your grades will be displayed as letters.

View

This option takes us to a page called **Grade Letters**. This page simply shows the range of percentage scores required to achieve one of the defined letter grades. The scores required are shown from **Highest** to **Lowest**. A screenshot of the **View** page follows:

Grade letters

Highest	Lowest	Letter
100.00 %	93.00 %	A
92.99 %	90.00 %	A-
89.99 %	87.00 %	B+
86.99 %	83.00 %	B
82.99 %	80.00 %	B-

Edit

On this page you are able to edit Moodle's default settings for grades as shown in the next screenshot:

Override site defaults

Clicking on the **Override site defaults** checkbox will enable you to change the default settings to whatever you feel is appropriate for the course.

Grade letter 1

Once the override setting is enabled, you are able to adjust the character used in Letter 1, by default A, to any letters or characters you desire. For example, you may want to give an A+ for students who achieve 98 percent or above. To do this, you would simply insert A+ into the **Grade letter 1** textbox. Using this option allows you to create special, predefined scales for use in your course.

This explanation applies to all **Grade letters**.

Letter grade boundary

This percentage shows the minimum number required to achieve that score. Again, if you would like to alter the percentage, simply press the drop-down button and select the desired percentage from the list.

The options available range from 100 percent to 0 percent. They also include an **Unused** option, which means that **Letter grade boundary** will not be used. You have fourteen options to work with, so chances are that several options will remain set to **Unused**.

Again, this explanation applies to all **Letter grade boundaries**.

When you have finished with all the changes desired, click on the **Save changes** button located directly below the last **Letter grade boundary**.

Import and Export

In Moodle, it is possible to import and export your grades.

Importing grades

If you need to import grades to your course you are able to use two file types: CSV and XML. The size of the file you are able to import to the course depends on the course settings and the maximum uploadable file size will be displayed on both **Import** pages.

For detailed information about how to import grades visit Moodle's site at `http://docs.moodle.org/en/Grade_import`.

Exporting grades

Sometimes you may need to have paper copies of your grades or you may simply want to physically store them on CDs. To do this you'll need to export them. Moodle offers several ways to export grades, from spreadsheets to plain text files.

The process is explained clearly on the Moodle grade export page found at: `http://docs.moodle.org/en/Grade_export`.

Summary

As you can see, Gradebook is a complex and extremely useful system, but it is not the most user-friendly one around. The ability to instantly access student grades can be very useful in helping students where they need it. Offering feedback via Gradebook can also add to learning by pointing out where the student excelled, went astray, or giving them additional feedback outside of the assignment itself.

In addition to you having access to their grades, students having constant access to their own grades can be beneficial as well. Students performing at a higher level may receive some beneficial backwash from the process. Students falling into a lower bracket may be inclined to approach the instructor or classmates to find out where they are going wrong.

The reporting features available in Gradebook, from grading simple assignments and forums to quizzes and tests, allow you to see the whole grade picture for each student in the class, in groups or as a whole in a complete, simple, or custom view. This is an invaluable tool in helping you see possible issues in instruction, materials, or any other issue that may have affected the students' work on the activity in question.

Categories and subcategories can help keep you organized, can help the students see where every assignment will impact their grades, and allow for instant feedback and/or changes, should they become necessary.

Gradebook is a powerful tool and something that, when used properly, will help you and your students track their progress and help you identify stronger or weaker members of the group.

Index

W

Thank you for buying
Moodle 1.9 Testing and Assessment

About Packt Publishing

Packt, pronounced 'packed', published its first book "*Mastering phpMyAdmin for Effective MySQL Management*" in April 2004 and subsequently continued to specialize in publishing highly focused books on specific technologies and solutions.

Our books and publications share the experiences of your fellow IT professionals in adapting and customizing today's systems, applications, and frameworks. Our solution based books give you the knowledge and power to customize the software and technologies you're using to get the job done. Packt books are more specific and less general than the IT books you have seen in the past. Our unique business model allows us to bring you more focused information, giving you more of what you need to know, and less of what you don't.

Packt is a modern, yet unique publishing company, which focuses on producing quality, cutting-edge books for communities of developers, administrators, and newbies alike. For more information, please visit our website: www.packtpub.com.

About Packt Open Source

In 2010, Packt launched two new brands, Packt Open Source and Packt Enterprise, in order to continue its focus on specialization. This book is part of the Packt Open Source brand, home to books published on software built around Open Source licences, and offering information to anybody from advanced developers to budding web designers. The Open Source brand also runs Packt's Open Source Royalty Scheme, by which Packt gives a royalty to each Open Source project about whose software a book is sold.

Writing for Packt

We welcome all inquiries from people who are interested in authoring. Book proposals should be sent to author@packtpub.com. If your book idea is still at an early stage and you would like to discuss it first before writing a formal book proposal, contact us; one of our commissioning editors will get in touch with you.

We're not just looking for published authors; if you have strong technical skills but no writing experience, our experienced editors can help you develop a writing career, or simply get some additional reward for your expertise.

PUBLISHING

Moodle 1.9
for Second Language Teaching

Engaging online language-learning activities using the Moodle platform

Jeff Stanford   PACKT

Moodle 1.9 for Second Language Teaching

ISBN: 978-1-847196-24-8   Paperback: 524 pages

Build robust and reliable persistence solutions for your enterprise Java application

1. A recipe book for creating language activities using Moodle 1.9

2. Get the most out of Moodle 1.9's features to create enjoyable, useful language learning activities

3. Create an online language learning centre that includes reading, writing, speaking, listening, vocabulary, and grammar activities

Quick answers to common problems

Moodle 1.9
English Teacher's Cookbook

80 simple but incredibly effective recipes for teaching reading comprehension, writing, and composing using Moodle 1.9 and Web 2.0

Silvina P. Hillar   [   ] open source

Moodle 1.9: The English Teacher's Cookbook

ISBN: 978-1-849510-88-2   Paperback: 304 pages

80 simple but incredibly effective recipes for teaching reading comprehension, writing, and composing using Moodle 1.9

1. Packed with recipes to help you use Moodle effectively to teach English

2. Create a different atmosphere to help students improve their writing skills using Moodle

3. Implement different techniques in the teaching of reading comprehension, writing, and composition using a variety of resources from the free and open source software available

Please check **www.PacktPub.com** for information on our titles

Moodle 1.9 E-Learning Course Development

ISBN: 978-1-847193-53-7   Paperback: 384 pages

A complete guide to successful learning using Moodle

1. Updated for Moodle version 1.9

2. Straightforward coverage of installing and using the Moodle system

3. Working with Moodle features in all learning environments

4. A unique course-based approach focuses your attention on designing well-structured, interactive, and successful courses

Moodle Teaching Techniques

ISBN: 978-1-847192-84-4   Paperback: 192 pages

Creative Ways to Use Moodle for Constructing Online Learning Solutions

1. Applying your teaching techniques through Moodle

2. Creative uses for Moodle's standard features

3. Workarounds, providing alternative solutions

4. Abundantly illustrated with screenshots of the solutions you'll build

5. When and how to apply the different learning solutions

Please check **www.PacktPub.com** for information on our titles